This is Mime!

THE SAN FRANCISCO MIME TROUPE

The San Francisco Mime Troupe: The First Ten Years

R.G.Davis

introduction by

Robert Scheer

Ramparts Press
Palo Alto, California 94303

Library of Congress Cataloging in Publication Data

Davis, R G
    The San Francisco Mime Troupe: the first ten years

    1. San Francisco Mime Troupe.

PN2297.S25D38   792'.09794'61   74-19934
ISBN 0-87867-058-0
ISBN 0-87867-059-9 pbk

Published by Ramparts Press, Palo Alto, California

        First Edition

LC 74-19943
ISBN 0-87867-058-0 (cloth)
ISBN 0-87867-059-9 (paper)

Printed in the United States of America.

To Sandra Archer, Matt & Robb

ACKNOWLEDGMENTS

Authorship, before this book, appeared to be a singular activity; it has been more like a shepherding. Thanks to Rocky Morowitz, Herman and Ruth Schein this book was begun; Sandra Archer and Robert Hurwitt ordered the first plunge into the data; after two revisions Martha Howard threw the whole thing up in the air and it came down in another order; Tim Drescher reprinted that version four times; then Elizabeth Stephans did the final edit and brought it into shape so that Russ Stetler could point up some discontinuities and Loie (Lois) Rosencrantz could organize it into a visual presentation. Ultimately of course this shepherd is responsible for the point of view.

Memorabilia and records of the *San Francisco Mime Troupe: First Ten Years* are archived at the State Historical Society of Wisconsin, 815 State Street, Madison, Wisconsin 53706.

Contents

INTRODUCTION

The San Francisco Mime Troupe, which began in 1959 as the R. G. Davis Mime Troupe, has been the most consistently energetic and responsible element in the counterculture of the Bay Area. Beginning with the Beats and continuing through the new left, rock and other explosions, there has scarcely been an event that did not feature the Mime Troupe. One of the real values of this book is to provide an important insight into the making of one of America's liveliest cultural periods, as seen through the eyes of the ubiquitous R. G.—a participant, not a bystander.

In my own memory, Ronny Davis appears more as a force than simply a person who blew through where I happened to be standing. This was literally true during our encounters in the early sixties when I was, for all practical purposes, imprisoned in a tiny triangle of books—a salesman in Lawrence Ferlinghetti's people-cluttered City Lights bookstore. Ronny hung out then with the younger Actors Workshop people next door in Vesuvio's bar. They were physically much healthier-looking than the disheveled *beatitude* magazine poets up Grant and they had much more self-control than the black jazzmen and white Negroes across Broadway at the Swiss American (made famous when Lenny Bruce fell out of one of its windows). Self-conscious leftists were scarce then and as one of their number I carefully preserved space in the magazine rack for the *Monthly Review* and *Studies on the Left*, which were not exactly in the same kind of demand as the *Crazy Horse Review*. It wasn't that our customers were apolitical—most of them were out to destroy bourgeois society. They just couldn't see the usefulness that political analysis might have for their work. Given the state of the left in the fifties, there was much reason for that dim view.

Ronny was the most frequent intruder in my little political-librarian scene, as I'm sure he was on many others. The results of all of his investigations and energy outbursts then and over the years were theater events—at the basement Encore Theatre downtown, where he subverted the prestigious Actors Workshop which had given him space, or the very hip Spaghetti Factory, or at the drafty abandoned church he found out in the Mission District.

For Ronny the move out to the Latino Mission area was not simply a matter of cheaper space (always a consideration) but also an attempted break—at first unsuccessful—with the artistic bohemian community as one's sole constituency. The more serious move in that direction came with the Troupe's free productions in the city's parks. Ronny became committed to that elusive goal of having radical theater touch and be defined by "regular" people, as opposed to patrons of the legit theater—a constant preoccupation with not selling out. Throughout all the changes and refinements, there was almost a religious reverence about the company's search for a process that would free it from dependence upon the powers that be. Later it sought a base from which to destroy those powers. (Awareness of that enemy began at a point of raw actor/director stubbornness about what an audience and theater company should be and do, for and to each other.)

Theaters that depended upon Ford Foundation subsidies for their existence would end up selling capitalism, or at best accepting its framework, no matter what promises company members made to each other. This is what was happening to the Actors Workshop, San Francisco's nationally celebrated company in which R. G. was a rising young assistant director. At first he guerrillered away with late-hour shows which were intended to startle the Workshop out of what was fast becoming a comfortable pattern of safe set-pieces. His counter troupe was bold, raucous and open to outrageous ideas. But the parent company didn't even quake—let alone change—and instead, in a rather familiar turn of events, Ronny was celebrated as "innovative." All of this fuss was actually going to be good for his career!

I believe that there is something physiological about Ronny's reactions in such situations that prevents his rational consideration or rationalization of the prospects for opportunism—he malfunctions. And instead of saying "uh-huh," and letting his brain retreat to safer ground, he smolders and then erupts.

His inability to kid himself into an acceptance that something would be "good for his career" is indicated by the deadpan Colombo style of the writing in many of this book's scenes. He gets to New York and meets the famous Becks, who think they are gurus and saints (which maybe they are), but there are serious contradictions in what they are doing with the theater. Something inside Ronny has to discuss the contradictions—push them further—as the Becks lapse into meditation. Ronny has offended yet another important circle of friends.

While Ronny can be funny, charming and certainly attractive, none of that is allowed to interfere with his persistent and unsettling denial of what is "in." And that quality has proved in the long run to be of greater significance than the hyper-outrage of the Diggers or other crazies who have at times been attracted to the Mime Troupe. It is a quality which Davis implanted in the Mime Troupe and which I think flourished after he left.

When the liberal press praised a Mime Troupe performance, Ronny wanted to know where they had gone wrong. It was not a matter of churlishness, but an understanding that there is a power structure and if it is not threatened by your theater, then your theater is shit. During the last two winters, years after Davis had left the company, the Mime Troupe received extremely favorable reviews in the *Times* and the effect was so unsettling that the company almost fell apart. All of this seems incredibly silly, self-defeating and childish—unless one adheres to a very different standard of success from that accepted by capitalist ventures, large or small.

This obsession with the power structure and not succumbing to it is only infantile if the power structure does not in fact exist or if its existence is judged a good thing. If bourgeois art and politics were honest, they would cop to this. But such an admission would also be tactically foolish, for the greatest weapon protecting bourgeois social relations is the obfuscation of the fact of their existence. The Ford Foundation was not set up to advance capitalist ideology, rather "for politically neutral philanthropic goals." Lincoln Center was not created by the rich to entertain themselves and preserve a safe culture, rather "to aid the struggling arts." The fact is that positions like these have either been accepted or talked around by most of those "concerned" with art, and it is precisely that bland acquiescence which compels the persistence of Ronny's opposition.

For Ronny and the others in the company, a preoccupation with the power of foundations and Arts Commissions soon broadened with the events of the sixties into a full-blown and well-thought-out appraisal of modern American monopoly capitalism. I say well-thought-out on the basis of my own participation in the company on several tours which frequently saw a hard day and night of performing in Albuquerque or Fargo capped off by a late night study session or just a serious discussion about Mao's redbook, the Panthers, or the Mideast.

It would be difficult to exaggerate the staggering number of hours that went into the ideas and form of new plays. Outsiders were brought in to give talks, reading lists appeared and endless committees functioned or malfunctioned. To be sure there were wine and spaghetti feeds and the best parties in town and numerous romantic affairs and occasional bouts with drugs and nature. There were also obviously periods of laziness, incompetence, trucks crashed, scripts losts, tempers thrown. In a certain way Mime Troupers, Davis included, didn't take themselves too seriously—they were (and still are) a ribald and genuinely non-pretentious group. You would want to go to a Mime Troupe party. They were just a lot more fun to be with than most other groups, given to impromptu bands, general spontaneity, and a more diverse and interesting bunch of characters

than one expected around the left.

At the same time this rag-tag beggars' army (the troupe actually lived off a glorified form of begging after each performance) was more responsible and less highhanded in its political commitment than any group which I encountered around the Bay Area's new left. I think it was an awareness of this that caused the normally fratricidal left to be united in its appreciation of the Mime Troupe (most had been visited more than once by Mime Troupers in search of material). I think Davis is correct in his brief assessment of the other countertheaters of the time that they did not share the Mime Troupe's political accountability. Their politics remained the private property of the key actors and directors of the company.

It is my own view that this eventually happened to some degree even in the Mime Troupe because of Ronny's very strong personal impact. Once he accepted a political and, indeed, Marxist criticism of the troupe's work, R. G. created the basis for his departure. He had helped the company to take seriously the ideas of Marx and the Chinese Cultural Revolution, while still seeking to maintain his individual prerogatives. It could not hold. I think it would have been better if (in the terms of the Cultural Revolution) he had been "rehabilitated," but as we should by now be painfully aware, there are limits to one's ability to transcend the restrictions of bourgeois life-style while still living within bourgeois society. If socialism in one country is difficult, then socialism within one little theater group (or commune) is impossible. Nevertheless, that does not negate the educational value of such struggles. I wish that Ronny would accept this, but I don't really expect him to. Any history that I wrote of *Ram-*

parts would contain the same defects. But the veterans should tell their stories, and I find this book to be an invaluable history of the troupe and a good slice of the sixties precisely because the author struggled through so much of it.

Ronny is an especially useful reporter, using techniques quite opposite to those celebrated in the new journalism. There is almost none of that obsessive "color" which delights in precise proportion to its irrelevance to the real subject at hand. For example, when Davis writes about the Living Theatre of the Becks he does not take their performance as an occasion for launching his own play. On the contrary, he wades right into their dressing room to find out what they think *they* are doing, then he retreats to the balcony to mull it over, then goes back again to the Becks. It is relentless, it may even be unkind or incomplete, but Ronny does something most journalists refuse to do about their subject—he takes the theater of the Becks seriously—horribly seriously. If they are right then he is wrong. He will have to change his own theater dramatically. But are they right in the *main* thing that they are doing—their theater? That's what he cares about—not whether they are having affairs on the side or whether they like him or whether they make funny copy. It is a journalistic restraint that must be very hard to live with, but it makes for very clean reading. Indeed, the whole of this book is so uncluttered by the preliminaries of stage-setting that at first glance it is disconcerting and may scare one off. But in a day of over-inundation of media and concern about chopping down trees this lean and essential style might just catch on. If that does happen, Ronny will no doubt perceive *its* inadequacies and get on to something better. In the meantime there is need for a note of caution to the reader that this is not a book designed for skimming. It is not constructed along the accepted model of a great lead and ending, to be completed on one toilet-sitting. Different sections do stand on their own, but there is no simple ordering of their importance and remarkably little fluff. R. G. Davis has always required a nail-scratching tension and discipline in his actors and that same demand is now made of those who would read of his theater. As he has always argued, if the play is important, then it warrants the discipline to put it on right, and that goes for the audience as well.

It is also true that Ronny's development spans a greater distance than most. He didn't go to Harvard and he didn't start out either a red or poor. In the pages that follow he traces in an almost detached fashion (all of his stuff has a Brechtian style as well as a Marxist vision that is slightly disbelieving as it dissects) his movements from Middle America through the bohemian substructure to the Berliner Ensemble. I don't know for sure where it ends up.

At a time when many on the left feel demoralized and cynical (and when much too much junk has been written about the sixties) I found this to be a stimulating and optimistic book. Although I would have liked to have seen more discussion of Ronny's final falling out with the troupe, the book is honest, free of self-serving embellishment and constantly zeroes in on the key issues as they arose in the practice of the time. It is optimistic because as one reads this history of our skirmishes with power it is clear that whether we want to admit it or not, we did in fact win—not the war, but at least the skirmishes.

ROBERT SCHEER

1

THE BEGINNINGS

Alternative theatre sprang not from its own head but from the unfulfilled expectations of elite and commercial theatre and the inordinate boredom of middle-class life; not merely to entertain, rather to educate, not merely to educate, to be an example; not merely to be an example, to create an opposition; not merely to create an opposition, rather to change to a reproduction of self for more than the privileged.

Where did all this come from? Where did it go? That is the purpose of this investigation.

A friend who read the manuscript asked, "What was *your* political development?" As I remember it, the first stage was boredom with middle-class life and a search for an occupation that was engaging. My family was full of FDR Democrats and I remember arguing with a public school teacher about conservative Herbert Hoover. I also remember reading and giving a report on Edgar Snow's *Red Star Over China* at the age of thirteen. When I got to college the McCarthy period was on and they told me, "You should have been here when the Korean War vets were around, the place was hopping." A few of us set up a Political Action Club to counter the misinformation of McCarthyism. The fear of communists was rank, but a sharp fellow dissident said about Ohio University in 1953 that "no self-respecting communist would come to this school." Moving farther from home to the University of New Mexico I associated with the anthropology students, who were the most progressive elements in the school and sensitive to the Indians. Although I studied economics—supposedly to become a journalist—the theatre was *the* attraction.

In 1951 I saw Jose Limon's dance company and thought: "That's terrific; should learn that." So I studied modern dance at: Ohio University, two years; University of New Mexico, two years; Connecticut College, six weeks (ten hours a day); and professional studios in New York for another year. As progressive as modern dance was at one time, its form had become limited. As I choreographed more complex dances I found myself at an impasse. The form inhibited my thoughts—or better, my thoughts had outstripped the probabilities of dance. Then I saw Marcel Marceau and thought: "That's terrific; should learn that." So I studied mime with Paul Curtis's American Mime Theatre in New York for two years and performed with them.

Paul Curtis taught a combination of Method (Actors Studio, Stanislavsky) and mime as he learned it from Etienne Decroux. Rejecting Decroux's non-Method approach to movement, Curtis developed a rational internal system unfortunately attached to a hodgepodge of American calisthenics. The American Mime Theatre, without intending to do so, produced modern dance with pretensions. The work was interesting, but I had to go off and study with the master. In 1957, with the aid of a friend from my college days, I obtained a Fulbright scholarship to study at the Etienne Decroux studio in Paris for six months.

As I begin to understand and respect it, the ritual of theatre involves a transference of sensual life energy from one group of people to another. This is not a mindless task; it requires rigorous imaginative expertise. At the Decroux studio in Paris much time was spent on isolation of the hands; the foot; the "poitrine, ceinture, basant"; and counterweights. There was little debate with the master as to one's interpretation; some discussion, yes, but not the freedom of "improvisation" we Americans feel so essential to learning.

Decroux's ability to present the counterweights or weight distribution of an ordinary activity through clear and precise movements (isolated parts reassembled for clarity) was his genius and contribution to the visual theatre. By exposing the entire detail of the activity he reproduced a cleaner picture."*

As a member of the Charles Dullin Theatre during World War II, Etienne Decroux, ex-butcher, laborer-turned-actor, worked with Jean-Louis Barrault on the science of literal movement. Barrault continued on in the theatre while Decroux intensified his research.

In mime classes both at Curtis's studio and later in France, my long hours of dance proved extremely valuable. As an indigenous American form, modern dance covered more space than the precise techniques of Curtis's calisthenics or Decroux's mime. The physicality and non-balletic use of space made it possible to utilize Decroux's

* About the same time in England, Rudolph Laban's scientific investigation of movement produced aids in Time and Motion studies and a rather complex means of notating dance called Labanotation.

science in a progressive manner.

In the Frenchman's studio the ability to execute an isolation or a weight change was based both on internal and external expertise. The quasi-ideological explanation for a stance or a gesture by Decroux gave the work a seriousness that few Americans could abide, yet Decroux's dictum, a pre-Cartesian concept, "Nothing in the hands, nothing in the pockets," cleaned the stage for the new concept of Mime Corporal, or expression through the body and ignored the existentialist turmoil under his window. The stage is not "clean," it is full of a person and other elements. It is this conjunction of existentialism, Method acting and modern dance that allowed me to create a seven-minute mime demonstrating a richer presentation than modern dance and with more content than pantomimic technical demonstrations.

"White Collar Day," the title of which represents the content of the piece, re-enacted the routinized daily movement and gestures of waking, washing, dressing, traveling, eating, working, the return home, TV, and sleep of a clerk-typist. Each activity was stripped to its essentials, analyzed for its purpose and the essence presented. These activities so analyzed contributed to the depiction of a person trapped. For example, lunch break: fast shoving gesture (of food) into the mouth ended with a real jab in the stomach, actually painful to the performer, thus producing the accurate facial and physical expression of eating on the job.

The Mime performs gestures within a motivated frame of reference. He has to act on himself, and uses everything that is present on stage in front of an audience. The tools are the elements: audience, light, air, sound, clothes, body, wall (or curtains), floor. These become props. The Pantomimist (who believed in what Decroux said, "Nothing in the hands and nothing in the pockets") had to indicate emotions, props and scenery. He had to learn facial grimaces which Method acting had discarded as nineteenth century melodrama. The Mime's use of the immediate environment produced a realistic (not naturalistic) depiction of life.

After six months of six classes a week, with the dedicated disciples of Etienne Decroux, I decided to present a concert at the American Artists and Students Center in Paris. Madame Decroux was surprised: "But you haven't studied long enough." "Should I wait until I'm sixty-five?" I retorted (Decroux's age at the time). I had studied long enough; begun dance at seventeen and at twenty-five I had to try my skill in front of an audience. As a practical and aggressive American, I couldn't wait any longer and I also believed that only half the work is done before it is presented to an audience.

My big half hour at the American Students and Artists Center was no smash success, although I performed works I had conceived and developed from costume to announcement card. When I tried for another show at the USIS center, I was refused. "Mime is a French art form," they said. Today, we would say they were imperialist-lackey-running dogs! At the time, I just thought they were narrow-minded shits.

Marcel Marceau was the popular image for all so-called Mimes. Even though he performed mostly in pantomime, his white-faced pedal-pusher act was hard to follow. He didn't make any noise, the reviews said. Yet there was an awful lot of music, and just enough squeaking from his shoes to make reality pop. From this contradictory squeak so much a part of his musty art, a theatre group was to emerge that caused a great deal of trouble and provided a great deal of pleasure for many people: the San Francisco Mime Troupe.

When I left Paris and returned to the United States I feared the big buildings, the noise and the terror of American commerce: landing in New York was like a slap on the head. I had shed some Americanisms that I wanted to keep shed so I quickly left for the only "French" town in the whole territory: Frisco. Stationed midst the seven hills, I set up shop and looked into various theatre groups, trying to find a place to fit in.

I was not overjoyed with performing alone, nor was I able to conjure up magnificent mimes without the aid of other people. The single performer is limited to his own self. Nice work if you can create magic, but solo performing eventually leads to self-manipulation or freaky tricks. I tried to see all the pantomimists and mimes to find out what they did to survive. I was fortunate to see the work of one Peter Lane. At the time he was performing at the Hungry I, a nightclub in San Francisco. He did four or five bits between the main acts. Over coffee he told me he had recently done a full two-hour concert in Los Angeles, where he had performed all his work: thirty-four animals, four eggs, three sandwiches and ten flowers. He didn't laugh, so I didn't either; nor did I succumb to the temptation of asking him to perform a soft-boiled egg right then and there in the restaurant. After all, we were sophisticated arteeests!

While I performed and taught classes in the Bay Area, I went around to many of the little theatres to see what was happening. I had heard about the famous Actors Workshop as far away as Paris. After warming up at one or two of the little theatres I auditioned and was accepted at the workshop as an assistant director.

At its peak, the Actors Workshop represented a positive, regional reaction to commercial Broadway and simpering college theatre. The repertory included plays by Whiting, Arden, Pinter, Durrenmatt, Genet, Shakespeare, Brecht, Frisch, Beckett. Over eleven years, its kaleidoscope of seventy European plays was dotted by eleven American originals. Herbert Blau, an English teacher from San Francisco State College who had studied chemical engineering, was most responsible for the repertory. Jules Irving, his partner, with the assistance of a dedicated company businessman, Alan Mandel, produced, directed and sometimes acted in shows by the workshop. Irving had been a director of Kampus Kapers, a seasonal amateur variety show at San Francisco State College, in addition to teaching drama. He kept the books of the company in the black with inexpensive, but profitable, children's shows.

In separating from academia and by placing their company amidst the community without debasing their intentions, they utilized the free artistic energy in the San Francisco Bay Area— talented people who no longer made their living from their art. This scramble operation sometimes created good work, but it never produced major innovations on the stage.

Blau forecast the fate of the Actors Workshop in an article printed in *Encore*, March/April 1960, under the title "Littlewood and Planchon in an Affluent Society":

> Dissent can be bought even when it is still dissenting. The great novelty of the Beat Generation in America is that its howls have made a pretty penny.

That is not to say dissent always wants to be accommodated. In America, where even protests get grants from the trust funds of Ford and Rockefeller, it can't help itself.

He also stated, "Assimilation is the secret weapon of the bourgeoisie." This was the year of their first Ford grant.

The transition to full-time professional company was accompanied by increased overhead and expanded cost for production, making the rush for foundation money inevitable. Rent in 1962 was fifteen hundred dollars a month for the Marines Memorial Theatre and eight hundred dollars for the Encore. These figures were outrageous when the majority of the people in the group were still volunteers. Production costs ran about ten to fifteen thousand dollars per show and advertising costs increased to five hundred dollars a week, while apprentice salaries, an innovation, were twenty-one dollars for a seventy-two-hour week.

In 1960-61 Ford provided $56,000 and promised $197,000 over a two-year period. For a while there was talk of matching funds but fund drives got bogged down because the community could not donate money and buy tickets as well. Eventually, the box office was used to match funds and Ford stopped trying to be a "community stimulant."

Following the stipulations of the grant, the Actors Workshop hired ten actors from New York and Los Angeles at two hundred dollars a week to work with members of the company who had, after years of labor, worked up to weekly salaries of from fifteen to fifty dollars. Irving increased production. The talent from the big cities didn't stay on for the second year. Some left because they didn't get the parts they were promised,

Circus Mime, 1960-61
Who's Afraid Mime, by Jonathan Altman, 1961

others because the cultural work in San Francisco didn't advance their commercial careers.

The exhausted company called for company meetings. Jules handled the dispute between the actors and the management personally and smoothed things out. When Equity came in with Ford (United Auto Workers and the Automotive Industry), Irving publicly maintained that there was no separation between the company and the management. People began to drop out and disappear faster than usual.

While working in the Actors Workshop as an assistant director, I also hustled up a small group called the R. G. Davis Mime Troupe.* We worked in my studio on Brady Street, a short street of slum houses tucked around light industry. Working three hours a day, five days a week, we created mimes from ideas I had in my head. We unveiled our results on October 29, 1959, at the San Francisco Art Institute with "Games—3 Sets" and two other numbers, plus a short talk on the subject of mime.

Our small company, comprised of people from the Actors Workshop and students from my private classes, created enough material to perform an hour-long show. We performed so rarely that

---

* During rehearsals for the third commedia, *Ruzzante's Maneuvers*, we changed our name. "R. G. Davis Mime Troupe" was too close to the concept of a dance troupe where the star dancer is usually choreographer and director. I couldn't see my name on a banner above the commedia stage. Mime stayed in the title because it was closer to the dance troupes yet apart from the regional theatres. We were to travel light and move around—thus, Troupe. San Francisco, naturally. Our stationery came out at the same time and it, too, signified our direction. Coming out of the jaw and claws of a griffin (chosen by Pat Lofthouse from the works of Jacques Callot), we placed the motto: "Engagement, Commitment & Fresh Air."

new material was difficult to develop—hardly anyone had seen the old material. Performing once a month at special events could not provide the necessary stimulus for growth. We needed somewhere to perform regularly.

The Actors Workshop presented two different productions each week at the Encore. They would strike one on Thursday night and strike the second on Sunday evening. I asked if we could present a free 11:00 P.M. mime show on Sunday (at no cost to the Workshop) just to have a chance to use the stage. The Encore was dedicated to experimentation and new talent, so we were on.

The 11th Hour Mime Show opened on December 11, 1960. It was the avant-garde event of the season. We didn't have much competition; who else was doing free mime shows at 11:00 P.M.? Donations were slim; none of us knew how to beg in those days. A hundred twenty people gave a big seventeen dollars, about fifty cents a worker. (The program appears on the facing page.)

We began to develop techniques. We would begin each show with some kind of startling shocker to dispel the coldness of the basement, the "artistic" atmosphere and the distance between the audience and the performer. Our most effective opener had the golden Encore drape slowly raised about three feet up allowing the audience to see just our legs, eight of us standing, ready for action. Then it would drop and you'd hear mumblings backstage: "stupid shit . . ." It would rise again with great difficulty and reveal the eight with backs to the audience. The entire group would then turn in unison with exquisite fluidity, à la Etienne Decroux, and lower their arms to their sides. Upon reaching this graceful symmetric position facing the audience, they

THE ACTORS' WORKSHOP
PRESENTS THE

R. G. Davis Mime Troupe
IN THE

11TH HOUR MIME SHOW

Each Sunday evening from 11 PM to Midnight the
program will consist of numbers from the repertoire
of the troupe. The program will change from week
to week as new numbers are created.

the troupe

Norma Leistiko
Robert Doyle
Susan Darby
William Raymond
Ruth Breuer
David O'Neill
Barbara Melandry
R. G. Davis

Pianist : Martha Karge
Lighting : Judith Harris Wolcott
Stage Manager : Yvette Nachmias
Costumes : Judy Collins
Poster Design : Robert LaVigne

When Jacques Copeau, one of the great innovators of the modern theatre,
resigned from the Comedie Francaise, he went literally to the country, to go
back to the soil of his art. He formed a young troupe, trained in all the instruments of the art of acting, among them Mime. The art of Mime might even
be considered the soil of the art of acting. It is made of muscle, and gesture,
and rhythm and motion, and may give birth by the devious route of internal
action to the unexpected Word.

Mime has not yet found its way in any significant fashion into modern
American drama. But we trust it will in time. As practiced by the R.G. Davis
Mime Troupe it retains, even when well-formed, a connection with its spon-
taneous and improvisational sources. It is young in spirit, and truly experimental. The people in the troupe have trained together, and the work you
will be seeing - though prepared for an audience is an original account of
what they have done together.

This special event is part of The Workshop's expanded activities under
the new Ford program. Actually, the task of completely matching the funds
for the current year of the grant is still underway. And though we have made
no charge for the "11th Hour Mime Show", we would appreciate any contribution you'd care to make, however small.

Jules Irving
Herbert Blau

An early program at the Encore Theater, 1960

would scream wildly. Blackout.

Later, when critics wrote of the "Mime Troupe's shock effects," I thought back to those days when we actually did try to shock people. It was difficult. We developed a return audience and couldn't use the same gimmick twice. We spent a lot of time inventing.

The work we were doing on classical, yet improvised, mimes and the production of *Endgame* with the Actors Workshop led us naturally into our next troupe performance, Beckett's *Act Without Words II*. Beckett's agnostic endlessness is the theme in this two-sack mime. Two characters, A and B, each in his own grey sack, alternate in waking, getting out of the sack, dressing, lifting the other sack and moving it two feet to the left, then undressing and retiring into his sack once again. Two different kinds of life are described, the lethargic thinker and the frenetic compulsive, each achieving the same results: sack moved two feet to the left. Two paths, same end.

This mime had no excess, nothing gratuitous, nothing that wasn't calculated to impart Beckett's ideas. What I learned in Paris training with Etienne Decroux and, eventually, from Beckett, was the necessity of scraping down. Decroux started from "nothing in the hands, nothing in the pockets." Beckett ended with "discard." His plays, since *Endgame*, have been a diminution of paraphernalia. All very un-American in this consumer environment and, therefore, difficult to teach actors who have grown up with the trivia of props, lights and costumes.

Painters at the San Francisco Art Institute had been helping us with our eleventh hour shows and Judy Collins suggested that we do a "happening" with them. Robert Hudson was the main contributor of material. He would give us an object or a prop and we would improvise with it. His sculptured and found pieces were metal frames, wire wheels, tractor tires, a stuffed bed with arms and legs, dolls, balloons, etc. We experimented in our studio then brought the results to the Encore for viewing. Everything was painted white or black, no other color was allowed except our blood-red mouths. Rehearsals began after Workshop shows, around 11:00 P.M. and continued until four in the morning.

The origins of improvisation as a modern technique have their roots in the social work of Viola Spolin in a welfare house in Chicago. She invented and catalogued exercise/entertainments for her welfare clients. As a technique it is a fine experimental and socially productive tool, the major emphasis being on individual participation in a group. The technique's value lies in providing participation with little preparation, instant experience, and in the probability of breaking mind logjams. The elevation of participatory fun to theatrical experience became improvisational theatre. The paradox of improvisation in the performing world is that there is hardly any such thing. Jazz musicians rehearse their riffs, just as theatre performers rehearse their bits and gags. During the performance, depending upon intuition or feel, these riffs or bits and gags are played out.

The approach used to create an improvisational scene is neither difficult nor mysterious. The instructor or director chooses a situation; the actors take on characters and decide the who, what, when, where and why of the situation; they then begin to talk to each other or "improvise." To achieve the full benefit of improvisational skitmaking, certain conditions are important. Obstacles are minimized; conflicts are few; people work together, allowing for easy flow of dialogue and action. In the professional theatre the director calls the shots and selects portions of the improv to keep or rework. After the first improvisation the same pattern, or rehearsal, takes place as in any ordinary play production.

In this work, Event I, and later in Events II and III, the approach was like jamming, but jamming when the logs were clogged up. We tried new impressions, un-completed images, ideas and intuitive notions when the creative spirit was locked into a conventional form and content. Thus, by exploring half-realized ideas, we opened the form to investigation without worrying about the content, purpose or message. The audience was guinea pig and, hopefully, helped us re-align whatever we did to mean something or at least to understand our process.

We used the whole theatre. In the lobby, there was a long, elaborate chalk talk given by filmmaker Carl Linder, a master of academic doubletalk. His conversation was repeated on tape to the audience as they descended the staircase to the theatre. The audience had to walk across the stage through a group of musicians to get to their seats. Artist Wally Hedrick put up a sound and light machine so that every time a loud sound blared it would ignite a light.

Dialogue was worked around a scenario that resulted from the improvisation with the props. Four people on the stuffed bed writhed and oozed over each other as they conversed about laundry as if they were in a laundromat. The Giacommetti frame-like structure was used by a white figure, while black and white tires and wire wheels were rolled across the stage. We were experimenting off the printed page with concrete visual images.

At the end of each show, we allowed writer and director Lee Breuer to introduce a completely new element. One night, four of us were on stage playing football with dolls' heads and sundry props when we heard a great crashing come from the men's john just off the main seating area. The crashing continued while we marked time kicking the dolls' heads around. It got louder and louder and then, suddenly, the door of the men's room slammed open and out came Bill Raymond dressed in white longjohns with a white hood, crashing and crashing. He had four ashcan covers tied around his ankles. The abominable crash-ashcan man stepped high, crashed around on the main floor and headed for us on the stage. We had to deal with him. He won.

The climax of every show was a dry-ice smokescreen laid down on the entire stage. I pedaled a tricycle to the center, dragging an ashcan full of dry ice and water. The smoke spewed out over the entire space, three-feet thick. Then, all ten performers moved in slow motion through the fog and froze as the show ended.

This playing around, taking images and working them over, always means an enormous struggle; each moment has to be explored. Why discarded? Why kept? As the decisions were made the difficulties in making the next choice increased, in that we had accumulated a particular set of conditions. In creative limbo, intuition is not enough, and certainly not in a collective production. No one could do whatever came to him or her without affecting ten other people who had to absorb or reject the input. Simplistic notions about intuition and improvisation were constantly questioned.

Toward the end of the run (one show per night for nine weeks), I began to understand the storm.

A
W

PRESENTS

11ᵀᴴ HOUR
MIME
SHOW

R.G. DAVIS
MIME TROUPE

SUNDAYS, 11 P.M. TO MIDNIGHT
ENCORE THEATRE
430 MASON STREET

WEEKLY FROM DECEMBER 11

✳ AN ACTORS WORKSHOP PUBLIC EVENT

Event I, Encore Theater, 1961

It was the madness of the early sixties on display. The entire show was never comprehensible to any one person since, operating on many levels with simultaneous events, the event was as complicated as the political and social realities we all felt. Frightened by instant atomic destruction we had accomplished a madman show for insane people who were struggling to present all of the world in one hour.

In 1962 Morton Subotnick and Ramon Sender acquired a Victorian house on Jones Street and offered a large room with sliding doors for theatrical happenings: poetry readings, plays, events, music concerts, environments for the Tape Music Center. I saw many of the events and learned to understand electronic music. One performance of a Robert Duncan play stuck in my mind and was to become the basis of Event II.

During the performance of the Duncan play an actor went blank and completely forgot his lines. The whole audience held tight as he changed from agonizing red to yellow peril to death white. He stammered, we did too; he choked, we did too; he held on, we did too; and WHOOSH, he remembered and continued the scene. The actor hadn't intended to give us the most interesting moment in the play but his accident, like other accidents I had seen in legitimate theatre, was real and cut through the conventions. Sabotnick and Sender asked me if I would take on an evening and create a theatrical event. I agreed, with this particular "mistake" in mind.

Event II, the first non-Workshop exploration, was an original piece designed and created by the performers. Looking back, it was sandbox time—still playing with the conventions and the techniques of bourgeois theatre. It was more a purgative than a creation. One friend thought it had

some charm and the reviewer from the *San Francisco Examiner* wrote a favorable column but did not submit his copy because he thought we'd have been busted for nudity on stage in 1962. I designed the show to make mistakes and to regurgitate everything. These motives do not always create the most interesting effects. There are some things that have not been done on stage that might as well not be done.

When the sliding doors of the main room opened on Event II, they revealed a mirrored closet with Judy Rosenberg and me imitating each other's movements (borrowed from Joe Chaikin's Open Theatre exercises). Judy and I had worked together in *Galileo* at the Workshop and this piece was built from the rapport and trust we had developed. The first time the doors opened, we were in full cover, moving mirror-like. The doors closed, opened again and we appeared in half-cover—bottoms, no tops. The doors closed and opened again to show us with no cover, painted bottoms, black over the crotch.

While we were inside the mirrored closet, Danny McDermott, in his first big role for the Mime Troupe, intoned all those things we hardly ever admit about stool and vomit, the unspoken but everyday functions of life.

> You know when you're just getting up from the toilet you look back at the shit floating, and wonder if the big pieces are full of corn or not, and see the little balls float. And the last drop flips onto your leg and you flush, noticing the toilet paper with the brown goo still on it. There's a little left on your hands, so you wash, but the soap misses and your thumb stinks when you pick your nose . . .

He usually improvised it. It was like verbal Zap comics, spoken as we performed beautiful moving images in the closet.

We placed the audience up against the walls on boxes of varying heights, so that they had to look down on the action, and we covered the whole room with a black cloth which had head holes cut out of it. I hoped the audience would fiddle around under there and get sleazy. Black cloth with heads sticking out, watching, literally united the audience, but rather than increasing contact, it merely made things cozy.

We were playing around with the items of boredom and mistakes. A recorded tape played selected important quotes, while some gross opposite took visual focus. Throughout the entire event, Ruth Breuer and Susan Darby, expert improvisationists, pushed a huge canvas and wooden pyramid constructed by Bob Hudson and Bill Wiley from the back of the room to the front. I never completely knew what they did, since I spent my time in the mirrored black silk box playing with Judy.

We had taken our clothes off in public, at last exposing ourselves, struggling to break with the commercial naturalism of regional theatres. Yet we had only presented the simple ironies of shit and beauty, rationality and irrationality, the poetic and the mundane, and fortunately we couldn't and didn't elevate our undressing to a theatrical style.

The small unstructured Events (I and II) and *Plastic Haircut*, a film I made with Hudson, Wiley and Robert Nelson, broke my head open to new visions. They served as a purge of old misconceptions and my interest turned toward more complicated modes of creativity. However, I had yet to rid myself of the pretensions of naturalistic theatre while integrating mimetic expertise. The first impulse upon getting on stage is manifested through naturalistic details. We walk on with our-

selves and "act." The same is true in movement. The first thoughts and gestures come easily in pantomime but when one wishes to interpret, to analyze, to inform rather than to mirror nature, naturalism is only the first step.

As we tried to join artistic and political influences, we floated from indoor theatre to outdoor theatre. The gusto of the outdoor performances gave our productions added energy and extravagance when the winter rainy season forced us indoors. We opened our indoor theatre on the ninety-sixth anniversary of the first performance of *Ubu Roi*, which we retitled *Ubu King*, on December 10, 1963.

The tension in the play as a result of my direction was the injection of social implications into avant-garde drama. As a new left agitator, my own politics were unprogrammatic but left. In addition, I related to a play in print as an abstraction, mere words on a page, which only actors in motion would make concrete. Although we created an interesting production and it was a good choice for the Mime Troupe, *Ubu Roi* is not a magnificent play. It holds a particular niche in French literary tradition: the first play with shit (*merde*), it stands as a pyramid (or pile of dung) in the anal-erotic desert of aesthetics.

In his notes on the play, Alfred Jarry calls for placards, one man representing an army and other elements in what we now understand as epic drama. Drawing from old English theatre and from puppet plays (*guignols*), he voided the tradition of legitimate nineteenth century drama. In 1896 the puck and dash of evil in *Ubu* was rather dynamic, but in the context of mid-twentieth century imperialism, it pales. Like Grand Guignol (ca. 1910-1940) a French super-real theatrical form, where "real" blood flowed from stabbings or garrotings and eyeballs popped out of heads, and which closed down after World War II's Auschwitz and Buchenwald, *Ubu Roi* lost its impact in the shadow of genocidal bombing patterns in Vietnam.

The launching of the new theatre with the presentation of this play was not meant to be a revival of Dada; rather, the cross currents of art and political activity appeared to join. We had neither a tight program from the new left, nor a new direction for art.

HANDOUT
Written by Milt Savage

This is the brink!
  ZAPP!
    THIS is the crisis.
      ZAPP!
        Over the edge!
  ZAPP!
    Theater is guerrilla war!
      ZAPP!
        Now, a desperate leap!
          ZAPP!
zeep,
  so who cares?
      ZAPP!
        War is risk.
          ZAPP!
            War is hell.
              zip,
                So what?
Every performance a night raid!
  ZAPP!
    Attack!
      ZAPP!
        Surprise!
          ZAPP!
Engage!
  ZAPP!

Run!
  ZAPP!
zoup,
    you're kidding?
      ZAPP!
        You're dead.

ATTENTION:
  Fellow citizens! We are all up to our chins in it. The fall season will open with Alfred Jarry's play, *Ubu Roi.*

  A state of siege exists! All members of the Ensemble share the income, classes, work and dangers. Whose side are you on? No tickets! Donations at the door. We can't carry garbage. Minimum production costs. People, not machines. Blood, not money. Sweat, not public relations. Professionals only: less than that, and we don't survive.

  A Kabuki actor starts at five, a Balinese dancer at six. In France, Jean Vilar's T.N.P. is completely booked by 2,800 factory workers, five times a year. Antonin Artaud's first theater was called, "Theater Alfred Jarry." Total theater is total risk. Over the edge!

There are so many variables in the theatre, so many elements to piece together, that a smooth running performance is unique. If the show is good, the lights don't work; if the reviewers and audience are receptive, the actors forget how to act; if the performers are riding along high together, the house is empty and in non-commercial theatre, where the actors take risks in performances (new styles, etc.), the possibility of failure is constant. The cast of fourteen played their fifty roles and worked furiously during the show to reach the "big names" in the San Francisco audience. Amateur groups are fantastic when it comes to hysterical possibilities. It was a smash opening, a rare moment in the theatre. The

Mere et Pere, *Ubu King*, 1963

The whole Polish Army, *Ubu King*, 1963

second night was typical—a bring-down. Amateurs (and sometimes pros) can't get it up for the second time around. As a big-time manager, I mistakenly invited the critics to the second night. Both Stanley Eichelbaum of the *Examiner* and Paine Knickerbocker of the *Chronicle* saw a dull show, but we offended them even before the boredom set in. They panned it with such obvious irritation that Morton Subotnick said, "If you were in a reasonably cultured country, those reviews would bring droves of people to the theatre." In San Francisco, it was different, but one friend understood, though his defensive claims of a full house were more rhetorical than actual:

December 15, 1965

Letter to the Editors
San Francisco Chronicle

Dear Editor:

Paine Knickerbocker's nose-holding reaction to the SF Mime Troupe's "Ubu King" has turned out to be an effective piece of criticism. The house has been full ever since. No one suspected Knickerbocker had such a large following among the avant-garde. If he pans some show, they're sure to go.

Too bad he left halfway thru the play and obviously didn't bother to read it before coughing up such a superficial condemnation. We expect more of a drama critic than the stock reactions of a Lucius Beebe or a slurban matron faced with a long-haired poet at a cocktail party.

Even if the plot wanders too much thru too many scenes, even if the play has an over-inflated underground reputation that needs puncturing, Ron Davis's direction introduced brilliant devices to overcome the script's worse faults. And the costume of Mother Ubu (to whose "foot-long" breasts Knickerbocker gloomily objected) was a marvelous invention, with the breasts tied by cords to the wrists, so that in whatever direction Mother Ubu gestured, the breasts symbolically pointed.

And also completely lost on Knickerbocker was Davis's Brechtian interpretation of the whole farce, making Mother Ubu into Mother Courage, and thus up-dating this old surrealist war-horse as a modern burlesque of all revolution, dictators, and violence. In this semi-civilized country where we still shoot people we don't agree with, it would be real nice if some newspaper critics got the point. The play would undoubtedly flop in Dallas.

Sincerely,
Lawrence Ferlinghetti

This period made up of choices, not always understood, influenced our future activity. In rejecting the bourgeois theatre, little theatre, regional theatre and the communist old left, we lifted ourselves out of the stagnation of the fifties. Unencumbered by party, program or theory we practiced escaping from the bourgeois doldrums. Inevitably, we drifted toward an alternative culture or a culture parallel to the powerful middle class. At points in the S.F. Mime Troupe's history, we actually crossed the divide between us and them—with commedia in the parks, with minstrel shows on stage and with *L'Amant Militaire* on tour. But we could only puncture, not take over; and, in some cases, not even take advantage of our successful insulting assaults.

Abandoned church Studio Theater, Capp Street, 1964

Chorizos, Duboce Park, San Francisco, 1964

2

COMMEDIA DELL'ARTE

Why commedia? The intrinsic nature of commedia dell'arte is its working-class viewpoint. Its origins are the alleys and corners of the marketplace. The Italian street hustler in the 1500s with an instrument turned medicine man, added a singer, picked up a few *jongeleurs*, jumped onto a platform of barrels covered with boards in the piazza and commedia became a recognizable entity (and a way to make a living). It pleased its audience by farting and belching at the stuffier stuffed classes. Commedia did not long remain a folk art. Once elevated to the stage it was taken notice of by the patrons of the art, who could view the marketplace from their elevated rooms. Whole companies were supported as every aristocracy since and before had hired the local yokels to clown for the court. Steady employment by the Duke of Mantua, or his like in France or Spain, was not to be refused by the socially mobile actor-beggars who were just one step above their brother beggars of the streets.

The scenario arranged by the lead actor or director loosely united the individual characters. Each performer played one role for life. He learned closing and opening lines, poetry and physical tricks, *lazzi* and *burla* (particular business, solo or duo). Seven or eight performers followed the scenario as best they could, performing on a platform with a back curtain for easy entrance and exit. Each exaggerated type (doctor, servant, lover, pedant, merchant, gambler or concubine) wore colorful and well-defined costumes and all characters, except the women and the male lover, wore masks.

During the early rehearsals of *The Dowry*, we were fortunate in meeting Carlo Mazzone, a mime from the Lecoq School. He had played Brighella under Giorgio Strehler at the Piccolo and possessed eight leather commedia masks made by Amleto Sartori. Mazzone showed the masks in operation and told us some of their history. The mask-making skill had disappeared with the Renaissance Venetians but Sartori unearthed the process and created these magnificent examples. Each mask, a fine sculpture, fixed the image of a face and needed only a turn of the body to make it come alive. The process of molding the leather to a wooden form was a Sartori family secret but the real genius was the characteristic sculptured expression. Sartori had carved useful props—Pantalone's nose was hooked and his eyes properly almond-shaped; Arlecchino, with eyes like small dots, had a strained forehead with nothing behind it; Brighella's perpetual wiseguy grin had room for shifty eyes; etc. We had our photographer friend Nata Piaskowski take meticulous pictures of the masks and had people copy them. Our papier-maché and cheesecloth imitations were often too heavy and the contours not sharp enough. Mazzone left us with a sense of some impossible magic about the masks. In the seven years of playing commedias, we found only one artist, Francesca Green, an Art Institute graduate and commercial designer, who could make a few usable masks. In 1968 I realized that there was a simpler method and sent a letter with a check to Sartori.

Commedia actors performed their memorized lines, jokes, ad libs and physical business much like traditional jazz, introducing current material as they could. The actor as performer/author kept the early commedia alive; but as commedia lost its social intelligence, writers came to the rescue. Molière and Goldoni, using original commedia scenarios, invested the plots with reason and rational dialogue.

We went to work on commedia dell'arte as we had on the Events—by jumping in and splashing around. We plowed through all the books, Italian, French and English. We improvised from old scenarios and plays by Molière and Goldoni; wrote our own scenes; tried different characters. We discovered that the stereotypical characters operated both as an escape valve for irritation and as an integrating force. To the liberal, they often appear to show prejudice. However, if you dig the people and the contradictions, the stereotypes are more accurate in describing social conditions than bland generalities. We eventually learned in commedia, and later in the Minstrel Show, how to make stereotypes carry the burden of social satire.

We worked our asses off researching, stealing, gleaning and improvising. When we couldn't find what we wanted, we wrote it ourselves. Bill Raymond and Ruth Breuer wrote their own scene. Joe Bellan and I worked on one scene from Molière's *Scapin* for months and put about two hundred jokes into one eight-minute sequence. Eventually, we had to slow it down so that the audience could stay with us. Bill Raymond, our Pantalone, moved like a dream. He could stand on one leg and wiggle all limbs in different directions at the same time. He was one of the few Pantalones we had who ever had the duck-like sense of the part. Unfortunately, Raymond's mind was slow and he couldn't figure out what to say when we improvised dialogue around him. However, he put his fault to good use: he would simply stare out front, dumb, and his mask held the tension. It was perfect. Ruth Breuer, who had flapped around various stages and in various parts, broke through her repressive acting training and flitted across the stage as a beautiful servant girl. Mazzone told us that most characters kept high off the ground, especially the servant types like Franchescina. Ruth played the whole show half-toe. Commedia didn't sit, it floated.

We kept our scenes and spirit of commedia focused around the 1600s and related to Jacques Callot images. Although few could move like the drawings of Callot, his spirit was what I wanted—rough, gutsy, and dynamic. The second stage was performing for an audience. In comedy the audience is master. If your joke works, they laugh; if it doesn't, they don't. A simple formula that anyone can live by.

In our commedia the performer had to be totally involved. There was no open fourth wall; in fact, there were no walls. Therefore, the performer had to keep his thoughts way ahead of the action. This commedia was "Brechtian" in that the stage play was a game. We posited that all action on the platform was fake, masked, indicated, enlarged show biz, while everything off stage was real. On stage we were totally committed to the dialogue, *lazzi*, pantomimic or mimetic play and could sustain the fakery of the

Commedia poster, *The Dowry*, 1962

Dottore and Pantalone, *The Dowry*, 1962

onstage commitment by admitting the reality of off stage. After exiting behind the drop an actor stepped off the platform, took off his mask and out of character walked around to the side to watch the other actors.

The Dowry opened at the Encore but when that theatre dried up as a source of "new work," we went off to perform at the Spaghetti Factory, a cabaret in North Beach, on Thursday evenings. We worked through the winter rains polishing and learning the show so well that real honest-to-goodness improvisation actually took place. After a few months inside, we finally got our chance to perform in the open air as commedia had done three hundred years before.

Our first outdoor performance, May 1962, was in Golden Gate Park. The whole thing was a whirl of excitement and I can only remember one important event. Yvette Nachmias, who had been struggling with her character—a matchmaker—in a scene we had lifted from *Scapin*, came off stage and yelled at me, "The reason for the large movements and gestures is because they performed outside." That's what it said in the books; that's what we based our exaggerated movements on; yet, inside in the beer hall and the small theatre it was not always evident. Once outside, theory and reality crashed together into a screaming joyous perception.

We played our second performance in Washington Square Park in North Beach. We set up our twelve-foot by twelve-foot wooden stage on the grass and three hundred old Italians stood with hands folded behind their backs, half-understanding what we were doing. They stood the whole hour, talking amongst themselves and watching. The names of the characters—Pantalone, Dottore, Silvio, Flaminia—meant something to them. Some

of the old country had come to the park which they sunned and talked in. It was their heritage we were throwing up on the stage.

The social content and text of *The Dowry* were minimally important; audiences returned to see the frenzied interaction of characters. It was during the constant reworking of the scenario that we came upon an important innovation. In a scene taken from Molière's *Scapin* my Brighella and Joe Bellan's Dottore worked out physical business that contradicted the lines. We performed pantomime activities which were in opposition to the text but which continued the intent of the scene. Brighella, servant to Silvio, tries to get money from Dottore. Brighella claims that Dottore's son, Silvio, has been abducted by the Turks and must be ransomed.

Dottore: Now, what's this about my son Silvio?
Brighella: Oh, I met him a little while ago, terribly upset by the break-up of the marriage. So, in order to console him, I took him down by the docks and there we saw a wonderful Turkish galley, and up steps a young Turk, and he invites us aboard and shows us the greatest hospitality. And he sits us down to a meal—a meal full of antipasto, pasta, pasta, pasta, pasta *[At this point, Brighella begins slapping his right hand over his left as if to keep a rhythm and also like sharpening a razor on a strop. Dottore follows the rhythm and nods with the beat.]* pasta, pasta, pasta, tortellini . . .
Dottore: Ahh tortellini . . .
Brighella: *[now full-scale sharpening razor]* Then we had white wine and small demitasse black coffee *[now pantomimic: soaping up Dottore's face for shave]* and some wonderful cigars—the long black ones, you know. *[now shaving his face with pantomimic razor]*
Dottore: Any more wine? *[head back—accepts shave]*
Brighella: *[while shaving]* Oh yes, then we had some more red wine, more cigars, chocolate crackers, more pasta . . .

Fracischina.   Gian Farina.

Scaramucia.   Fricasso.

Commedia figures, seventeenth century

Dottore: [waking up abruptly, hits Brighella's hands away] So what harm did this do you?

Brighella: [mock tragedy] Ahh, while we were eating this meal, the boat pulled out of the dock and once we were on the sea he dumps me into a skiff and sends me to you to say that if you don't give him five hundred guineas he'll ship your son off to Algiers.

Dottore: Carrrumbaaaa!!!

The above is a *lazzi*, a set routine in which two actors act upon each other through dialogue and activities to further the plot and illustrate their characters' (masks') characteristics. A *lazzi* is like a riff of jazz and can be used from show to show. We used *lazzi* of getting money, of seduction, of fear, of jealousy, etc., not as individual stage tricks, but rather *as a means to advance the scenario* and delineate attitudes of stock characters.

In Etienne Decroux's researches, just as with Kabuki theatre, one sees a visual presentation of an activity or an emotion. Both have analyzed and dissected, then reassembled and created a clear activity (Decroux) or a precise emotion (Kabuki). Decroux tends to idealize the activity and Kabuki freezes the emotion into an ideogram. Our discoveries in *The Dowry* were not pure delineation of activity nor pure ideogram. Rather, by manifesting the inner con game with visual illustration (from mime to pantomime) we clarified the objective of the con man, thereby combining the precise activity of Decroux and the image-making of Kabuki.

By the time we opened *Tartuffe* in 1964, we had created our own theatre out of an abandoned church. The rent on the theatre in the Mission District was eighty-five dollars a month and we did not have to worry about packing them in. Nevertheless, after a month of performing four nights a week, we decided to perform only when the audience outnumbered the cast. Outdoor performances in the parks relied on a ready crowd and drumming up trade was easy. In the Mission, tucked away on a side street, we had to advertise and stir up publicity. Not always successful, we struggled through a season of "little theatre" hoping word of mouth, a "great show," luck and tenacity would increase our audience.

From the first commedia our opening format was designed to help the performers warm up in front of an audience and let the audience in on the "secrets" of backstage.

We would set up the stage, get into costume and makeup (or masks), play music, loose and easy, gather into a circle and do warm-up physical exercises while singing songs. At first, the songs were from an Archive record of the Central Middle Ages, often simple rounds, Christmas tunes, and eventually, tunes from Wobblies and political songs from Italy, Mexico and even some we wrote. When inside we sang behind the drop or "off stage" in the dressing room. In the park, we sang and played to one side of the stage. By 1966-67 the singing and playing (tambourine, recorder, drum, castanets, hand clapping) were interesting and the audience usually joined in. We opened our circle and taught a three-part round, like "Scotland's Burning," but with new words:

L.A.'s burning, L.A.'s burning, Watts out,
Watts out. Fire, fire, fire, fire.
Pour on money [or, Pay your taxes]*

We learned to work with audiences before the show. By 1967 we knew it was a necessity when

Cap. Esgangarato.   Cap. Cocodrillo

Commedia figures, seventeenth century

---

* Another song of this genre, sung to the tune of "Alouette," goes like this: "Alioto, Mayor Mafioso, ..."

Setting up the stage, *Tartuffe*, Big Sur, 1964

performing indoors to create a less suspicious relationship between "us" and "them." After the
group singing and physical warm-up, the performers began a Renaissance melody (see example): recorder first, followed in succession by
other instruments and completed with voices. At
the height of the tune, we paraded toward the
stage. Once behind the curtain we stepped onto
the platform, then leaped into view in front of
the curtain, bowed to the audience, circled on he
platform and as the cast exited, one person spun

out from the group and began the introductions.

Signor, Signora, Signorina!
Madame, Monsieur, et Mademoiselle!
Ladies and Gentlemen . . .
Il troupo di Mimo di San Francisco
Presents for your appreciation this afternoon
An adaptation of Molière's great play by Richard
Sassoon
Directed by Nina Serrano Landau and R. G. Davis
An adaptation called . . . TARTUFFE!

Despite political analysis or intellectual mes-

Tartuffe, Civic Center, San Francisco, 1964

sage, the job, especially in commedia, is always to "get to them." In our "openings" we ad-libbed good and bad jokes, cornball and marvelous, then introduced each individual character with some appropriate wisecrack. The openings took us much time to develop and never were finished until the last moment. We wanted the audience to see and learn about the characters prior to the play (exposition) and we also wanted to get used to each other on stage.

Commedia characters are not simply assumed by an actor; they are characters with a history and a mask. The mask is not only the papier-maché or leather object one puts on one's face, but also the stereotypical gestures, attitudes and individual pieces of business. Mariane, the young daughter and lover in the Orgon Family, was a traditional "mask" placed in the more developed context of Molière's play. Young, skittish, quick-tempered, she is a jealous lover who diddles with her emotions. Silvio, her lover (the son of Dottore), the male counterpart of the ingenue, is romantic, brash, heroic and hysterically incompetent. These *innamoratos* attempt suicide, revenge or separation but always return to the same place—love.

In a highly stylized play, the actor usually has one task—to play the character. In our adaptations we gave our actors three jobs: play yourself, play the character, play an Italian who was a commedia performer. The person was to act himself while reading the script, simply to understand the situation, the conditions, the motives of the character and the point of the play. This is then simple Stanislavsky technique where actions and objectives are discovered without trying to perform the text.

The second layer of refinement or the development of the mask requires physical characteristics such as a duck walk for Pantalone; a swinging bravado for the lover; snap, crackle and suspicious looks for Brighella. And accents—French (for lovers), Italian (Dottore and servants), or Jewish and Mexican with their concurrent gestures. The personal attributes of the actor were changed or extended to create the mask.

The third level—historical imitation of Italian actors—required some study of commedia dell'arte and preparation that would produce a rich stage characterization. Each modern actor was to find his/her Italian counterpart. Francesco Andreini played Capitano Spavento (ca. 1600); Guiseppe Biancolelli as Dottore; Isabella Andreini as first lady; Tomasso Fortunati played Brighella; Domenico Biancolelli as Arlecchino.

These levels of reality, one concrete (self) and the other two assumed (mask and Italian actor), allowed for constant shifting of characterization and play. When the actor lost the character's believability or failed to make the audience laugh,

he could change to the Italian role and say, "Well, I tried thata one, no?" Or when a dog walked across the stage, the performer could break character as Italian actor and comment from his own vantage point or if he was skilled enough he might stay inside the mask (role) and deal with the intrusion as the character. The ad lib (improvisational wisecrack) was the oil of transition.

Why go through this elaborate structure? In the twentieth century all three levels made up only an approximation of the sixteenth-century form called commedia dell'arte. There was no way of deluding the audience or creating an illusion that we were really commedia dell'arte performers just in from the Duke of Mantua's palace.

Directors in academic theatre usually emphasize the literary style of their productions. Since I had not spent years and years being impressed by the grandness of language, I viewed the text as only material for mime. I had always approached the actual performance as more relevant than the text. The existential reality of a performer in front of an audience required that something happen—even if the text could not do it. In 1964 we put our trust in the content, and our adapter, Richard Sassoon, would not let us discard the text of *Tartuffe* for some silly trick. He and Nina Landau were strong enough to impress our work with discipline.

We had, with the vibrance of commedia, attracted people to the company but more often the excited overworked themselves and left. Fortunately, the cast was composed of four old timers (those with some experience) and three new, highly talented actors. We had promised to perform the first preview of *Tartuffe* for the San Francisco New School. We were only able to finish the first half; nevertheless, our first per-

Rushing around before the show, *Chorizos*, 1964

formance was a night of magic! The first half ended with a song which illustrated our multiple-image style and our new political consciousness. Using a modern tune (see example) Tartuffe sang the chorus and spoke the verse as three female cast members stood off stage echoing the chorus in puppet-like frozen poses.

Chorus [3] & Tartuffe [sung]:
　Evern night and every morning
　Some to misery are born.
　Every night and every morning
　Some to misery are born.

Tartuffe [spoken]:
　Not from any lack of fortune
　Nor of features fine and clear
　It is something deep in nature
　That through ages perseveres.

Chorus [3]: [repeat last two lines]
Tartuffe [sung]:
　Some possess the need to punish
　'Tis virtue and needs no excuse
　Others thrive on pure misfortune
　To torture them is no abuse.

COMMEDIA THEME

for recorder, percussion, and la la

The opening and closing theme of most commedias
From a minstrel tune of central Europe, thirteenth-fourteenth centuries

Tartuffe [spoken]:
> Laws are made for men to live by
> Morals make us all believe
> But to speak of good or evil
> Is a mask that does deceive.

Tartuffe [sung]:
> For men concoct the wildest fancies
> To warm their lonely beds at night
> 'Til at length their dreams deceive them

Chorus [3]:
> Oft repeating, they believe them
> Oft repeating, they believe them.

[Lyrics, Saul Landau]

We believed in *Tartuffe* enough to want to tour and embarked on a plan of renting semi-professional locations rather than staying in our little abandoned church or moving to a larger building. Traditionally, the next step would have been to rent a fixed space and build up a large stock of flats. Rather than that, we wanted to go to the people, to expand our own neighborhood and to make contact with the rest of the country. We discovered that touring was not so easy. At first we did not have a stage manager. The actors set up the stage, the lights, the costumes, the props and then performed he show. On our first venture out of town with *Tartuffe*, the conditions were such that we had to prop the stage up five feet off the ground. Half the cast became fixed with acrophobia and the other daredevils frightened the shit out of the audience. By late '64, we expanded to include qualified technical help, designers, writers and composers. We transcended the "little theatre" circle and became involved through our art with he growing Bay Area radical movement.

The years 1964-65 for the San Francisco Mime Troupe were spent creating our own material and rehearsing at a leisurely pace. I did not burden myself with a "season." We had no official business manager, nor "organization." We had abandoned, after a six-month trial, the hope of bringing an audience to the Latin American ghetto in the Mission. We never had any Latinos come through the doors. Our relations with the community were more apparent at the Donut shop on the corner of 20th and Mission than on the stage in the abandoned church.

My friendship with Saul and Nina Landau produced a dream of a white elephant and a concrete black extravaganza. I had played a small role in a radio play which Nina directed; Saul wrote a scenario for a commedia the troupe worked on; Nina co-directed *Tartuffe;* Saul wrote the song and assisted with production business for the troupe. I assisted with the San Francisco New School and arranged some bookings for the San Francisco Opposition, a "pinko" front whose motto was, "Opposed to everything." The San Francisco Opposition invited speakers to San Francisco. Susan Sontag, Paul Baran, Paul Sweezy, Clancy Segal, and Marc Schleiffer were presented at the ILWU Hall or at our own studio. The *coup de frappé* was "I. F. Stone at the Palace."

A more elaborate scheme developed when Bob Nelson and Saul put together a midnight movie series on Friday and Saturday nights in our abandoned church. With Nelson's advice and with help from our Mimers, who sang, took tickets, and gave away free wine, Landau got into the movies by creating a successful underground midnight series that eventually brought the fire department to condemn our Capp Street Church.

Since our labors crossed, we decided to go big time and find a place to house both the Mime Troupe and the San Francisco New School. We

II

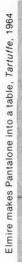

Elmire makes Pantalone into a table, *Tartuffe*, 1964

V

VI

III

IV

VII

VIII

wanted to purchase the Palace Theatre opposite Washington Square Park in San Francisco's North Beach to house live shows, movies, New School forums, classes, speaker events, poetry readings and anything else that might come along. The twenty-four-hundred seat movie theatre was smack in the middle of North Beach. We planned to take out a few rows of seats to expand the stage area and create magnificent events. Our first offer was $150,000 (we paid $85.00 a month rent on the old church). We got pledges up to $50,000 for a downpayment. The owners eventually countered with $250,000.

We looked into other theatres, like the Haight Straight Theatre, but thought it was not in such a hot location (sic). Marshall Naify, the chain theatre mogul, kept the Palace Theatre counter at $250,000 and we ended up with lots of pictures and interesting plans. We dropped the white elephant dream and Saul and I commenced work on the most outrageous production the Mime Troupe ever created—*The Minstrel Show*.

Poster for *A Minstrel Show*, 1965

3

THE MINSTREL SHOW

In 1964, when I first thought about doing a show on racism, *The Blacks* by Genet came to mind. I had seen the New York production and was fascinated by its possibilities. Although I was dubious about the relevance of the play, I thought if I could find Black Muslims (not knowing what they were like at the time) or black activists, I could achieve a quality not obtained in the New York production. I hoped to reach a strength and depth rarely achieved by using non-political actors. Roger Blins's production of *The Blacks* in Paris had used politically hip actors and reports of the performances indicated a far greater confrontation with audience consciousness.

My search ended for a number of reasons: the lack of performers; Black Muslims and Black nationalists were not about to consider Genet's play; we couldn't mount a production like I envisioned without some organization and we had none; and the rights for the production had been sewn up by the New York producers, who made sure that no one did the production unless they profited, which, of course, meant few productions. The choice of play faded from possibility,

but the hope of using politically active people as performers stayed on.

The search for relevant material on civil rights continued until one of us (either Nina, Saul or myself) happened upon the idea: why not write a play—write a minstrel show. The idea was nurtured by finding out that minstrel shows were a part of our cultural heritage from 1830 to 1920 and, at its peak, there were three hundred floating companies, from town to city, amateur and professional, rapping out: "Mr. Bones, who was dat chicken Ah saw you wid de odder night?" We realized that by doing an original minstrel show, or an adaptation of an old one, we would be following the line we had established with commedia: adaptations or returning it to 1600s commedia; and, of course, we would get right into the problem of racism—ours and everyone else's—by unearthing those stereotypes, clichés, cornballs and all that Uncle Tom jive.

Our first cast was memorable. I placed some ads and sent out a few press releases, announcing we were holding auditions for a minstrel show. In 1965, racial activists were for integration. The first call was attended by about fifteen people— some white, some black—who came to our Capp Street theatre. I told them we were going to go through some difficult personal and political confrontations and I wanted to be as out-front as possible. I said, "We are going to unearth the garbage of our culture and sort it out. For example: we would like to open the show with something like 'eeny meany miney moe, catch a nigger by the toe . . .'" This little rhyme had been taught to me as a kid, probably by my Negro maid, and we were going to get it up and out and use it for what it was worth. I blushed on saying that rhyme in front of blacks, but that was the essence of the minstrel show.

Selecting performers for a show that was not yet written was difficult. Although none of us had seen a minstrel show, Amos and Andy, the Marx Brothers' darkie movies, Stepin Fetchit and Rochester were in our consciousness. We knew much of the stereotypical racism was pounded soft by WASPish thinking and we expected to have a rough go.

We auditioned and auditioned. Finally, one day Roy and Willie Ballard walked into the studio with a group of black-bereted street politicos. They had been famous in demonstrations at the Sheraton Palace and now were working the Cadillac sit-ins. (Cadillac sold more cars to Negroes, and, it followed, why not demand Negro Cadillac salesmen! Some of us saw the Cadillac Row issue like Paul Jacobs, who said: "And the difference between a white goniff and a black goniff?")

I didn't discuss political tactics with Roy or Willie Ballard because they brought along Willie Hart and Jason Marc Alexander. Roy looked particularly macho and interesting as a type, but was no stage performer. His brother couldn't keep a beat. But Jason was flash and Willie was a natural. I think they auditioned by singing. Willie Hart led them in one of those intertwined quartet sets that black kids do on the street: four voices in four-part harmony. Willie Hart underplayed his character, Hokus, who was a country Stepin Fetchit; while Jason played a snappy urban street hood. Both guys were essential to the creation of the show and stayed in the entire two-year run. We never did find a permanent third black to match these two, although, in the early rehearsals, we worked with a great performer who was five feet wide and six feet tall, played piano, could dance and sing, and was a fine actor. He left. The show

was merciless and each joke was self-critical. He couldn't stand up to the scrutiny of the form: racism, white or black. He did not dig the politics or the jokes at his size. He would not admit that he was twice the width of any one performer and we found out later that he hadn't noticed he was Negro until the age of twenty-one.

We collected a number of whites from various sources: John Broderick from commedia days, the curly-haired kid who could bullshit back at Jason. Both about twenty-two, they didn't give a shit for racism, so they would just slam insults back and forth. More sophisticated, I found myself embarrassed by John's slinging, but it was great for all of us. Jason got hit sometimes and he did some hurting in turn.

I had presumed that I would play a part, but I could not. It took all of my time to try and figure out the show. We finally got Kai Spiegal, who had played Père Ubu, to take on the endman, Klinker. Six minstrels, three white, three black, all in black face, powder satin-blue tails, black fright wigs and white lips and eyes. They were out of sight. In the dark, they were crazy. We decided that we would use blacks and whites—yes, integrated—but all playing in black face, so that the audience would have to struggle through the performance trying to figure out which were black and which were white. The process would unnerve them and fuck up their prejudices.

The spirit of commedia ran through the Minstrel Show, stereotypical characters, exaggerated gestures, masks, in this case blackface with white parts that were particularized by each performer, and the whole show was done in presentational form. The element that made the show particularly American and in part an American commedia, was that it was based upon the many years of

The cast of *A Minstrel Show*, 1965

minstrel show history in the collective theatrical conscience of the United States. We not only knew of Amos and Andy, the Black Crows and a few solo comics, but we discovered that the country had been criss-crossed for eighty years by traveling groups. At its peak three hundred-odd companies performed in blackface doing musical numbers and nigger jokes. Minstrel types were imbedded in white unconsciousness: even though the books didn't talk much about popular forms, we saw the show's stereotypes in oppressed ghetto characters. Whereas our commedia poked holes in American stuffiness, the minstrel show upchucked the unmelted pieces from the melting pot.

The Interlocutor in rehearsal was played by Saul, but it was important to have an older man, someone with a deep voice and a presence like the traditional ringmaster—a circus ringmaster. The only example of an Interlocutor I had seen was in the Russian circus, an adult figure to the childlike clown.

For the minstrel show we found an older man who was a little slow but who had a deep, rich voice. While the kids squeaked, he would bellow. Somehow or other, money got in the way and he expected to get paid for each rehearsal. About a week before we opened the show for in-house previews, he quit. As always, I found myself on stage in a top hat with some stupid make-up, trying to play a basso profundo. I could make some of the bullshit, but I knew I was on only for a short while. We needed a taller actor, too, somebody who could look down on the six-foot Willie Hart.

Robert Slattery worked on the waterfront as a longshoreman and had been involved in political activity in the Bay Area. He walked in, looked down at me with his great, mature, stone WASP-ish face like a fine Clark Kent, tough and determined. I can't remember auditioning him. It was a miracle, and how can anyone audition miracles? Slattery was so hard and cornball that he was almost impossible to replace. When he got tired of us, we tried others who gave different interpretations, but when Slattery came out on stage, you knew white America was in the middle of these screaming, ranting darkies and that he was the thing to be attacked. He was no paper tiger, he was strong, imposing and he had the show in his hands. He was the perfect ringmaster.

We placed our stereotypes (Stepin Fetchits, even radical blacks) in conflict with Mr. America. The stage conflict had to reflect the observable social conditions, otherwise it would have been fantasy and dream therapy, rather than politically relevant. The movement had yet to develop a strong radical leadership. Malcolm X was just clearing the ground for many blacks and some whites. The Panthers had not begun to talk tough yet. We had to investigate why the civil rights movement objected to Uncle Tom.

Uncle Tom, it turns out, was not as horrible as I imagined. The minstrel show darkie is a variation of a Tom, either drawl outside and quick-witted inside (Stupidus from Roman mime, Pulcinella from commedia) or the snappy, urbane dude (Sanio, Roman; Brighella, commedia). The lower classes develop great means of survival and Uncle Tom, even in Harriet Beecher Stowe's novel, is a survival character. A Christian slave who, rather than tell on his escaped companions, suffers a beating (the martyr), yet he doesn't flee. In struggling to leap out of the slavish obedience to racist America, civil rights lambasted the Uncle Tom; however, not in this show. We raised him to smart alec, to wise conniver, to brute threat to white man's existence, and learned to respect him.

In addition to our social analysis, we had to deal with the personal liberation of each actor; not only to incorporate some material we might find in each performer but also to make sure that the individuals would present the collective point of view. I asked each actor to talk privately into a tape recorder about the time he first realized his black, white or ethnic identity. We learned a lot. Jason and Willie had torturous early experiences. Willie saw his father run across the path of a milk truck. The driver, furious that he almost hit the man, yelled out: "You fuckin' nigger . . ." His father didn't say anything. Marc Alexander lived with his mother, who was a mammie to some white kids. He went to play with the black kids down the road and they threw him in a box and called him "whitey," while they kicked the box around. Don Pedro Colley, at twenty-one, walked into a dining room in some college in Oregon and didn't sit at the table with all the blacks, but with the whites. They pointed to the black table. White-Spanish-descent kid, Julio Martinez, said, "We were never prejudiced against Negroes. Of course, we were never taken for Negroes."

All of us heard these important "coming-of-age moments." Those who had realized early their skin color or ethnic origins understood our show and created its whip-like intensity. Performers who had not experienced the existential racial twist until very late never stayed on long.

We worked on the show for nine months, constructing it slowly. After the fourth month, I increased rehearsals to twice a week and there was a demand for money. Jason and Willie needed it; the whites looked on with interest. We began to pay five dollars a week to each performer. Increasing the number of days of rehearsal, but keeping the pay the same, we finally got our show moving enough to see run-throughs and rehearsals

of the whole thing. Music was put together by various banjo players. The choreography or scene management I put together with the help of Jason and some stuff by John Broderick. We did a tambourine, shoutin', stompin', cake-walk for the opener that was a minstrel show version of a commedia warm-up. It was practiced till everyone was swinging together. It opened to a roar of applause and when the Interlocutor came on and gave out with the glib, "Gentlemen, beee seated. . . ." (the traditional opener), we had warmed up the house.

Minstrel shows had a particular format which we simply imitated. The cross-fire was quick, rapid-fire cornball gags between minstrel and interlocutor.

[Viz: Read very fast in minstrel lilt; Interlocutor—straight white man; Minstrel—exaggerated Tom]

Talk:
Inter: Gentlemen, be seated. *[All sit except Gimme.]*
Gimme: Wish I was rich, wish I was rich, wish I was rich.
Inter: I heard you the first time, Mr. Gimme.
Gimme: Did you? But de fairy gimme three wishes, and dem was it.
Inter: Where did you see a fairy?
Gimme: On a ferry-boat. *[All guffaw. Gimme sits.]*
Inter: Mr. Bones, are you a Republican or a Democrat?
Bones: *[jumping up]* Oh, I'm a Baptist.
Inter: Come, come. Whom did you vote for last time?
Bones: Robinson Crusoe.
Inter: What did he run for?
Bones: Exercise. *[All yuk yuk; Bones stays standing with Interlocutor.]*
Inter: Now, cut out the foolishness. Are you a Republican or a Democrat?
Bones: Democrat.
Inter: And your wife is also a Democrat?
Bones: She was, but she bolted.
Inter: Bolted the party?
Bones: No, just me. When I come home late, she bolts de door. *[All guffaw.]*

A Minstrel Show, 1965

A Minstrel Show, 1965

Although there was some original material in the show, brilliant stuff improvised by the minstrels or written by Saul Landau, the basic format and material had been "gleaned" from the old minstrel shows. I read hundreds of pages of crossfire, picking out the most appropriate gags I could find: those with a bit of political relevance and ones we could make funny. There were probably tons of garbage done in the old minstrel shows and only some of it was usable in 1965. Crossfire, the heart of the minstrel show, was actually no more than a traditional routine between two performers: the straight man and his clown. When minstrel shows faded away, vaudeville took their place with duos like Weber and Fields or Gallagher and Scheen, who did cross-fire dialogues, but without the other six or ten minstrels.

We followed the cross-fire with a traditional Stump Speech on Evolution, done by John Broderick in the style of a Southern senator (couldn't tell if he was black or white), then a great song: "Old Black Joe" first sung in part by the minstrels, who turned their backs to the audience in pseudo-piety, bowed their heads as the Interlocutor recited. One of the minstrels didn't bow his head completely and began to masturbate (simulated) as the dramatic recital continued. There was the complete opposition of elements working toward hysteria. The tone and presentation of "Old Black Joe" by Bob Slattery was superb, something like Laurence Olivier or Paul Robeson, and directly behind him this blue-coated crazy whippin' it off. The cops could barely write it all down fast enough, the heavy ideologues winced or winked at the childishness, but thousands got hysterical.

The Interlocutor finished off his portion of the song with a rendition of "Old Black Joe" in flamboyant Spanish:

Se fueron los dias buenos
Cuando mi corazon era joven y feliz
Se fueron tambien mis amigos buenos
De las sueldos de algaodon.
Se pasaban, se pasaban para una tierra mejor,
    eso lo se.
Escucho las voces suaves llamando me
VIEJO NEGRITO JOSE.

He dissolved in tragic tears and was led off center by one of the minstrels who took pity on him. The others began to march around and Klinker jumped up on the chair and shouted in platdeutsch (à la Nazi), to the marching minstrels:

Grammaphone gesellschaft,
Volkswagen uber alles;
Hansel und Gretel in der Schwarzwald.

They stopped marching. He came down stage and ended the number with a bark to the audience, "Alta Swartza Jeuden." The minstrels jived him back to his chair and we resumed the "rational" format of the minstrel show.

Bones asked the Interlocutor for permission to tell the folks something and, of course, the Interlocutor allowed:

Bones: I am here, my friends, to speak before you, one and all, to honor a very festive occasion.
Group: Yeh, Ho hum. *[yawns]*
Bones: For it has been proclaimed throughout this land by the President hisself, as sure as he is the leader of this humble band of people, that one week will be set aside every year at the same time so that we can *all* take pride in the accomplishments of the past. So, we for you are going to retrace back through the years and the ages the history of the colored race as glorious as the Bible's pages. Yes, at times, things looked very

bleak for the black man—
Group: And very black for the bleak man!
Bones: But it is changed, for Nego History Week will tell
you all how it really happened. How we balance out on
the great ledger book of time, and who was who in
literature, so that we looks mighty fine, and deserving
of a week unto ourselves.
(Note: Negro has no "r" in the Minstrel Show text, we
said *Nego.)*

Nego history went on with mimetic and verbal
demonstrations to portray Crispus Attucks, the
first black man to be killed in the War for Inde-
pendence; Toussaint L'Ouverture, an articulate
spokesman of black revolution; Booker T. Washington and his relations with Teddy Roosevelt;
George Washington Carver and the peanut; black
soldiers in Vietnam; and a jail scene with Martin
Luther King, which ended in a rising tide of black
power images. We punctured some of the exaggerated claims for three of the heroes, cut into the
Uncle Tomism in Booker T. and the absurdity of
a poor black man killing yellow men for an imperialist (racist) power.

Nego History ended with the minstrels banging
chairs on stage, yelling at the audience, "We're
brave. We're strong. Black is beautiful. Blood in
the streets. Revenge." About to get out of control, the Interlocutor rushes in to calm the darkies. We picked up the tempo with cross-fire. Then
the Interlocutor suggested that Gimme and Snowball "improvise" a "chick/stud scene." (Terrible
ruse, but in fake minstrel style, we could yassa
boss it to believability. Nothing was assumed as
truth.)

The chick/stud scene was the breaking point of
the show. If Nego History didn't bruise emotions
and hidden treasures, then the sight of a black

stud picking up a white chick in a bar and taking
her home to bed usually succeeded. The magic of
the show was the unearthing of stereotypical
images, placing them on stage, making them move
rapidly from cornball black jokes (minstrel racism) to radical black (radical puncturing) jokes
thus transforming a stereotypical image into a
radical image. The speed of the performance and
the shift from level to level, cornball to cornstalk,
caught prejudices offguard and exposed them.
The through line, of course, was the general apprehension about buried prejudices, which the
search for the white performers amid the black
faces constantly irritated. When the white and
black (three of each) performers played the stereotypes exquisitely, people got confused and
were likely to go away shaken.

To make sure we were on the right track, we
had many previews at Capp Street for invited
audiences. After each show, we asked people to
talk with us. We listened to Joe from CORE tell
us it wasn't correct; and I heard Jason and Willie,
who had sat-in and walked the streets, tell Joe
where the show was at. We heard a young black
kid ask us, during one talk-back session at the
Capp Street studio: "Why do you have four black
guys and only two white guys in the show?" (I
was proud of that question.) Mike Miller from
SNCC wanted to take the whole show and especially the white chick/black stud scene Saul had
written to the SNCC offices all through the
South. Liberal and establishment Negroes were
afraid that their "people" wouldn't understand.

Our best critique came from our friend, Juris
Svendsen, who worked in the theatre, was famili-
ar with Marx, Freud, Brecht, Genet and spoke
Latvian (being one), French, German, read Latin

and Greek, acted and directed. He saw a preview and then took Saul and me through the show, point by point, and made us clarify each political development. The cornball cross-fire was unimpeachable, but Nego History and the last few skits always presented political questions we only solved under the close scrutiny of friends like Svendsen or that ever-present grand inspector, the public.

In addition to playing one of the minstrels, I took over arrangements for the first out-of-state tour. Bill Graham, who was hired to help us tour from location to location (we had no stable theatre), had promoted himself to "Bill Graham Presents" and was on the way out of our company when we went to the Northwest. We played eight shows in eight days and I came home to stay in bed for two months.

Close to home, our maneuvers with *Tartuffe* had not prepared us for the realities of a show on the road—we knew little about touring. We packed the show in trunks for airplane travel, rented cars and did a whole fancy trip not knowing the actual costs, since contracts were being made up as we were on the road. Percentages were expected and it wasn't clear if we would have to pay for rooms or get them free. I had rushed to arrange dates and, at the last minute, asked someone to be stage manager, even though he did not know the show or its technical aspects. With only three technical cues called for, it was characteristic of this tour that no matter what place or what night, every show had one technical mistake, and a standing ovation.

The third day in Washington, April 3, 1966, we were engaged by St. Martin's, a small Catholic college. The booking had been arranged by two people who ran a help-Mississippi brigade in Olympia, Washington. The big deal contract was three hundred dollars for one shot. We arrived on a Monday afternoon for an evening show and came upon two kids who had been expelled for drinking wine on campus! By this time, dope had hit half the country and we, from the big city, couldn't remember what wine meant. Sniffing the air, I put up one finger and warned the other minstrels that perhaps this little school and our nice civil rights friends didn't understand what kind of event they had booked. We set to work anyway. The theatre was like a small summer-stock house. The show opened well, although the audience hadn't taken splendiferously to the banjo music and cross-fire. They seemed a little distant during Nego History week.

The chick/stud skit started to turn people over in their seats. Saul had written the main dialogue from an idea worked on by John Broderick and Jason Marc Alexander. The chick, with mask, wig and skirt, was played straight. The minstrel used his own voice. (There was no way to create an illusion. At all times, minstrel as girl was present.)

They tittered as the pink-faced doll entered, but didn't know what to make of the black stud picking up the white girl in a bar. When we pantomimed his room and he began to paw at her (touch, now), death rose up out front and after the simulated screwing scene, fleeing heels beat out a taps. During the dialogue, as the young black plays the macho-stud to nausea ("You ain't nothin' but a white chick—you're pussy and pale skin and you know no white man can satisfy you like I can") and the white chick takes emotionally embarrassing turns ("I feel sorry that so many bad things have happened to you. I want to love you because you need love"), the two figures were in individual spotlights while the rest of the

Chick-Stud scene, *A Minstrel Show*, 1965

THE CHICK-STUD SCENE

[As the dialogue begins, the minstrels turn their backs to the audience to give better focus to the chick and stud, who are standing in spots separated by ten feet of empty space, both facing into light and audience.]

Stud: For Christ's sake, if you got something to say, say it.

Chick: What's wrong?

Stud: Nothing's wrong, baby, you got a problem and I was just solving it for you. Felt pretty good, didn't it. Yeah, the white man invented that problem for the black man to solve.

Chick: You really can't have a relationship with me just as a person.

Stud: Baby, you came up here with me willingly, and lay down on that bed and spread your white legs, and humped up and down and moaned in my goddam ear. You was horny for black, baby, a black body on top of you, and now you think it's disgusting and cheap.

Chick: Well, I didn't need you!

Stud: What? What was all that moaning and groaning and oh-how-I-love-it about? Tell me you didn't like that.

Chick: I wanted you to feel good, but you're not man enough to accept it. You can't even be a good lover: if you can't take you can't give.

Stud: That's a cliché. You don't know who I am.

Chick: And you! You may have the body of a man, but emotionally you're a child. You can't know me as a woman.

Stud: Woman! Ain't no body tole you baby? You ain't nothin but a white chick. You're status and satisfaction and revenge. You're pussy and pale skin and you know no white man can satisfy you like I can. Now me, I'm different; I'm all NEGRO, with the smell of Negro, and the hair of Negro, and all the goddam passion of Africa and wild animals. I haven't got the same hang-ups, have I?

Chick: I feel sorry that so many bad things have happened to you. I really want to love you, because you need love.

Stud: You're a whore.

Chick: Don't say that!

Stud: You're a whore. You're trying to sell me something. You want me to buy what you've got. You've got guilt and you're selling it to me under a different label. You love Negroes, but I'm a man, and you can't love me if you love Negroes.

Chick: But I can. I want to. I lied. You did satisfy me. You were majestic and you were tender. Did you think I wouldn't notice your tenderness. You do want to love me. You need to love me.

Stud: Sheeeeet, you been reading too much James Baldwin.

[*Mimetic reaction: She takes off mask and skirt, holds them before her, moves tenderly, pleadingly toward stud, offering herself. He becomes cool, frightened. Mask and skirt continue toward him, swinging and coming on. Angry, Stud lunges for the imaginary neck of the mask and skirt figure. He strangles the image, as the other minstrel lowers the image to the floor. Stud discovers that the skirt is not filled, is empty, kicks it. First minstrel still has mask on hands, begins to laugh, as other minstrels laugh and scream, he pursues black stud off stage with threatening pink mask. Blackout.*]

cast, with backs turned to the audience, were in the dark. Onstage, I could hear the heels, but when I turned around I did not expect to see half of the small audience gone. We stuck it out and continued, until some jerk stepped onstage and another ran to the light board. Blackout. We had been cut off. In the dark, we had no voice, so I ran to the front of the stage and yelled "Fire! Fire!" The lights went on immediately. General pandemonium. The student body president, a nice clean-cut Catholic, stepped to the front and asked why I had yelled "Fire!" It was illegal. I said, "Get off the stage." He announced that the show was being stopped by students. We found out, of course, that the head priest agreed. He said: "Just last week, we talked about sex, but this is going too far." I responded, again, with "Get the hell off the stage and we'll finish our show." We tried.

When a performance erupts into a confrontation like the one we were in, there is a choice to continue, if you can make it happen, or to take on the confrontation and prove them wrong. We took on the confrontation, but I'm not so sure we shouldn't have performed in and around them and forced them to yell, scream, fight or act more stupidly. I took off my black fright wig, still in blackface, and said, "O.K., let's get to it. This is an example of suppression of freedom. Free speech is bullshit at this college. These people don't trust you in the audience to make up your own minds. All those who want to see the show, we presume, are seated and want us to go on." Shouts of "Continue the show, let them go on." Then, Jason started to talk and he rolled along beautifully. A few others guys got into it but somehow or other it all broke up and we could not continue. Some little motherfucker from the

surrounding area wired AP and sent in a terrible story about obscenity and other politically perceptive trash.

As the newswires hummed, so did our anxiety. From the little town of Olympia, Washington, the capital of the state, we sailed into Seattle and immediately called a press conference to counter the AP story. We were in it up to our necks and not quite clear how to move. I acted straight and read a statement, while two actors came in complete costume to show the press what we looked like. The press conference was no different from all the reviews we received: the conservative papers doubted us; the liberal papers praised us; and the underground called it far out.

The news of the show spread, unearthing various worried liberals. One such junior executive ran the cultural affairs program at Western Washington State College in Bellingham. He came down to Seattle to see the show before letting us on his campus. He took me out for a drink: 7-Up and Four Roses! And he talked officiously, finally explaining that he and the cultural committee wanted to print a one-page statement explaining their position on the show—a disclaimer. "Sure," I said. He then asked if we would do a modified version. I said, "No, absolutely not." Worried, but not beaten, he agreed to honor our contract. We went up to Bellingham a few days later and there was an eight-by-ten statement posted about how they didn't believe it was their right to censor, but the cultural affairs committee wanted to warn the audience. . . . With that kind of statement, the audience was looking to be "shocked." No show in the world can come up to the excitement level of a nervously expectant audience.

To compensate and void the effect of this disclaimer, Bob Slattery agreed to go out on stage and say in his most stentorian, serious tone:

> Ladies and Gentlemen: We are happy to be here through the gracious invitation of your Cultural Affairs Committee. With due respect to their position, as stated in the flyer, we don't wish to create any trouble and will perform the *modified* version of our minstrel show. We hope you enjoy it.

We then went onstage and performed the whole fucking thing as done in all the other performances.

The first half of the show was never drastically changed, because it was a gem; it moved, slapped and disturbed. From the cornball, hoky opening to cross-fire, jolly jokes, to stump speech, the show was a fast-paced parody of traditional minstrel and monkey logic. The song "Old Black Joe" loosened the screws and Nego History was a solid piece of historical satire, the chick/stud scene got under the skin and was topped off by Watermelon.

Bob Nelson, Landau and I, with members of the Troupe, conceived, wrote and played in a movie about the life and death of a watermelon or thirty ways of doing in or getting done in by a symbol. The film, "Oh, Dem Watermelons," won award after award for its rapid-fire hysterical insight. In the production, the live sound was made by the cast, who chanted a Steve Reich repetitive round, as the audience viewed the film. "Watermelon, wa-ter-mel-on—WATERMELON, etc." The repetition of sound increased as the film came to a close, and the watermelon started chasing people up streets and up steps. The Interlocutor came to center stage and announced:

> And now, ladies and gentlemen, there will be a fifteen-minute intermission, during which time we will have dancing on the stage. The minstrels will go among you and take a partner. . . . . house lights, music, please."

The minstrels leapt off stage into the audience, whooping it up. The music turned up a rhumba, the Black Muslim song, "White Man's Heaven is a Black Man's Hell." We wouldn't even let them get away during the break.

The minstrels picked up blond women to dance with on stage and, of course, made approaches to the various women. The intermission was designed to illustrate blacks and whites dancing and spill the action from stage to the audience. Most of the actors did it with gusto. They picked up chicks and copped onto the sexual energy aroused by the show. The chick/stud scene was a theatrical depiction of a symbolic scene; however, the realities of the dancing section bothered me.

The second half was composed of two playlets: a cop/kid scene, based upon the Gilligan killing in New York's Harlem that touched off the riot of 1964; and a bathroom scene written by Saul and worked out by the cast in a clear and precise depiction of the social problems of the period. The cop/kid scene was always improvised and was difficult to recapture. The bathroom scene takes to print more easily.

[Bones, Inkspot and Gimme come on with signs: "Nigger" apron, "White" and "Negro" vests. Two minstrels set up door and one is flushing a toilet. Negro and white approach the bathroom door:]
White: After you.
Negro: No, after you.
White: Oh, go ahead, I can wait.
Negro: No, you were here first, I insist—
White: No—*[more ad libbing by both]*
Nigger: [enters, listens to debate, anxious to get inside, pushes through] After *me*. Shit, you goin' to stand there and debate who is going to take de first piss?

Negro: [enters bathroom] Where's your manners? You're the kind that gives our race a bad image.

Nigger: In dat case, I moves on over since you have to go so bad. Dere's room enough for two.

Negro: That's not what I meant.

Nigger: Oh, who gives a damn what you meant. [flushes toilet, pantomimes combing hair]

White: Maybe I should leave and that way it would be less crowded.

Nigger: Wait a minute, boss, you mean you didn't even have to go? What de hell you come in here for and cause all dis trouble? You one of dem peeverts?

Negro: [to white] Pay no attention, sir. He's probably drunk.

Nigger: Fuck you. Why you got to kiss de white man's ass?

Negro: Watch your language. Remember where you are.

Nigger: I know where I am. I'm in de pissin' room and I come in here to take one. I don't know what you come in here for, but it sure wasn't for pissin'.

Negro: If you were any kind of civilized human being, you would move aside and let the customers use the facilities first. I'm going to report you to the manager.

Nigger: If you like de manager so much you can go ahead and piss in his room.

White: I can see what you're up against. It's very difficult to deal with an uneducated person.

Negro: I agree.

Nigger: [to white] Shit, man—you need an education to learn to piss more than one in a commode. And you [to Negro]—you need an education, you white ass-kisser.

Negro: I resent that, you street nigger! [Goes to punch him. White man intervenes.]

White: Now wait a minute, let's be reasonable about this. Use some reason.

Nigger: [pulls out razor] Here's my reason. I'm gonna settle something with Mr. Ass Kisser. [Negro hides behind white] You chicken shit, Mr. Ass Kisser, you ain't no nigger no more. Don't even carry a blade to defend yourself. Mighty educated.

Negro: Cool it, baby—we're brothers! Dere's de white man!

White: Don't kill me, I didn't say anything. Honest.

Nigger: Yeah, no one says nothin' to me except clean dis and do dat. Well, now I'm saying something. One of you is goin' to get it, and maybe both. All I gotta do is figure out which one of you I hates the most. [freeze]

People thought we were on their side, thought it was a civil rights integration show. Not so, we were cutting deeper into prejudices than integration allowed. We poked not at intolerance, but tolerance. We were not for the suppression of differences; rather, by exaggerating the differences we punctured the cataracts of "color blind" liberals, disrupted "progressive" consciousness and made people think twice about eating watermelon.

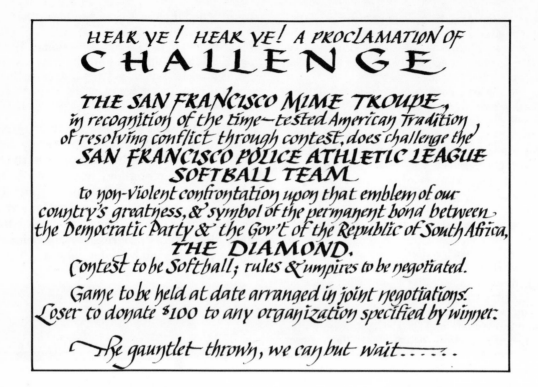

HEAR YE! HEAR YE! A PROCLAMATION OF

CHALLENGE

THE SAN FRANCISCO MIME TROUPE,
in recognition of the time—tested American Tradition,
of resolving conflict through contest, does challenge the
SAN FRANCISCO POLICE ATHLETIC LEAGUE
SOFTBALL TEAM
to non-violent confrontation upon that emblem of our
country's greatness, & symbol of the permanent bond between
the Democratic Party & the Gov't of the Republic of South Africa,
THE DIAMOND.
Contest to be Softball; rules & umpires to be negotiated.

Game to be held at date arranged in joint negotiations.
Loser to donate $100 to any organization specified by winner.

The gauntlet thrown, we can but wait......

SAN FRANCISCO

MIME TROUPE, INC.
a non-profit corporation

450 Alabama Street
S.F., California 94110

415
431-1984

Our calling card, 1967

4

FROM ARREST TO BUST

We had come a long way from the days of a classical mime company performing at the Encore in 1961. Besides our passion for bringing theatre to the outdoor public, the Mime Troupe had engaged in a host of cultural activities—FM radio programs, San Francisco New School (a new left hot-house), Midnight Movies (underground film-makers), Beatnik Benefits, Happenings, a theatre season indoors, one in the parks every summer and a touring schedule just begun.

The dispute over the shows we did in the parks was not without its reason. We were not using an artistocratic cultural form to perform in the parks, but a low knock-about "dirty" form; not Shakespeare in the parks but Milt Savage/Machiavelli, Milt Savage/Angelo Beolco, Saul Landau/Tom Lopez and, now, Peter Berg/Giordano Bruno. Not only were the above not recognizable literary figures; we performed with color, movement, and without fear on the grass to a mobile public. If the Park Commissioners got past the style they stopped at the content.

To perform outside in 1962, we had to apply to the Park Commission for a permit to play shows in the park. Walter Haas, chairman of the commission (Levi Strauss Board Chairman) with his eight equally affluent commissioners told us, "There is a precedent that a group can only use the parks twice in one year." Milt Savage, Al Dela Rosa, and I heard the statement. We rode back to our Capp Street studio on my three-wheeler in our blue suits ("straight" costume) knowing we'd been buffaloed, happy that we could test our commedia. *The Dowry*'s results were positive.

To obtain more dates for our second show in the parks, *The Root*, Milt Savage's 1963 adaptation of *The Mandrake*, I learned to play "politics" with the commission. I contacted a friendly supervisor in the city administration who recommended me to one or two friendly commissioners who were given a sheaf of recommendations from friendly notable San Franciscans. The now friendly commissioners sponsored our request for the dates at the Park Commission meeting, making our request go through with ease.

The third commedia, *Ruzzante's Maneuvers*, played twelve or fourteen performances in the summer of '63 to finish out a larger schedule than even we expected. The vision of a theatrical alternative became a reality.

As our touring program became a probability it was obvious that we needed a promoter/business manager who would handle the various complicated arrangements. Sandy Archer, Elmire in *Tartuffe* and the company bookkeeper, introduced me to Bill Graham. Graham agreed to take the job on a percentage basis, rather than at a fixed salary like the other people in our company and insisted on maintaining a distance from our politics. Although he stood aside from our political direction, his isolation made him a good front man and sometimes a more energetic publicity seeker than a radical could be.

The Minstrel Show was just about on its feet,

Exception and the Rule had opened with Bob Scheer talking about Vietnam for the second act and we needed a play for the parks when Peter Berg happened by in his computer-job suit. I made a deal with him to pay fifty dollars for a commedia. We both thought it was a good price for a first play, neither of us having dealt in big business before. The play we chose to do was *Il Candelaio* by Giordano Bruno. Peter adapted and I directed. Berg loved the intricacies of the plot and emphasized the brutality inherent in the unmanageable play. I got lost but relied on the fact that Giordano Bruno had been burned at the stake for not recanting his Copernican views. The selection and occasional scenes were fitting for the upcoming spectacle.

Before opening in the parks, we invited Marshall Krause of the American Civil Liberties Union and Ephraim Margolin, both civil rights lawyers, to look at the show.* They thought it was a little brutal but not obscene. In our request to the Commission, Krause and Marvin Stender, our attorney, warned the commissioners not to become censors. The Commission granted us use of the parks for forty-eight dates on the condition that the show met their approval. After the third performance they sent us a letter revoking our permit. We called a special meeting, the lawyers repeated that our constitutional rights to freedom of speech were being tampered with, but nothing affected the moguls of San Francisco. I left the Park Commission meeting shouting, "We will see you in the parks and in the courts."

---

* When we had received permission to perform *Ruzzante* in 1964 the Park Department overseer had warned that the content of the show would have to be reviewed by the Commission. We had ignored the unconstitutional threat; nevertheless, we decided it was time to come to grips with their nonsense.

On the morning of August 7, 1965, we got to Lafayette Park early. We had announced our intention to perform at 2 P.M. in the glen and by 1 P.M. the place began to fill up. We had decided that I was to be arrested for this "showcase event." I took Luis Valdez's role for the pre-show spectacular. He was playing Brighella and usually was the first onstage. If it looked like there would be other arrests, then we had agreed to pack up.

They all came and even more: the cops, Stender, Graham, James Lang from the Parks Department, sign carriers ("Mime Troupe Si! Park Commission No!"), all of the troupe—even two Minstrel Show performers in full tails and blackface, Marvin Garson, Skip Sweeney, Herbert Gold, Paul Jacobs, Alan Myerson, Lawrence Ferlinghetti, Francis Heisler and a thousand other people. Graham had publicized the spectacular. Stender was on hand to coach with the legal details. We had prepared for years and it couldn't have been staged better: Sunday and a full house.

We began slowly with Jim Lang quietly conversing with me, then Graham, about the revocation of the permit. Stender arrived and so did the cops and we then changed directions and began to address the crowd, first explaining about our permit and the Park Commission's revocation. Lang countered, followed by Graham's description of the events. Stender worked on the cops.

The cop on hand was a Sergeant Eagan, by then the only smiling cop left in San Francisco. He was forever trying to quiet everything down and wanted us all to go to the station to talk things over. Graham and I got louder and included the public in every statement while we tried to figure out what they intended to do. Lang was pulling the cop strings, but what was their plan? We didn't quite get it clear but it looked like they would stop us if we set up the

The Miser, 1966

stage. Rather than be "stopped" for putting up a wooden platform, we cleared a space and the cast began to warm up: first recorder, then song; and, as the group sang and paraded together, we moved toward the proposed performing area. I danced into the cleared spot and announced:

Signor, Signora, Signorini
Madame, Monsieur, Mademoiselle,
Ladieeeees and Gentlemen,
Il Troupo di Mimo di San Francisco
Presents for your enjoyment this afternoon . . .

AN ARREST!!!

On the last line, I leapt into the air and the cop dutifully grabbed me before I landed.

Pandemonium: Marvin Garson, then of the *Express Times*, said later that he could not resist the opportunity, so he knocked a cop's hat off in the melee; Skip Sweeney lunged at the cop who got Marvin; people screamed and threw grass at the cops; photogs, warned in advance, filled their cameras; the press got their story. We three, Garson, Sweeney, and I, went into the waiting paddywagon. Two hours later, I got out on bail, charged with parking on the grass.

We had planned our side of the show well and the cops and the Park Department played to our calculations. As I went off to jail to be bailed out by Marvin Stender, the cast started singing and announced that they would perform. They hustled up four friendly bodies and had them stand in for a backdrop and entrance curtain. Two cast members who, for various reasons, couldn't afford arrest, had Ferlinghetti, Jacobs,

August 7, 1965

Gold and Heisler (the human curtain) in turn read their parts until the place cleared of cops. The audience stayed cheering and donated heavily for the legal fight to come.

In the following months we tried to make clear a multiple message—why we chose to perform shows in the parks; that the parks were owned by the people; and that the Park Commission could not act as a censor. We sent out press releases, held news conferences, wrote stories and even pamphleteered while the papers headlined the Park Commission's objection to "obscenity" rather than the fundamental issues of our trial.

The trial began with Stender stating that we had performed without a permit and that we would prove the Commission could not revoke any permits, save by violating constitutional guarantees. We spent four days clarifying the issue to the judge. He listened, then instructed the jury to decide whether we had performed with or without a permit. He sentenced me to one year probation, sixty days suspended sentence. The whole constitutional issue was avoided. Despite our loss in court, we stayed in the parks all summer and appeared again every year after.

To cover our legal fees and make more out of our arrest than the Park Commission wanted, we organized a benefit in our own studio on November 6, 1965. The entertainment was as varied as we had offered in other benefits. We had the Committee, Sandy Bull, the Fugs, Jefferson Airplane, the Family Dog, Lawrence Ferlinghetti, John Handy Quintet, and others. Two thousand people came. When I got there the lines were around the block and the firemen were just entering to tell us that we had to limit the intake to five hundred people. We quietly cleared some of the space and told others we couldn't let them in, collected $2,000.00 in donations, paid out

$400 for oranges, apples, bananas, one ad and $20.02 for a Fire Department fine.

Appeal II held at the Fillmore on December 10, 1965, again for the legal defense, was a big one that made rock promoters drool, music critics hop and Graham rise. The whole idea of electric music and dancing was, I think, suggested by someone from the Family Dog. Jefferson Airplane, Grateful Dead (originally the Warlocks), Mystery Trend, the Great Society and two to three thousand people were inside jumping and dancing, shouting and yelling. It was unbelievably joyous not only because of the music but also because it was a meeting of people concerned with pushing the establishment off their backs. I saw painters, musicians, politicos, theatre people, old friends, unknown long-hairs, straights all mixing, having given two bucks for a worthy fight.

The Benefits at the Fillmore were to support the legal battles of the free Park case. (Graham called them Appeals, an interesting difference.) We were collecting money to support both operations—the theatre in the parks and our legal hassles. Graham, hired to promote and sell our shows, had done his job well. There was one more appeal, Appeal III, January 14, 1966, for more "legal defense" funding. It netted little money and lots of lost time. Graham was hot to go for more money and we ended our working arrangement one day when on the phone Graham said, "Ron, the Mime Troupe can sponsor another rock show . . . we can make a lot together."

The body of the future Digger energy walked into our studio one day wearing Italian-American chic clothes. With a faint aura of Italian hood, Emmett Grogan, from Brooklyn and, most recently, from a U.S. Army hospital, told us of his expulsion. "They asked me to work in the dark-room and I went in one day and printed five hundred pictures of myself." Grogan came to us as an actor, explaining he had done some work in Italian films and liked our free spirit. He played in two commedias, *Olive Pits* and *The Miser*, a cop in *Search and Seizure*, and, later, went on to play the mindless computer operator in Peter Berg's play, *Output You*.

Berg's influence on Grogan and Grogan's influence on Berg coupled with the activity of the Mime Troupe and the energy of the Haight produced the Diggers. Their first known overground activity was providing free food in the Panhandle, a part of Golden Gate Park that runs the length of Haight-Ashbury. Free food (commandeered or stolen) was as electric as free shows; in fact, more directly related to the needs of runaways from boredom who were hungry. The whole process was gobbled up and the Diggers became social activists of the street. Once free food took hold, the notion of free expanded to free dope, free clothes, free city. As "free" things became improbable, abstract free thought replaced them.

The key elements in the Diggers' ideology were their insistence on anonymity and their literary idealism. Digger papers and communication-company flyers floated down Haight Street at least once a week during the high days of 1965-66. Each paper had important news, a poem or some psychedelic vision of Nirvana relating more to the immediate street population than the anti-political *Oracle* and the other flamboyant underground hip papers. The Digger Conspiracy eliminated "ego tripping" by circulating anonymous papers and thus eliminated leadership and organization. All practice and no theory made group action impossible.

While the Robin Hood/ Diggers were stringing their bows and Graham was building his castle, what was the Mime Troupe doing? Some of us were wandering around the theatre, whatever the hell that was in 1965. I had written a long essay on the workings of the company and an analysis of what we had done in the past few years. The article was read to the company in May 1965, just as we moved from Capp Street in the Mission to our new large downtown loft on Howard Street. Graham heard it and liked the toughness. Berg understood it and called it "Guerrilla Theatre." I had described what we were doing and made motions to implement that program of working outside the established institutions, supporting the movement, SNCC, CORE, SDS and so on.

In 1965 the objective of our group was to teach, direct toward change and be an example of change. We were to exemplify the message that we asked others to accept. We had yet to solidify the organization that could carry out the description of our program. We had no income and few probable markets for our product. Our product was different and the markets were new. The company was paying but five bucks per show per performer and small salaries to the office people. We were struggling on all fronts at once—aesthetic, political and material.

It would be presumptuous to assume that we were the center of all the action; nevertheless, we must understand where our ideas came from and where they went. We were as antibourgeois bound as the Diggers. Alternative theatre, guerrilla theatre, all the things we worked on and tried to create opened a Pandora's box of social action. However, although Berg had adapted *Candelio* for the Park spectacle and Grogan was attracted by the action, they forgot that the Mime Troupe had done free shows *with donations*, the Fillmore benefits were to pay the extra legal costs, not all the costs. We wanted to be supported by the people we played for.

5

FROM BUST TO BUST

In between busts we sometimes did shows, but the busts became more dramatic, dangerous and costly. The money and energy consumed in each successive trial began to outweigh its political value. The first bust in 1965 in the parks for performing with a revoked permit opened up the parks to free theatrical/cultural expression and got us on the front pages. By Christmas 1966, the issues were less clear and the publicity only a few lines.

Christmas, if you happen to be anti-consumer, is a season to annoy the shoppers. Christmas is also the season to sing. We thought caroling on the streets would be fun and we put our expressions of joy together with our political consciousness to develop the Gargoyle Carolers: twelve people in Hieronymus Bosch and Bruegel costumes went out and sang well-rehearsed Christmas carols with a few word changes. There was an ordinary hump-backed midget, a gap-toothed witch, a syphilitic monk, a few general uglies and other odds and ends. We came upon a bear's head, placed it on one of the carolers, gave her a tin cup and told her to go out and get carfare. We didn't

work for nothing! The group sang in front of a few department stores, then took off to North Beach and Broadway, a well-touristed spot in San Francisco's nightclub district. They sang in a circle on the sidewalk, blocking traffic, of course. The cops came and told them to move. They did; moved and sang; then they gathered around a busy corner and did their small show in front of the Bank of America. The tin cup was pushed into the watching faces and hands, and sometimes came back with change. The cops got pissed and busted the whole group. They were hauled off in costume to jail, which immediately netted a news story. Rarely do pock-marked priests and hunch-backs (the bear got checked outside) get arrested. They were booked for illegal begging. We demanded a jury trial and called a friend who had just begun to cross over the fence from the District Attorney's side in Richmond to the people's side in San Francisco, Richard Hodge (later involved in the Defense of the Oakland Seven and Los Siete). Hodge in court got the cop going on, "Did you see the bear ask for donations?" "Yes." "Who was playing the bear—can you point that person out in the courtroom?" The jury could not make up its mind and hung on the case. We won it, bear head and all.

The next bust was more serious. We had maintained the Minstrel Show in repertory as a money-maker and had exploited its political value in the Bay Area to the fullest when we set it loose. Peter Cohon took over, re-directing a new cast for our first cross-country tour, as I busied myself with booking contracts. We made the Minstrel Show into a trunk show. Everything broke down into trunks and each performer, musician and interlocutor carried his own suitcase, plus one other piece. We had nine people, eighteen bags, and they all flew. Most of them flew half-fare to boot. Those six-feet-four-inch darkies blew into the airport with the half-fare cards of nineteen-year-olds and the white midgets looked like twelve next to them and got on too.

The first leg of the cross-country travels began in Denver with three shows; then, to Madison, Chicago, etc. I was to join them in Philadelphia and head on to Town Hall and a big show with Dick Gregory in New York. We had made booking arrangements with a friend to perform two nights for the Young Democrats in Denver at a rented hall and then to go to Fort Collins and perform on the campus of Colorado State University. The second night in Denver, with two judges, ten notable Democrats and assorted officials in the audience, the cops busted three members of the cast.

Although we always wrote tour itineraries with the address and telephone number of the nearest ACLU office, we had played the Minstrel Show so often in the Bay Area and up the coast that we no longer considered it dangerous. The first night in Denver, they played to a moderately interested house. The second night was better and the show was running along when the cops came backstage during the intermission and said that the performers had to stop the show. The performers went out onstage and said, "Come out here and arrest us. Do it in front of the crowd." The cops did not want to do it onstage, so the Minstrels completed the show with a wary eye on the fuzz in the wings, then got off the stage into the audience and almost got away. The pigs grabbed three Minstrels and the Interlocutor demanded to go along.

They arrested the performers for "simulated acts of perversion" and sex and other crimes against the city of Denver. Generally, state obscenity laws are more rational than municipal codes; therefore, the city of Denver decided to try its own code and it could not have picked a worse night—half the town's Democrats were there. Walter Gerash, a formidable attorney in Denver, took on the case with Leonard Davies, who later turned up on Panther cases. Both good trial lawyers, they swamped the district attorney's office with those two judges and other notable witnesses, in addition to some evidence which demonstrated that simulated acts were not even done by the persons arrested. The cops, in their haste to arrest, couldn't tell the difference between one darkie and another and had got the wrong guys. They even had difficulty finding any of them in the crowd, despite the fact that they were in blackface, with black fright wigs, and wore sky-blue tails. The publicity helped, although here again the papers featured the "obscenity issue" rather than the content. The content of the show was volatile and the obscenity was mild compared to other shows around. Leroi Jones's famous plays *The Toilet* and *The Slave* had been performing in every major city with one hundred and fifty uses of the word "motherfucker" (in one or both of these plays) as compared to our "simulated acts" and a few sprinklings of the same. We, however, were doing stuff on white chicks and black studs, niggers and whites and digging beneath the surface of some heavy white prejudice. Thus, the content of the Minstrel Show's "obscenity" was much more dangerous to the protective consciousness of racism than the black poet's intense psychological assaults on whitey.

They were busted on a Wednesday night, September 28, 1966, and on Thursday were out on bail playing Fort Collins. The Police Chief at Fort Collins saw the show and said, "I don't know what the boys in Denver got so excited about." They flew off like birds, winging across the States, played heavy shows in Wisconsin and then continued on the tour.

In February of 1967, the three—Peter Cohon, director/actor; Earl Robertson, who played Snowball; and Bill Lynden—had to return to Denver to stand trial. The prosecution tried to prove that a string of obscenities, simulated sex acts and other garbage was sewn together and *covered* with free speech (or civil rights). Our lawyers, Gerash and Davies, tried to show that the string of obscenities, simulated sex acts and other garbage was sewn together for the *elevation* of free speech (or civil rights). We won.

Ominously, we had begun the year of 1967 with a vision of guilt and condemnation; that is, with a play by Jean-Paul Sartre called *The Condemned of Altona* in which I played Franz, a guilty German torturer. In a neo-naturalistic role like Franz, I had to internalize the part. I attached his characteristics to my personal past and, thus, assumed the guilt of individualism, capitalism, my father's crimes, the war in Vietnam and any other handy American guilt lying around. Although our production of *Condemned* only lasted the month of February and ended its real life in an article written by Peter Berg and me, "Sartre through Brecht," in the *Drama Review*, I carried around a little replica of the play inside my head and waited to be condemned.

The times were confusing. We were part of a movie; the documentary *Have You Heard of the San Francisco Mime Troupe?* was just being completed. *Olive Pits* was being rearranged with Peter Cohon and Arthur Holden, yet we still had forty-five energetic actors to utilize. The big catch-all for the rest of the company was called the Vaudeville Show. We had rented a large old shriners' temple on Geary Street, three doors down from Graham's Fillmore Auditorium, to present *Condemned*. With the empty seats and empty nights, we decided to present a vaudeville show, too. The temple had a stage with twenty elaborately painted drops that flew into the flies (the space over stage), depicting the life of the shriners (or the gift of the gods?). They were hokey backdrops which we supposed could be used for a vaudeville show. Sandy Archer and Joe Bellan tried to run it, but I heard the cast revolted and changed the conception. What conception I could never figure out, since we had almost no concept of the show except to use the drops!

The last tour of the Minstrel Show came up in March. I did not want to play in it and in fact had not planned on going. One healthy, Haight Street hipster who joined the Minstrel Show and swore on the tour split at the last minute to sell dope and, again, I had to fill in.

After two years of keeping the Minstrel Show alive we decided to pack it away. It was exhausting to perform and began to drain the energy of the company what with new cast members, costume repairs and text changes to keep up with changing political developments. The final tour was to be a quick trip in March booked by Robert Slattery who was doubling as business manager. We were to fly directly to Buffalo, pick up two thousand dollars for a week's work, flip to Canada on the way back, play Winnipeg, Calgary, Vancouver and then home. We didn't make it.

The promoter in Winnipeg, a big-time student booker, had decided not to announce our second performance at the college until we had done the first one and had not bothered to secure the hall for the show either. The first night, we played in a legit theatre in Winnipeg like the vaudeville traveling days—taxi from the airport to the snowbound theatre, back door, brass handles on the front door, big red plush gilt house. About two hundred people showed up and we couldn't figure out where or who they were. Still groggy, we went through the show, got to sleep and the next day had to face up to another political problem that we hadn't planned for. The complications about the arrangements didn't come to the surface until the end of our stay. We called a rally, made speeches, gave a partial dramatic reading of the Minstrel Show in a lecture hall with no costumes, no make-up, just blah, blah, blah. Another

political rally in no-man's land, neither wanted nor enjoyed. We left Winnipeg after two horrible days. Tired, we plunked down in Calgary, Alberta, met at the airport by two college kids who were pleasant enough and turned out to be police agents. (Ralph Gleason said when I came back to the States, "Calgary . . . man, don't you know bands never stop at Calgary. They go from Montreal to Vancouver, over it.")

We got off the plane with these two nice kids, girl and boy, loading our luggage into a stationwagon. We drove through the sunshine and snow of Alberta to the University of Calgary. We found that the performance area was here, also, in question; but by this time we were very groggy. I didn't want to fight for the right to perform in

Chronicles of Hell, 1965

the best places anymore. Just do it and get it over with.

We all looked at the gymnasium as a possible "theatre," played a little basketball, then went over to the cafeteria and looked at that. The guys went to the bathroom and jived around the toilet area—twenty-five urinals, twenty-five toilets, mirrors, all that American compulsion right there in Calgary. While in the bathrooms jiving around, the two pleasant kids assumed that people who jive in toilets must be on dope, so they called the vice-president who then called the sergeant. That evening, the cops searched the performers they found around. Three of us were watching a movie when a messenger arrived and said that one of the guys in the show had been arrested for possession.

What? We ran to find out what the problem was. They were talking very nicely, the pleasant uniformed tall blue-eyed monsters. Lee, who had stuffed some seeds and twigs in his sneakers years ago, had taken the fuckin' things along in case he should play tennis! (In the snow?) They found the baggie full of waste and arrested him for possession. We stood around jawing lines like search and seizure, constitutional bullshit, immigrants: nothing. We settled down to the telephones and called lawyers, got in touch with the National Democratic Party (NDP) and the left in Alberta. We realized that Alberta, run by a Social Creditor, was more like a feifdom than a province. Ernest Charles Manning, the leader of the Social Credit Party, had been elected early in the depression

The Condemned, 1967

years on a pseudo-FDR program: money to the people, take the oil profits and share it. He was not only head of the party, but also head of the Province. Every Sunday morning, he preached biblical fundamentalist sermons on the radio for his parishioners. We called about fifty people, asking for help and we came upon the notorious lawyer, the Melvin Belli of Alberta, Milt Harradence. All the guys in jail told me he was great. I never understood why they believed that, when all his clients were inside, not outside.

The first step was to establish legal defense. Harradence was hired by phone. We went into our guerrilla action roles. Each of us was to operate in some way during an emergency: publicity, legal, demonstration, rehearsal and show set-up. Everyone worked smoothly in Calgary. Even Slattery, who was not our age nor our temperament, stiffened his jaw and headed into the wind. We planned for the next day.

School sponsorship had disappeared along with the student who hired us. We decided to do the show; screw the Canadians, they couldn't stop us. We planned a noon-time rally right in the main cafeteria of the school. After the rally, we would go separately by different cars to the theatre we had booked downtown—not a theatre, but, a Shrine Hall. We had been refused a number of places but had secured this one at last. With only Lee out of the cast, we figured that we could do it with the stage manager, or a mannikin; whatever, we would do the show.

The rally or speak-in opened well. We sang songs, a kid came to the mike and introduced us (he didn't mention his own name), some teachers came closer as we began to talk of free speech, freedom of expression and all those nineteenth century liberal ideas we in America had fought

for against the Tories and British Empire. The kids kept on eating. Slattery spoke and I rounded it off with some pungent remarks. RCMP, the famous Royal Canadian Mounted Police, slunk around the back of the dining area, slithering out of the kitchen in big black overcoats and dark hats. We decided to split—fast. We stepped off sideways, got around a couple of doors behind the kitchen, zoomed into the dorm area, ran down a tunnel out through the backdoor to waiting cars provided by friendly students. Dividing into two groups in two different cars, we headed downtown, driving pretty rapidly, basking in the one well-executed maneuver of the whole tour. We came to a red light. ZAP. "Come with us." I couldn't believe it, our cars must have been marked, planted, set up or something. It was perfect. We were completely surrounded. How? We never saw the drivers nor the kids who led us to the cars again.

They called in their big-time experts to take us down to the RCMP lock-up. They told us we were going to the Immigration Office, but a narc is a narc all the world over. Searched there, they "found" nothing on Kent Minault, one seed on Ron S., and some residue on me. Ron S. and I were booked for possession and began to think about three years in jail (those were the sentences they were giving out in 1967). Then they told us they weren't setting bail and that they had no intention of doing so.

The bust in Canada raised a host of friends on our behalf, just as our 1965 park bust had. Our friend, Digger Grogan, called a press conference and sent out press releases that hit the Canadian and U.S. press. He organized a demonstration at the Canadian consulate in New York City with Allen Ginsberg and Gregory Corso. Both Ginsberg and Corso got in to see the head man. Corso is reputed to have jumped up on his desk and howled, "Let them go!" Anne Bernstein, actress and ex-Vietnam Day Committee member, ran the office while Sandy Archer and Bob Hurwitt planned benefits. Bob Scheer got in touch with Bobby Kennedy people and we got advice from them.

Don Duncan, doing a stint with *Ramparts* magazine in between the Green Berets and the Movement for a Democratic Military, came with Sandy to visit me in jail in Canada. So, too, my older brother. All helped except the attorney, Milt Harradence. Harradence attended more press conferences than court actions and did little else on the case than spend the three thousand dollars paid him. Eventually, through the good work of my brother, we got a notable Canadian to front our bail. With his name as security, a Supreme Court Judge set bail for Ron S. and me at twenty-five hundred dollars each. Through our anonymous benefactor, we posted bail from the proceeds of the San Francisco benefits. Lee had been released earlier on one thousand dollars bail and went back to San Francisco. Returning for the arraignment, he had been delayed by Customs officials at the airport long enough to get arrested again, this time for non-appearance in court, and forfeited his bail. Ron S. and I after two weeks in cages at the RCMP and the Spy Hill Gaol, finally got out and were given two expensive business suits to attend a court hearing the next morning. We got on a plane that afternoon and have never, never set foot in Canada since.

It was inevitable that we would be, at one time or another, busted for grass. When we were busted for all those other offenses, we never got busted on political grounds. We tried to argue "prior censorship" in the park case; freedom of the streets in the Gargoyle case; "free speech" in the Denver bust; yet, we were busted for trespassing, jaywalking, stopping traffic, obscenity and pandering to prurient interests. We were never arrested for the "crime" we committed.

It was clear then that the most dangerous thing we could do was to break into the smothering totality of their illusions, and insist upon our version of reality. In a way what we had to do was easy. If by exposing a little of the hidden injustice of the system, we could be threatening enough for the RCMP to spend hours of its time chasing us around Calgary, there was a crack in the wall. Sitting there in jail cleared my head and I could see us telling the truth and making the crack grow.

Centerman, 1966

Street hustling, *Candalaio*, 1967

6

COMMEDIA ON THE ROAD

While we were busted in Calgary, the Vaudeville Show was going on back home. It was not at all like the Minstrel Show in that it did not make a political point. In fact it was simply a stop-gap measure to take up the variety of energies in the company—tap dancers, tumblers, singers, dancers, half a rock-and-roll band, an old Vaudeville skit. The worst Eddie Cantor movie ever made topped eight acts.

We spent little time analyzing what a Vaudeville Show meant. We simply pet-talked it into existence and thereby blew it out of proportion. When Calgary exploded forcing everyone to devote all their energy to raising twelve thousand dollars for bail and legal fees, reality popped the pep talk. There were two paths open to us; to go back to Canada and fight or to reorganize the company. Immediately upon returning from Calgary, I spent two weeks on the phone trying to drum up support for a return bout in Canada. I wanted to go back and fight.

While I was busy working the phones, Bob Hurwitt arranged a benefit, affectionately called "Appeal IV" on April 12, 1967, at the Fillmore Audi-

torium. We netted six thousand dollars on a Tuesday night with the Grateful Dead, Jefferson Airplane, Quicksilver Messenger Service, Moby Grape, and the Loading Zone. I spoke at the dance and tried to say some cogent words about cops to the group of rock fans who had never heard of us. It was like speaking into a cotton candy machine. Some of the musicians remembered us from the old days, but the new rock fans, only two years old, knew the bands but not the Mime Troupe. We paid Graham back the money he loaned us to put up the bail and left the benefit business once again with lots of good feeling and no solutions.

There was a lot going on in the Haight in the spring of '67 and some of us viewed it from different perspectives. We had come off the high days of the 1965 arrest with a notable public accomplishment and believed ourselves to be the political artistic voice of the community. To carry through our community work we started an organization called the Artists Liberation Front—designed to stop the creation of cement mausoleums. The foundations discovered "the arts" in 1966 and everyone wanted a Lincoln Center. The Artists Liberation Front, a collection of San Francisco artists, was to put political savvy into the public mentality. It was composed of fifteen Mime Troupe members and about thirty other people. ALF was successful in voicing a certain type of foundation rejection but the Mime Troupe's castigation of Cement Cultural Complexes didn't provide us with any support.

We had no handle on any rational means of survival. We sent out shows to tour colleges but our college business had not coughed up enough to cover the total expense of the Minstrel Show. Our park shows were eking by and we were just developing new material for a cabaret theatre circuit. Our doors had opened wide to all comers, yet there was no centralized organizational means to handle the many people who came. Our classes in dance, acting and such made less and less sense to people who were attracted to the democratic notion of amateuristic total participation of "do your own thing." Our politicization program made no headway against a tide of long hair, electronic music, Digger fantasy and "action in the streets." Many of the members of the company were ignorant of our political history, having joined because of the noise we made in public. They had neither any stage experience comparable to the Minstrel Show nor enough theatrical talent to want to continue struggling with the Mime Troupe's alternative theatre.

In order to find out where people were at, I had conversations with groups of five over coffee and asked what each person in the company thought our direction should be. The majority were interested in a commune/theatrical/action troupe. Many wanted to buy or rent a house and live together. I couldn't believe that our problems could be answered by moving in with each other but others had one ear and foot on Haight Street and that was the message. What were we supposed to do with those fifty people out there in the big loft? After spending some days composing the letter, I sent a note to thirty-five people.

May 1, 1967

Dear   ,
    I am cutting the company down to manageable size. This is an arbitrary move which has some specific motives. If you want to hear them, please let me know, but I have decided to cut back to those people who are now performing and working in this company or who will be performing in the immediate future.
    To thank you is to negate much sweat and love, but I thank *you* not only for myself but us, those and the rest, who have benefited from what we have done together.

Ronny

The confusion of the past months was clarified and the immediate work became the central focus of all involved. The dismissal (we couldn't fire, since we did not pay) was accomplished without rancor for it was apparent that we could not supply a total lifestyle for more than ten to fifteen people. Of the thirty-five let loose, some went home, a few went to Digger street life, Ann and Bill Lyndon put together the Free City Puppets; and one or two whom I had wanted to stay left for traveling experiences. The remaining nucleus began work on the play which we had tentatively decided to perform, *L'Amant Militaire*.

The production was the outgrowth of seven years of innovative theatrical techniques, fortunately in the hands of four experienced commedia performers, three directors and three writers within the context of immediate political significance. This anti-pacifist play (for some an antiwar play) was performed by people who appeared to believe in the content of their message and were also able to take on the additional roles necessary for a radical touring group—accommodations, stage managing, publicity, prop, mask and costume maintenance.

Arthur Holden had been directing the preliminary stages of *L'Amant* while I was making calls to Calgary. When I left the phone and moved in as director of the show, it was a cooperative venture. Sometimes Sandy Archer directed and if she couldn't figure out what to do we dumped the problem into Peter Cohon's hands. The writing followed the same process. Joan Holden adapted Betty Schwimmer's original translation and re-wrote scenes upon rehearsal demand. Peter and Arthur continued to work on the script through-out rehearsals while Sandy and I wrote our own transitional scenes as actors had done in *The Dowry*.

The process was fluid for we were cross-examining our own views on the war. Our liberal pacifism came to the stage and was punched around by some radical thoughts. More interested in telling the audience what to do or "where it's at" than delineating the process within antiwar positions, we wanted to deliver a heavier punch than we had previously within the commedia structure. I suggested we present our directives with a puppet outside the play, off the stage, who spoke directly to the audience. Punch, the puppet (who later became Punch the Red), was the "radical" voice outside the play.

The addition of this outside voice, or puppet, with a commedia play was an tension of the polit-ical intensity we were beginning to require of our shows. Punch was supposed to give the audience direct actional information, i.e., come out and precisely say what the stage action only implied. Our first Punch in *L'Amant* was played by Bill Lyndon, who was given the role and asked to write his own lines. Eventually we thought it more appropriate if the actors, in turn, played the puppet, everyone getting a chance to make his or her own political point. The whole thing was cumbersome. Finally, the job fell to Arthur Holden and Darryle Henriques, who not only had time to get the puppet box in hand, but were also good at executing the part. They eventually re-worked the lines to suit audience response.

No matter what the line or how gross the Pup-pet statement, the "message" was always tem-pered by the image of a puppet box with legs (see illustration). The one-man puppet stage was such a lovely complex image that it softened the heavy "left rap." The audience could see the workings of the puppet and the puppet was permitted out-rages that we, as masked characters on stage, were hard pressed to commit.

L'Amant Militaire was originally a play about two lovers caught in the web of warfare. Not only did we shift the emphasis from their personal problem to the social situation but the performers who played the roles never dominated the action. In our productions, because of their non-meticulous and improvisational nature, those who could improvise and hold their own beyond the script dominated the stage—sometimes to the detriment of the production, script and political message. The lovers could not take the ring away from Peter Cohon, Sandy Archer and me. I moved well, controlled space; Peter had the character of Pantalone at his finger tips; and Sandy Archer could do three emotional turns between someone else's lines.

Just as the legs on the puppet box contradicted the "left rap" of the puppet, so, too, the comic spirit of individuals on stage interrupted the mes-sage of the play. We had been contained by Sassoon and Nina Landau during *Tartuffe* but we were feeling our own oats and I had a hard time repressing comic invention which I always felt to be more popular than *political* messages. Our openings warmed up the audience and the players, and presented the characters prior to the play.

Da Pope, *L'Amant Militaire*, 1967

Generale, *L'Amant Militaire*, 1967

Performance
at Stanford University
Palo Alto, California — 1967

Introduction, music, song, parade—"Il troupo di mimo ..." Capitano did introductions with Coralina.

Capitano: ". . . L'Amant Militaire"

Coralina: [enters on applause] Yes, that's right, L'Amant Militaire.

Capitano: Ah, Coralina, do you know where we are?

Coralina: He asks me if I know where we are. Do I know where we are! *[chuckle]* No, I don't know where we are!

Capitano: Portland State College. Where do you think?

Coralina: What? No, Generale Garcia, you got it all wrong. We are at Stanford University and we are sponsored by the Free University.

Capitano: Ah ha, so they are our sponsors, huh. Well, why didn't they fill up the house?

Coralina: They're our sponsors, not our supporters.

Capitano: You know today I heard, over there, that the Free University is taking a field trip. Six people are going to the Haight Ashbury.

Coralina: You mean like a sociological study? What are they going there to find out?

Capitano: Nothing.

Coralina: What do you mean, nothing?

Capitano: The Haight Ashbury is wiped out—completely dead. The Haight Ashbury is a demilitarized zone.

Coralina: You telling me that it's been dead and I didn't even know it?

Capitano: Yes. Today, October 6th, is the death of Hip.

Pantalone and hand, *L'Amant Militaire*, 1967

Coralina: Oh, I could have sent flowers.

Capitano: Let's introduce someone. . . . Introducing that sergeant, that Spanish sergeant, the green hornet from Harvard, our own Sergeant Brighella. *[Brighella enters doing a Spanish clap/stamp . . . bow]*

Coralina: And, following right behind him, in the Spanish tradition of right following might, of tall following small, Corporal Espada . . . *[Espada enters singing/ dancing . . . "Oh, dem Golden Slippers, Oh, dem . . ."]*

Capitano/Coralina: No, wrong show. Stop it dimwit . . .

Capitano: Introducing that philanthropic financier, the Venetian merchant, the only paranoid whose fears are completely justified, the great Senior Pantalone.

The plot of *L'Amant* was intricate. The Spanish army had been occupying Italy to protect the Italians from their own rebellion. The first scene between Pantalone, mayor of Spinacholla and father to Rosalinda, and General Garcia, Spanish commander-in-chief, gives us some idea of the workings of the play. Garcia announces that the war is coming to conclusion and the mayor suggests slowing down for the profits are good. Garcia warns that if they were to stay too long it would look like imperialism. Pantalone doesn't care what they call it—if there is a danger of a pull-out, he will sell his goods to the rebels. Garcia becomes suspicious. Coralina, servant to Pantalone, enters to tell him that Alonso, a Spanish lieutenant, is visiting his daughter. Garcia smart as a whip assumes that Pantalone is after all un-patriotic.

Alonso, Rosalinda's lover, is ordered to report

to duty in preparation for Operation Guinea Wrangle. Rosalinda, in despair and shock, collapses and sets off a *lazzi* of revival; Pantalone sees her, orders water, vinegar, help, then Alonso leaps in to music. Pantalone kicks the spic out and warns him not to return. Sergeant Brighella and Corporal Espada, in the following scene, recruit their quota, one wop Arleccino. Coralina discovers him in his new uniform and tries to make him see the war. He plays tricks and finally sees himself dead. He tries to quit, they rough him up. Garcia announces the new offensive offensive. Rosalinda thinks to talk the Generale out of the war. Alonso is torn between his love and duty. His dilemma causes his arrest for dereliction of duty. Garcia exits with Alonso prisoner.

Arleccino, disguised as a woman, enters fleeing from the army. Espada comes upon the woman, then discovers "Private A. Battacio" and takes the deserter off to be buggered, then executed. The penultimate scene is the execution of Arleccino and Alonso. The Generale yells: "Ready, aim," and suddenly a trumpet blast is heard from the top of the curtain and a figure appears above the set. Coralina, in a conical hat, serious face, then smiling, says, "I'ma da Pope." Everybody freezes. "But, first, I'ma sing a little song." (ALL) "When the moon hits your eye like a big pizza pie, dat's amore." Gods have come down from the heavens, but I have never heard of the Pope as the deus ex machina, played by a servant girl. It was the mind blower of the show.

Coralina spouts some Latin and Rosalinda, in recognition, exclaims, "Il Pape." Alonso says, "Who?" The answer comes back sharply: "I'm da Pope, dope." Coralina, as Pope, goes on to save the day. Reading a Papal Bull, she declares the war over and so, too, the killings and the executions. Garcia runs off the stage, exiting through the audience, shouting he will reappear (and we know he will). The Pope tells Pantalone to marry his daughter to Alonso. All exeunt to music and dancing, leaving Arleccino lying on stage. Coralina descends to wake him. Seeing her in the costume of the Pope, he exclaims—"Oh God, it's Dio. I'm dead." Coralina says, "No cretino, get up—look—it's Coralina!" (They hug.) "What you think this was, a fairy tale?" (Steps forward.) "Listen, my friends, you want something done? Well, then do it yourselves!"

End song and the whole cast returned to the stage singing and stamp/clapping "Marat we're poor . . ." to bows and applause.

Once again, the final image of the play was a total utilization of the conventions of the theatre for progressive purposes. The image of servant as Pope is compounded by bringing Coralina down to the wooden stage and upon showing Arleccino that she is Coralina, she exclaims what is intrinsic to the device (servant as Pope) and intrinsic to the image (device as shock) and intrinsic to the Mime Troupe's performance—"If you want something done, do it yourself."

Commedia requires a happy ending, much like epic drama. The commedian attacks or runs from fate. The epic character may even stand still, but the audience learns that fate or environmental conditions are changeable. Our commedias were bound by real politics, thus satire was our forte, not slapstick. We always related our joke to something tangible, rather than developing comedy from fantasy. The exit of Generale Garcia from the stage through the audience was no slight exit. We had avoided an inevitable end by using a traditional theatrical device, deus ex machina, but the war continued. The play intended to expose a pacifist's impotence, it did not intend or pretend to stop the war.

7

OUTSIDE AGITATORS

While we were working on the production of *L'Amant* we were booking a national tour to surpass the 1964 Minstrel Show adventure. In our first jaunt cross country in 1964, we played a flashy blackface show but we returned with no extra capital and couldn't observe or take advantage of the social effect. By 1967 we were an example of the new left Digger "acting-as-lifestyle" group. Unaided by government grants, foundations or big city bookers, our commedia guerrilla group of ten tramped across the country —a do-it-yourself kit in motion.

We flew and drove to our first date in Minneapolis. Flying all the time was too expensive and although rapid, it forced us to adapt our traveling time to flight schedules. We decided to fly a few to Minneapolis and drive the rest with the stage, a heavy metal but compact unit which fitted into our newly purchased panel truck. We were going to do this one right.

The booking business is as complicated as directing a show. Planning the transportation of ten people from one side of the country to the other with equipment for two shows and sundry instruments for lectures and parades took all my time not devoted to rehearsals. We had to create three or four options for one date to be able to chart a consecutive traveling pattern and I tried to average five hundred dollars a day but often accepted deals for two shows in one day for three hundred fifty dollars—"with donations."

Overpaying for the truck and overloading it didn't matter. Four of us were to fly, some with half-fare cards. For me, with grey hair, mustache and old lines on my face, to do the half-fare card trick, I had to bandage my head completely to look like I'd suffered a brain concussion, tie up my writing arm in a finger brace and bandage, put some red rouge under my nostrils, black lines around the eyes for bags, to get my ticket. Rather than waiting for the other passengers, this crash victim was escorted onto the plane first.

Our first booking in Minneapolis was at the Firehouse Theatre. Sidney Walters and Marlow Hotchkiss put us up for a few days, in addition to getting us a booking at the University of Minnesota for lots of cash. We wanted to make deals like this. We wanted to see all the other independent theatre groups, talk, show our stuff, and get them to help us on the tour. Our first stop was exemplary. We made friends with he Firehouse people. They got us a university date. We met street people and gave a few workshops. The Diggers in the group, Cohon and Minault, led the workshops. The message was, more often than not, "tune in, turn on and fuck it up."

We purchased another car in Minneapolis from an ex-cop. The Midwest appeared human after riots and shootings in the Bay Area. We rove our new three-vehicled caravan to the University of Wisconsin at Madison. The University of Wisconsin was like a crammed Telegraph Avenue in Berkeley. The student radical cafeteria, the rathskeller in the basement, was full of old army jackets, long hair, beards, levis and fur coats. It was dark; the food was bad; the crowd was intense. Upstairs, where the straights ate, the view was magnificent. We talked with the heavies, but some of us stayed upstairs with the view.

We were preparing our performance in their large, fifteen-hundred-seat auditorium when a few curly-haired, old-army-jacketed kids came up to ask if we would announce there was to be a demonstration against Dow Chemical the next day at noon on the "hill." We discussed it, said "sure" and suggested that we might go there to help. At the end of the show, we marched in a line, cast of seven, stamping and clapping together down-stage, full-phalanx, and I said:

> We are from another area, but would like to help you all here. We were told there will be a demonstration against the Dow recruiters tomorrow at twelve and we thought that you and we might all be there. We have learned through our experience that, after all, this country is our country and if we don't like it, then we should try to change it; and, if we can't change it, then we should destroy it. See you at the demonstration.

Standing cheers. The next day, two hundred people showed up at the demonstration, many more than had been anticipated. We began to understand the real power of outside agitators.

Tired from the night's work and rising to a cold freezing day, a few of us agreed to go, grumbling, to the demonstration. I remember going to the blue truck and getting some instruments out for Charlie Degelman, Arthur Holden and Darryle Henriques. I was planning to go off to the library and work on a speech to be delivered at the next date in Iowa, but I walked over with the group to the hill and joined the "millers" (milling around before a demonstration is a prerequisite). Organizers of the demonstration were speaking or growling into hand megaphones only heard by a few people in front of each growl. Few knew what all were supposed to do. Charlie and Arthur knew. They were supposed to move! To demonstrate! A bugle call, blat, blat, blaa . . . a drum roll . . . and the whole crowd followed the incipient marching band up the hill to walk around the building that the Dow recruiters were using.

During the demonstration, a few sat and blocked the entrance, others marched around. I suggested that the "band" lead, but not get trapped in the action. We had other colleges to stir up and I went off to the library to steal a book on *The Art of War* by Sun Tzu. When I got back, the tear gas was just clearing, paddywagons were driving away and kids were running in different directions. The city cops had escalated.

We were to give a lecture demonstration in a room opposite the tear-gassed area; but, instead, we had an assembly meeting with the Mime Troupers as meeting managers. This was not a time to discuss guerrilla or radical theatre—the students obviously had to figure out what to do now that their friends were going to jail. The meeting was hectic, but instructive. There was no clear line, many of the students, as usual, didn't know about Dow's involvement in the war or the complicity of the university in it but many were disturbed that their fellow students had been bashed by clubs, gassed and dragged off to jail. Personal assault was more important than any of the protest factors. We stood by, watching and listening. It was instructive to us as well. What would the organizers come up with?

A mass meeting was called for 9:00 P.M. in the Student Union. At the appointed time, the place was overflowing, so they moved the whole thing outside to a space behind the library. About three thousand people sat in the cold, listening to various points of view over bad microphones. Not one speaker, from professors to the Trotskyite students who were talking about American Imperialist Power, could or did speak to the anger or imagination of the three thousand people assembled. The grad students complained but clearly did not want to jeopardize their positions. The professors were meeting elsewhere to decide what they would do and by the time someone came up with a reasonable idea, about an hour and a half later, only fifteen hundred people were left to declare a strike. The strike's aims were typical: amnesty for those arrested, no more recruiters, etc. The action was exciting, but had no links to the rest of the college, had no spearhead, just a vague bunch of torsos and arms.

The next day, the strikers were handing out leaflets and we drove off to Iowa to see what mischief we might help stir up. Like good outside agitators, we were most often only additions to already volatile circumstances. We, too, had no network that fed us information or directed our attention to develop action where there was none. We happened to be on the spot when the college kids were moving.

We went tripping off to the University of Iowa for the Second Biennial Conference of Modern Letters on the subject: "The New Grotesque Or Is There a Post-Realistic Fiction?" We had booked this one months in advance and I remember the apprehension which we all had about attending the conference, wondering if we were up to the calibre of other participants. Despite four months of collective inspirational rehearsals and rewrites of our show, we had been surprised by the positive reactions in Minneapolis and Madison. I was to give a talk on "Saturday Evening Post Realism." I had not won too many friends with my previous talks about the Mime Troupe Guerrilla Theatre, but I prepared rather carefully for this one, planning a more formal presentation.

Getting very close to the people, to the parks and lower classes, makes dealing with the privileged and celebrities seem awesome. We had played to large crowds in the parks where we shared apples and wine and were now going to perform in a very upper-class conference. In part our fears were unfounded. Our best effect came after we had demonstrated our abilities.

Theatre is a drag in most places and the only comedy the kids saw at that time was run by Hollywood tripsters. Once in a while an artsy-craftsy troupe toured each college—dancers from New York, pick-up French acting companies, Japanese koto players, violinists, sopranos and piano players. Rarely had those students seen an American contemporary company, a group close to their own feelings and ideals. We were unknown until we did our show, after which the kids jammed us and we were culture heroes with rights of passage not even offered to some of the hip professors. We didn't have to be rational. We were lefty stars in Iowa and we used it well.

The talk I gave on "Saturday Evening Post Realism" dealt with thoughts about drama and art that we had developed ever since our company began. I suggested that there was no possibility of naturalistic parody if one looked and used one's eyes in a progressive aesthetic manner. No parody made better sense than LBJ's own words:

We have one sixth of the world's population and half of its wealth.

[or the more explicit]

They want what we got and they ain't going to get it!

The only way one could show it up for what it really meant was to change the context, which I did and they all laughed.

After I spoke, Robert Creeley followed with some nice comments about the Mime Troupe show. He was followed by an academic from Harvard who talked about "the significance of furniture in the works of Dickens, Wadsworth and James." The accent was irritating and the pleasantries boiled us over. Peter Cohon and I ran out looking for the sound system or the lights or the air conditioner; anything to fuck the guy up. We failed. Lots of desire but no knowledge.

As we left the University of Iowa, we heard plans of a huge demonstration against the Iowan branch of Dow. Grinnell College in Grinnell, Iowa, was our next stop. It was called the "Harvard of he Midwest." We had played the Harvard of the West, the Harvard of the North, and even had a Harvard graduate in our cast; but when we arrived at this dump we got bad treatment and shortchanged. It was Pete Cohon's old school. We stayed with his ex-teacher and understood why Peter left school with only his guitar, Kerouac's *On the Road* and a few extra baggies.

We had booked into Grinnell because it was on our route towards the East. I can't remember if we were supposed to get donations and a fee or didn't get our fee because we had no contract. In any case we had no lights for the show, the time was wrong and the audience throught it was free and that no donations would be asked for. All in all we spent a lot of time hassling and weren't enlightened by any of it.

When booking our shows I used any contact— family, old school chums, friends of friends— anything or anyone who would give us a lead. I sold the *Olive Pits* show alone or in a package

with *L'Amant* or the lecture without *L'Amant* or the whole thing for two days. We rarely received aid from any administration's entertainment or cultural committee. We were too small, too radical and didn't come from New York City. We had to rely on the one or two radicals in the English Department to get us on the campus and scrounge up money to pay for the different events. We seldom were invited to a college through the Drama Department—except in one extraordinary case at Carnegie Tech's Institute of Drama and Speech.

I had finagled the second-in-command of the drama desk at Carnegie Tech to put up three hundred dollars for a lecture, "to hear the world of the alternative theatre." He agreed, if we included a demonstration. We had a perfect number for the time and the place. It was called, rather plainly, *Eagle Fuck*. It was not meant to be subtle.

An eagle arrives onstage, circles and leaves. Enter a large Vietnamese puppethead holding a baby; eagle back again with two-foot-long penis; knocks down lady, bangs her, kicks the baby and stomps off. Four peasants come to take the dead woman and child away. Then, little freak-like images of helicopters come on, whizz around, and chase the peasants. The eagle enters with puffed up chest and goes off.

After that number, we were serious for a few minutes. Then I began with a piece of advertisement ripped off a Hertz brochure: "When you're enjoying the theatre in Minneapolis driving your Hertz back to the airport from the Tyrone Guthrie Memorial Theatre . . . Zo den mine Studenten, der theatre is zimply a means by vitch to rent a ccccaaaarrrr? Ya!!!" I then wrote Che's phrase on the blackboard behind me. "The duty of every revolutionary is to make the revolution." I also read from the second guerrilla theatre article I was working on.

By the time we got to Carnegie Tech in Pittsburgh, Pennsylvania, about midway in the two months of travel, we were living, breathing guerrilla theatre freaks. Carnegie Tech houses one of the most important and largest drama departments in the country and is a major supplier of fodder for regional theatre. I didn't know before we got there that they were especially interested in the Guthrie Theatre in Minneapolis. We attacked, in turn, the idiocy of the drama department training people in outmoded technique for bourgeois middle-class theatre, not giving them information (life) to create from, and, of course, denying bourgeois prejudice with bourgeois liberal crap-out "objectivity." I don't think many of them came to see our show.

After Pittsburgh we took a few days off, saw the middle of Pennsylvania, then headed for the final leg of the big journey: Central Park, New England and the Box Factory. We had made elaborate arrangements to play at the new theatre to be opened by the Film Coop on Wooster Street in an ex-box factory. We were the first item to play at the new theatre and, of course, when we got there the place wasn't ready.

I had calculated while arranging the tour that if we pulled a "freebe" in the middle of Manhattan we would get the necessary splash to make our box factory appearance known and cover the mistakes made by inexperienced promoters. We played Sheep's Meadow (the Hippie Hill of New York City) with *Olive Pits* prior to the New England section of the tour and two weeks before the New York run. The show not only drew the hipsters but every camera freak in the underground. I was busy the whole performance banging into New York name photographers trying to keep them away from the front of the stage.

There was one shutter-freak who paid for the right to shoot us. NBC contacted me and wanted to get shots of the troupe for publicity. Of course, everything is for publicity, after all, the world is full of opportunities. I said we would pose—for cash. NBC paid a hundred dollars and 499 other camera flickers got it free.

From Central Park we went into New England: Harvard, MIT, Boston U, Brandeis, Goddard, Bennington and Yale. At Harvard Charlie Degelman was a hero; a Harvard grad who dropped out and came back to piss on the institution; at MIT we were more radical than Noam Chomsky; at Boston U we helped agitate for a strike; at Brandeis we hit the Jews with all the Pantalone gags we could muster; at Goddard the hippies won, they were so stoned they couldn't understand our accents; at Bennington we sang a famous dirty song arranged by Minault and Cohon in the president's house with dissident students.

Oh, the roving sex offender is coming to your town
And if you treat him nicely, he'll pull his britches down.
He'll tantalize your children with candy gum and toys
And introduce the secrets of sexual thrill and joy.

By the time we came back to the city for our two-week run in lower Manhattan at the Film Makers' Coop Theatre, our Central Park free show was on the front pages of the *Village Voice* and we had enough publicity to carry us through the first few days until word-of-mouth and reviews brought the crowds.

We were attractive not only because we were hip, aggressive, artistic, alive, knowledgeable and funny but also because we were out-of-towners. We could be praised and then would leave. We did not bother the New Yorkers; only the hip career critics like John Lahr, who couldn't believe white long-hairs were as radical as blacks or browns. As the house filled up, our last week was completely packed (three hundred to three hundred fifty sitting, standing, bending eight shows a week); the careerists thought something must have been wrong. Reviewers and critics are to be avoided if possible; however, when the box office is dependent upon their notices, one must be attentive to them. The *New York Times*'s reviewer saw a bad performance and asked me if he should write about the show. I asked him not to, bad publicity was never any good for our box office. What may confuse some is to read critics as if their columns contained anything more than mere publicity. When we toured the Minstrel Show and received reviews from the conservative press, it was something like "the audience seemed to enjoy it, but I was bored . . ." Boredom was the last word in don't-pay-for-it. The liberal critics wrote "not always in good taste, but then . . . heaven . . . hell." *L'Amant Militaire* in New York City elicited favorable responses. The *Times* of London compared it to Yale's showcase event.

I wanted to turn our notoriety into something more tangible than a single event soon to be forgotten. If radical theatre was to have any effect on this country, others would have to repeat our success and to this end I suggested that a radical booking agency be formed.

The agency began with a meeting in New York of a number of groups. Open Theatre, Pageant Players, Gut Theatre and the New Lafayette were interested. Saul Gottlieb, writer and itinerant dramaturge, called a second meeting and invited others from La Mama and groups I didn't know in the New York area. At that meeting, I asked La Mama Troupe to leave since it represented no alternative to commercial theatre. Eleanor Stuart admitted that she was only "giving actors, direc-tors and playwrights a chance." Hers was an apprentice program for off-Broadway. I conceived of radical theatre not as a training ground for the bourgeois world but rather as an alternative. Because of our isolation, our ideological strength and the social environment we worked in, ex-Mime Troupers did not feed the off-Broadway theatres nor the commercial movie industry. In most cases, we directed activity away from what Eleanor Stuart and the New York crowd wanted.

The booking agency was run by Saul Gottlieb by default rather than through long-range political insight. He also saw the agency as a way of facilitating the Living Theatre's tour of the United States. They had been negotiating with the U.S. government to pay back-taxes and Gottlieb, who was also writing a book about the group, was interested in arranging their return. Unfortunately, we did not know a tour of the Living Theatre arranged by the Radical Theatre Repertory (its official title) would take over the major work of the agency and sink it.

The same problem of organization and ideology that hobbled the Mime Troupe afflicted the Radical Theatre Repertory but the Repertory had one additional burden—New York.

During our two-week, sixteen-show run at the Film Makers' Cinematheque (box factory) we were offered various deals—ice cream cakes Off-Broadway; go uptown/Lincoln Center and the Forum Theatre; how about a movie. I talked with agents and people with money, all very nice chaps sunk into the liberal world of cocktail parties and name droppings. We were going home! Our outrageous show, almost animalistic, couldn't be placed easily off-Broadway. We were not union performers, and Equity actors couldn't do commedia. In addition, a few of us had grown up in and around New York.

THE TIMES, London, December 18, 1967

San Franscisco anti-war play beats Yale one hollow

From Henry Popkin
New York Drama Critic

Just recently the San Francisco Mime Troupe brought an anti-war play to New York. At the same time the repertory theatre of Yale University, a few miles away, staged an anti-war play. A comparison of the two suggests that Yale University could profitably go to school to the San Francisco Mime Troupe.

The Mime Troupe is a rowdy, vulgar—I am sure they would insist upon this epithet—bunch of actors who spend much of their time on the road, some of it in court, and a little of it in prison. They boast that one of their shows has been performed "in courtrooms of Denver, Colorado, and Calgary, Alberta." (The charge against them is usually obscenity.) At its founding in 1959 this group apparently had some sort of connexion with the San Francisco Actors Workshop, which can now be said to have become transformed into the eminently respectable repertory theatre of Lincoln Center. To call the San Francisco Mime Troupe respectable would be to administer the most cutting—and most unjustified—insult. These actors' intentions are best expressed by their leader, R. G. Davis:

> We have tried to cut through the aristocratic and square notion of what theatre is by bringing movies into stage performances, presenting speakers who are sometimes far more dramatic than plays, applying broadly comic forms (the minstrel show, commedia) to serious issues. We have embarked upon a guerrilla scheme of living off the land and travelling, trying to provoke change.

As for technique: "Mime is the point of departure for our style, in which words sharpen and refine, but the substance of meaning is in action."

The play that Mime Troupe brought to New York was Carlo Goldoni's *L'Amant militaire*, translated by Betty Schwimmer and adapted by Joan Holden, who was subsequently introduced as the "dramatist." (I cannot tell why the title was given in French. The play is normally called *L'Amante militaire;* it does not belong to the period of Goldoni's Parisian exile.) J. S. Kennard's *Goldoni and the Venice of His Time* inadvertently explains its appeal for the Mime Troupe. Disparaging the play, Kennard complains: "Goldoni could not represent or understand patriotism and militarism. . . . His *Memoirs* evidence his pacifism." Anti-patriotic, anti-militarist, pacifist, how could Goldoni fail to interest the San Francisco Mime Troupe? The situation is ideal for the inevitable contemporary parallel: Spanish soldiers are fighting in Italy, fraternizing with some natives but alienating others. *Commedia* half-masks are worn by all the character men, and everyone speaks with a comic Latin accent, except for Pantalone, the major of Spinachola, who speaks with a comic Jewish accent.

It is made perfectly clear that the Spaniards in Italy are the Americans in Vietnam. The plot is still basic Goldoni: a Spanish lieutenant courts Pantalone's daughter, but Pantalone favours an amorous Spanish general; to avoid military service, Arlecchino disguises himself as a woman, but is found out and charged with being a "prevert" (a word admirers of *Doctor Strangelove* will recognize). The *deus ex machina*, however, is basic San Francisco Mime: an actress wearing an ecclesiastical headdress puts her head over the back of the set, announces "I'ma da Pope!" and puts an end to the fighting.

Other additions include free-wheeling jokes and contemporary allusions. The Spanish general promises "to pursue peace with every available weapon," and Pantalone once adopts President Johnson's voice. "McNamara lives!" someone explains, à propos of nothing in particular. Between the scenes, Punch somewhat superfluously and quite emphatically points out parallels to the war in Vietnam, at one moment leading the audience in chanting: "Hell, no, we won't go." Even without Punch, the Mime Troupe gets its ideas across unmistakably. The actors contribute their abundant physical exuberance and a very skilful use of the basic language of American popular comedy—the vaudeville dialect. In an excellent cast, I must single out Sandra Archer, who plays the soubrette and "da Pope," as an actress who could make her mark in the "straight" theatre any time she wants to abandon her guerrilla principles.

Yale's anti-war drama is *We Bombed in New Haven*, the first play by Joseph Heller, author of *Catch 22*. I should explain that, in the parlance of American show business, to "bomb" is to fail and that New Haven is not only the home of Yale University but also the home of many pre-Broadway tryouts. Ambiguity is, to a degree, preserved in the play, since we are aware of the main characters both as bombing pilots and, Pirandello-fashion, as actors. Possibly, they "bomb" in both meanings of the word; as pilots, they begin by bombing Constantinople and end by bombing Minnesota. Something of the *Catch 22* quality is conveyed by rebellious Sergeant Henderson, the Yossarian of the occasion, who cocks a snook at authority and keeps trying to find out if his companions are really soldiers who fight and die or only actors who retire to their dressing rooms when their parts are finished.

Mr. Heller's wit is sporadic in the first half of the play but almost entirely absent from the second half, in which the Pirandellian element also withers and hard-jawed didacticism takes over. The captain, who was a young man in the first half, now encounters his 19-year-old son who is now ripe for death in battle and who turns to ask us: "Why didn't you do something? Didn't you care?" This cry from the heart is in no way prepared for; it belongs in another play. *L'Amant militaire* transmits its ideas more effectively precisely because it maintains the same rude tone throughout. It is, ultimately, more serious because it is never entirely serious. *We Bombed in New Haven*, on the other hand, becomes finally too serious to be taken seriously.

8

FROM GUERRILLA TO RESIDENT RADICAL

When we came back to San Francisco with ten thousand dollars in the bank and a good reputation there were those who thought we had done it, and that was enough—out. Others were tired. I interpreted the whole thing as a chance to get moving and create a large organization. Creating an organization is no task to begin with old tools. The tools need to be refashioned and an examination of existing conditions should be undertaken. By interpreting our hysterical achievements as the signal to charge forward I overlooked a few problems we needed to face. I was convinced we could forge on and double our output. We could hire new people (and pay them!) and broaden our effect on the community. I presented to the group a plan for a hundred twenty-five shows in the parks of the Bay Area. Two different commedias with two different casts. Too much, too soon. The group's eyes rolled in their heads. How and who was to do it?

We had pared the membership down to an essential cast for touring. In order to perform a minstrel or commedia character, our actors had to be both politically and esthetically trained. When good performers left they took their expertise with them. The shock of their leaving was difficult to take. Only four out of the ten people from the touring show stayed. We auditioned and found new actors who were to play roles in both commedias, *Ruzzante* and *Patelin*. Even though this was enough work for twenty people, we began work on another kind of "show"—one that proved to be valuable in numerous movement situations.

One day Frank Bardacke (People's Park activist, writer) burst into a room where I was talking with friends and said, "It's great, we're winning!" "Who?" "The NLF are kicking the shit out of the Americans." Flash image. The Vietnamese, NLF/PRG, Chinese, Cuban, Russian and all socialist and revolutionary movements around the world support the people's war of Vietnam. We support the people's war of Vietnam. They represent half the world's population. We are not alone. Guilt and depression inherited from the old left were at times washed away by the new left radical thinking. For a moment, instead of feeling torn between defeat for our country and hoping for victory for the "enemy," we could side with those who were hot-fighting imperialism. How to concretize this image?

The process by which we arrived at a Guerrilla Marching Band is important since most Digger, Yippie or psychedelic visionaries create images that are interesting and exciting but are flashes easily absorbed into the mainstream. The marching band attached to a theatre was a new innovation and the mountain of rags with politically twisted tunes made the band utilize, once again, a popular mode of entertainment and return the form to its progressive origins.

Our idea of a marching band was loose, but not

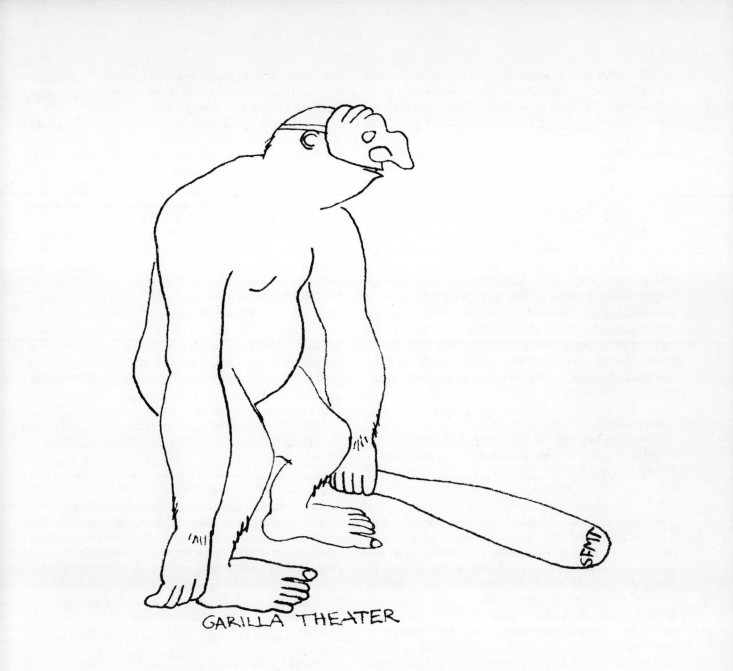

GARILLA THEATER

Original drawing for Gorilla Marching Band, 1968

as loose as a few long-haired volunteers who came to see Charlie Degelman, musician and, now, bandleader. "I want to join the band." "What instrument do you play?" "None. I don't play any instrument, I just want to join the band." Our rehearsals were chaotic. We had no money to pay anyone and I made a lengthy explanation about how, if we did get money, we would pay one dollar, five dollars, and so on.

Our first outdoor rehearsal was in the parking lot for delivery trucks of the *San Francisco Chronicle & Examiner*. We twenty assembled en masse and set up rules for stopping and turning. We had expert girl twirlers. About one out of every three women in the company had been a cheerleader or a booster. The group warmed up and took off around the parking lot. The drivers came out of their trucks and watched, smiled and then cheered. We stopped. I had the group sing "Avanti Populo," the Italian Communist Party song, and the drivers cheered louder. "Italian. Get dat." We knew the idea was a success. Everyone loves a parade.

Creating a style for the band took some time. Only two images came to mind worth using. One, a black high school band I saw in an AmVet parade in New York City in the forties; and the other, the Hamilton Air Force Base Drill Team. The first was ragged and out of step, but on beat. The second, led by boney Sergeant Moon, was spit, polish, fancy braid and comic skits on the street. I doubted we could spend as much time as the Air Force drill team in perfecting our act, but I calculated that we could attempt to march in step and the failure (or lack of interest) would result in a humorous conclusion. Our costumes were mountains of rags and imitation Mummers' outfits. We used a fake World War I helmet piled with rags and a tunic made of strips of colored cloth. The flying-clothed long-haired out-of-step marching band was always a blast.

Eventually, we filled our various musical spots with members of the company. We purchased glockenspiels and bugles to add to our drummers. Our specialty was the national anthem, which we made into something of a theatrical anti-American tune. At the end we flipped up signs that said, "GET OUT OF VIETNAM."

Our official debut was the Peace and Freedom Founding Convention, March 16, 1968. We marched into the hall at 9 A.M., played the national anthem, flipped the signs and they stood on the chairs and cheered. We repeated our success at the Great Beaknik Poetry Reading a month later in San Francisco. Ginsberg, Ferlinghetti, Meltzer, McClure and Welsh gathered on the stage, the audience waited, the band struck up in the lobby, twenty mounds of rags filed down the aisle and proceeded to wipe out the place. It was a hard act to follow.

In July of 1968 we changed the Troupe's location from a downtown loft to a larger building in an industrial district between Potrero Hill and the Mission. We hired a techman and a costume designer, established a formal office, a library, a kitchen and a roof area for breathing. Even though the organization of the organization was never as effective as I would have liked, we recognized the need to operate a company with many people, not just a family. We did a little better than Peter Schumann or Luis Valdez and a lot better than most of the other alternative groups. We had fewer illusions—about the secretary, the tech, the design, the p.r., the booker, the books and the writers.

We had functioned under an occasional leadership called a Gerontocracy whereby the oldest members became a committee of decision-makers. It didn't work. The oldest members were not all interested in taking responsibility nor were they involved in the day-to-day running of the company. Once in a new space Sandy Archer and Joan Holden delivered a yellow paper declaring a need for a new organization beginning with an Inner Core, a group of five to be elected by the company at large, to decide on the direction and policy of the company. An Inner Core was elected and suggested salaries for all members. An across-the-board twenty-five dollar salary was established. We had been paying five dollars per show and two and a half dollars for children's puppet shows but were confused about the rate for two shows in one day. There were some loopholes in the twenty-five dollars per week for all members—the techman/wife team, booker and our secretary received more.

Toward the end of 1968 salaries were aligned down rather than up. I resisted having the secretary's wages lowered since her work was the keystone of the office and her continuity was enormously important. Ann Riley, from the English working class, worked for us for two years. She received no other source of income and the seventy-five dollar weekly salary we paid her, I felt, had to be maintained. Our own salaries of twenty-five dollars per week were below livable minimum—only manageable if one could get money elsewhere. Equal salaries eliminated most working-class people, certainly anyone who supported a family.

As a company of twenty paid members it was imperative that we develop new material for new markets. The New York Radical Theatre Repertory at first seemed a door to new markets but

after a month in San Francisco I realized that it couldn't help us three thousand miles away. Short trips to local schools were too complicated to arrange through New York. I wrote to Ota Jurgens, the new director of the agency, suggesting that they concentrate on the areas around New England and Pennsylvania and not attempt to book across the country. We would try to take care of ourselves. However, the group running New York Radical sent out countrywide mailings. The brochure looked exciting. Unfortunately there were obvious distances between the groups, not only in technical ability but also in political positions. Active for about two years, primarily with the tour of the Living Theatre, the radical booking group ended its short life with a mimeographed listing of the addresses of all radical theatre groups, mailed to all radical theatre groups.

My own attempts to solve our survival problems were not so hot either. I hired an "outsider" as an overall administrative aide, a skill that would not work its way up through the rank and file. The imposition of a person into our closely macroméed group was possible if the group took to the outsider. This was not the case. Neither radical nor able to function in the penny-pinching atmosphere, he left. I next hired a booker who would have only one job, to book advance dates and thus supply the company with income. I thought it would be helpful if the booker were not a member of the company but just one who did a good job and let us mash out the rhetoric and the political position of the company. Once the Inner Core fixed our overhead, we had to do some hard thinking about income. If one beat the bushes and panhandled hard, the parks netted ten thousand dollars for a two to three month period.

L'Amant and Pits had earned that much; however, it was only one-sixth of our yearly budget of sixty thousand dollars. Patelin and Ruzzante performed one hundred twenty-five shows but despite our increased production and selling outlets, income dwindled. The times had changed and our presence in the parks was no longer unique. Rock bands were giving free "Summer of Love" concerts to thousands.

By not traveling to Europe in 1968 and rejecting New York, we lost the opportunity to impress the community in Seattle, Portland, and the Mission District. While producing, directing, acting and playing hotshot, we failed to realize that the news from the Big Apple impresses all Americans and that Europe impresses New Yorkers. We didn't even notice that Nixon and Reagan had come to power.

We went diligently from park to park, playing colleges in Oregon and Washington, begging and being "honest," with less and less effect. Our honesty was not the best policy. It was liberal martyrdom. We had begun by going to the people and serving what we thought were their needs. As the events of the sixties developed, we found ourselves in repetitious struggles.

In 1965 we had done the San Francisco Park and Recreation Commission; in 1966 we had a small fight in Berkeley; in 1967 Richmond was a problem; and in 1968 we were almost stopped from playing the sacred parks of Mill Valley. By then the Procedure was well known. We applied. They refused. We went to a council meeting: "Freedom of Speech." They refused. We swore to do the show. They swore to call the pigs. We went to court. They gave in halfway. Although the situation was changing, we did not change our methods. Thus, what was once a real struggle and

called a publicity stunt became a publicity stunt even though it was a real struggle. Fighting for the chance to present a radical show became a boring confrontation.

The summer of '68 did not move along with any grace or positive feeling. We had always relied on the outdoor summer season to keep our spirits up. Playing in the open air is usually exhilarating. At the very least, the sky, trees and green grass are pleasurable; yet the summer increased our squabbles as the plays and the performers were overworked.

We had a tradition in the Mime Troupe of associating with groups outside and inside our organization. We had shared space with the San Francisco New School, SDS, then the Diggers; and in the summer of '68 we took in the San Francisco Newsreel. Our association with the New School and SDS was progressive. We were expanded by them; we didn't threaten their existence and we helped each other. The Diggers left and came to annoy us, while SF Newsreel haunted the place.

SF Newsreel was formed by a few filmmakers who saw the use of film as a political tool. Almost immediately the few filmmakers who had training left and the organization took a heavy political turn. The basic ideological lines running through their organization were a rabid American variety of Maoism and an aggressive activism which stemmed from a New York group called "Up Against the Wall Mutherfucker," affectionately called the "mutherfuckers." Both the doctrinaire sloganeering of Maoism and the anarchic Mutherfuckers implanted seeds of chaos that sustained a general feeling of discontent.

We had also collected some psychdelic dropouts who were attracted by our Digger leftism and a few people from the middle class who had never heard of the new left and had joined the "movement" just as it began pulling itself to shreds. Always trying to pull a rabbit out of the hat, I suggested we organize a radical theatre festival that was composed of the few groups we respected. Perhaps I thought from this association we could come up with some magic to keep us going.

The Radical Theatre Festival, sponsored by San Francisco State College through the efforts of Ken Margolis, paid for minimal expenses, allowed people to see the Teatro Campesino, Mime Troupe and Bread and Puppet Theatre. After the festival, the Mime Troupe Press, a new thing, published a booklet on the festival with the following epilogue by Juris Svendsen:

EPILOGUE
I

"... when you establish one, you can establish two and then you can get three. One, two, three Vietnams. One, two, three, many radical theaters ..."

II

The guerrilla theaters that met for this festival refused to be called revolutionary, with both Valdez and Schumann stating explicitly that "revolutionary" was a qualitative term. How is this to be understood—"guerrilla" yes, "revolutionary" no? And how is "revolutionary a qualitative term?

First of all the festival was a meeting of artists in the theater, of individuals who had survived as identifiable groups long enough to be called theaters. Each group had an artistic basis established by its founder, each founder had a personalized view of his relationship to society, that is, a political stance. Diverse crafts and persons had been invited and assembled to express this stance.

These groups exist within a basic dialectical formulation: how to achieve artistic identity as a group, and how, as an artistic and social unit of discrete individuals, to understand and effect a common political consciousness and select the means to enact it. The balance of this dialectic differs in each group at present. The list of differences is too long to argue; it is enough to enumerate the variables; degree of artistic control by founding personnel, crafts and talents available, economic requirements of individuals and of the group, sociological location of the group, kind and degree of political awareness of their public and continuity as a group in the face of external political changes.

Other determinants enter into the dialectic of artistic identity and communality of political goals before their "revolutionary" identity can be considered but one thing is clear—regardless of what revolution each group is looking for, they are "guerrilla" in their very existence as identifiable artistic groups opposed to the prevailing society and its political views.

Now, that is not saying much: every artist is a guerrilla in that, in bourgeois conception, he is always outside of society. The difference here is that the guerrilla identity has all the logistical complexity of a political focus behind it. Yes, any theater could be called guerrilla if the distinction were a matter of economic struggle alone. All theaters have to con, crawl, beg, plead and promise. But the non-revolutionary theater does so to get back into society and their personnel use one another to crawl or vault back onto the heap.

Revolutionary theaters, on the other hand, are true guerrillas, artistic focos, in that they remain outside to become one with a new society. These guerrilla theaters want to get into a society: one with which they are one, because it is also of their making. To that extent these guerrilla theaters are revolutionary.

How is "revolutionary" a qualitative term? Members of the groups would, in general, agree on the social and political nature of the society they want.

So "qualitative" does not here refer to the quality of the society they seek or the revolutionary tactics needed to get there but rather to the condition of each group in the present historical moment.

The groups agree on the inadequacy and unlivability of the present and on what must be commonly achieved, but each sees a qualitative difference in its identity in this transition. If the matter were merely one of simpler linear logic, in which each group was the copula between A, the present state, and B, the state to come—they would all be revolutionary.

But the trick to reading one's revolutionary existence is to realize that you change your living present as you work toward the common future. We disagree as much in our reading of the present as in our projection of the future. It is a common observation that we drag our pasts with us and, as adages go, that is right. But the point with theater is that those who participate in it drag with them, and are encumbered by, the ever-living now as they work their way out of it.

To the three groups, "revolutionary" is indeed a qualitative term because it refers more to their present existence and less to their common tactics or views of the future. The shared goal is plowed back into the everyday, tactics become a matter of daily affairs and not a collective operation to be programmatically pursued by all together. (That is what festivals and conferences are for: to check up on each other's successful means.)

In the end, you must live your own life. Tactics are to be argued and revised, goals to be commonly viewed and changed. Tactics and goals are revolutionary in these theaters, but the quality of what is revolutionary in them now is the separateness of their existence as individual groups.

These groups are guerrilla, that is clear. And if their revolutionary being is not clear in definition, it certainly is in existence.

The objectives of the festival were both exter-

Cranky, *Patelin*, 1968

nal and internal. I hoped by presenting ourselves in concert that we would declare that Radical Theatre was an entity. One group's farting in the wind made no noise. And with enough space between performances each group would be able to see what the others were working on and gain from the entire experience. Thus the public presentation was as important as the internal cross-fertilization.

Puppet Box, Children's Show, 1968

We gave workshops and open-panel discussions while presenting shows at night. Bread and Puppet demonstrated how to make puppets, bread and produce banners; El Teatro Campesino presented their first full-length play, *Shrunken Head of Poncho Villa*, which was wit, spit, speed and incision into a Mexican/American life; the Mime Troupe presented everything we were doing—commedia, crankies, puppet shows. In an attempt to theorize on the cultural revolution as part of our act I read from an article I was writing.

The Bread and Puppet Theatre and El Teatro Campesino were nothing new to us. Luis Valdez had been with us in 1965 and I had seen Peter Schumann's work before that. In 1964 I happened upon Schumann's theatre, a cold downtown ex-moviehouse in New York City, and watched a Christmas pageant play. It contained some of the most interesting shapes, hand puppets, masks, live bodies with fake props, trips of scenery and action that I had seen. It was epic in its simplicity. Props were used as suggestions for total pictures. Images were conjured up in our minds through the use of a mask, a gesture or an element of the real thing. I watched and absorbed.

The Bread and Puppet Theatre, more than the Mime Troupe, performed on the streets. The first few shows, much like a one-man band (Peter playing the bass drum, announcing the puppet show, putting drum down, then doing the hand puppets), occurred on Third Avenue in New York. Having no parks as we did in San Francisco, he used street corners and cleared space on the cement. The Mime Troupe later used a puppet-punch in *L'Amant Militaire*, "cranky" or paper movies in *Patelin* and developed a whole line of Gutter Puppets all directly descended from Schumann's creations. The Teatro Campesino, after the 1968 festival, branched out into Aztec puppets, all brown and furious little madmen. The influence of Schumann's images throughout the radical theatre world is enormous.

El Teatre Campesino was much closer to us both geographically and aesthetically. Luis Valdez came to the Mime Troupe after seeing us perform *Tartuffe* on a street in the middle of San Jose State College in 1964. He was attracted by the shouts, the noise, the spirit and the guts and we were attracted to his bounce, insight and humor. He worked with us—played one role in *Candeliao*, did pieces of *Shrunken Head of Poncho Villa* in our workshops and read and studied playwriting. Then he disappeared one day and turned up with

Protesting the TAC Squad, San Francisco City Hall, 1968

one of the most important theatrical inventions of the 1960s. He put together a group that combined theatre and organizing, workers and culture, performance and lessons. His base was the Delano Grape Strike, "la causa," and his first skits or *actos* were done for striking grape pickers. The meteoric rise of El Teatro Campesino was due in part to the sentimental and racist attachment white people have for their "unfortunate" brown brothers. El Teatro Campesino was so "right-on" in 1965 and 1966 that by 1967 they were touring the nation and played the Senate Committee on Migratory Labor in Washington.

In 1965 while performing for farm workers, Valdez characterized his group as "somewhere between Cantinflas and Brecht." The *actos* are rapidamente, funny and at times crazy. The *acto* or short skit with placards identifying each character was developed to communicate to the farm workers the purpose and elements of the Grape Strike. The early skits were put together on the spot for a particular issue. Others later on described overall conditions of contracts and contract negotiations. The name-plated characters are like pre-commedia masks, or medieval morality play figures. Morality plays contained characters like Good, Evil and Chatterbox who were as familiar to the community in the twelfth century as El Patron, Don Coyote and Esquihole are to the farmworkers.

The audience, familiar with the types, attends to the characters' relation to the situation. The necessity of unionizing in order to obtain a contract is made clear in *La Quinta Temporada* by illustrating the exploitation of the farmworkers by the contractor and the contractor by the grower.

Liberal playwrights often try to make their

Gorilla Marching Band, 1968

plays more "political" and turn their naturalistic people into abstract moral figures, viz. the "downtrodden," the "social changer," the "political anarchist," and the "morally good." This rarely clarifies social conditions. In the intrinsically political skits of El Teatre Campesino, designed for roadside communication to workers in the field, the performer of Farmworker was a living, breathing farmworker. This person, not an actor, didn't need to emphasize his psychology; he focused on the details of the conditions in question. The problem for El Teatro was to offer a political and economic analysis that would convince workers to join the union. At their peak of union worker theatre, Luis Valdez, Augustin Lira, Danny Valdez, Felipe Cantu (the original farmworker) and Donna Haber created *actos* that were so exquisite as to make it possible for anyone to understand the social and economic conditions of migrant farmworkers.

When El Teatro showed up at the festival with a full-lenth play they began to deal with issues facing the entire Mexican-American community. They moved from Delano to Del Rey, California, and then to Fresno. Once in Fresno they took up the question of the Chicano in Vietnam and the social role of the Chicano in middle-class America.

The Festival was a means by which we got a closer look at and inside of each of the three companies. We hadn't planned or even considered operating any closer than we had so far. Personnel from the Mime Troupe later on went to work with the Bread and Puppets, and we continued to work closely with El Teatro. However, nothing more formal was considered.

The Mime Troupe had done an anti-pacifist play, *L'Amant*, in '67 and was struggling in '68 with the issues of capitalism from an anti-capitalist view. The Bread and Puppet Theatre sustained a rock-like pacifism that appeared to be supported by some joy, El Teatro Campesino floundered in Fresno against the Brown Berets, hysterical activism and the ever-constant Huelga. Yet it reached into its urban Chicanismo and came up with an enlarging "Shrunken" head. We exchanged information and became friends.

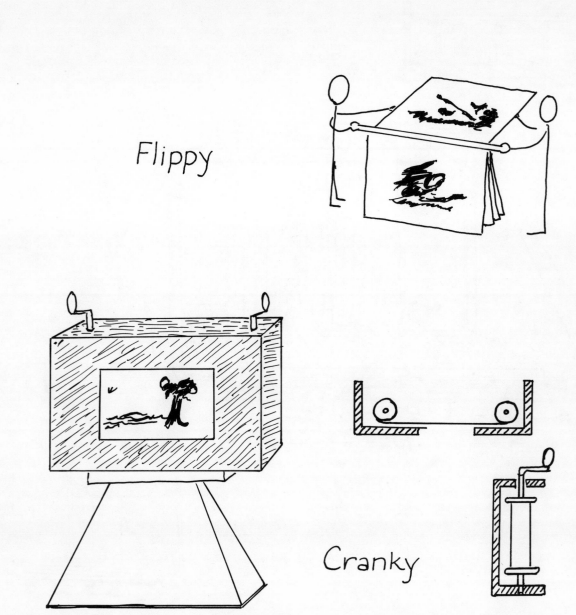

Flippy

Cranky

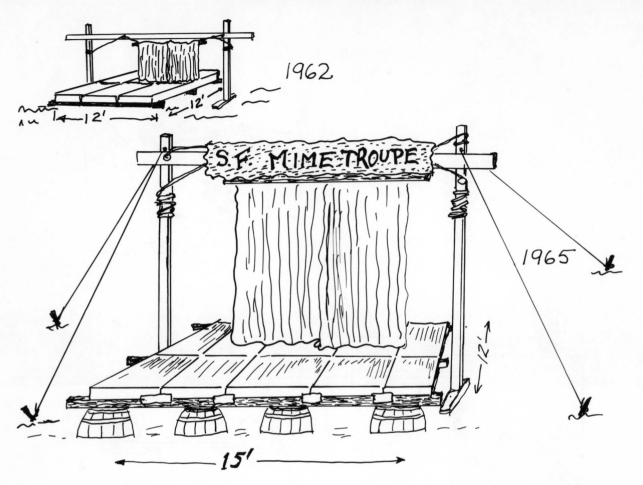

1962

S.F. MIME TROUPE

1965

15'

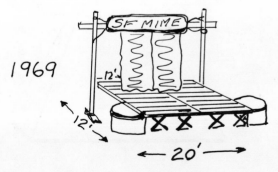

1969

SF MIME

12'

12'

20'

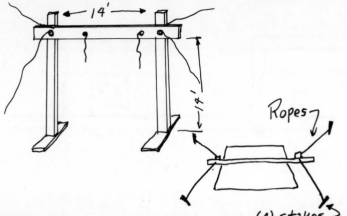

1962

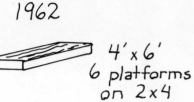

4' x 6'
6 platforms
on 2x4
on ground

Ropes

(4) stakes

1965

3' x 6' - odd shape
1 x 3 T & G - top
on Underpinnings
on ½ barrels

1969

1 x 6 planks
with cleats
bolted together
Underpinning's
on x's

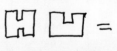

Backstage

H ⊔ = ✕

For underpinning secret
plans, write, otherwise the
above don't woik

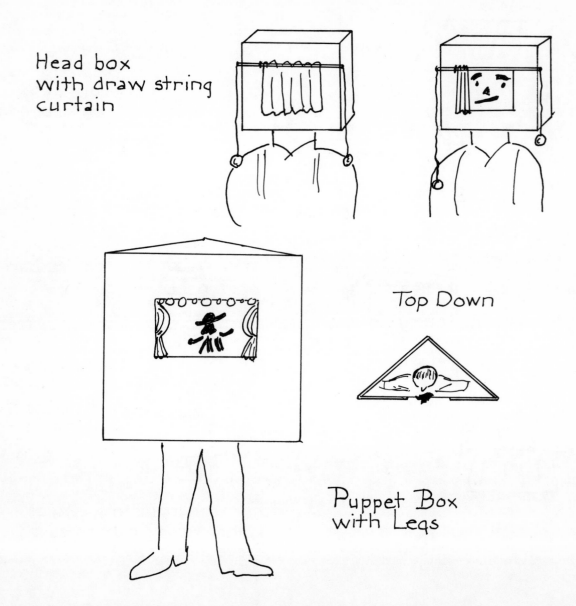

Head box
with draw string
curtain

Top Down

Puppet Box
with Legs

9

BITS AND PIECES

As a result of the festival cross-fertilization we began a series of vignettes, skits and puppet plays we labeled Gutter Puppets. It became a part of our repertoire by the summer of '69 and toured as the second act with a short commedia.

A puppet stage that folded up, props that packed inside the puppet-box trunk and a few people who could travel in one car made it possible to send the Gutter Puppets to demonstrations and emergency calls for "political" skits. The first good puppet play, by Eric Berne and Charlie Degelman, was called "Little Black Panther." A little Black Panther, anxious to off a pig, is about to be womped on by a porker but is saved by Bigger Black Panther, who gets the little Panther out of the scrape and suggests that he organize before going ahead with his intentions. Eric composed one more on draft resistance and went off to work with Peter Schumann. He sent back to the Mime Troupe a "flippy" on the Presidio 21. This flippy was made up on ten painted canvases, three-by-five images on canvas hung over a pole, and as each image-picture was flipped into view, an actor would tell the story. The Pre-

sidio 21 were twenty-one soldiers under indictment in the stockade at the Presidio San Francisco, who sat out. Protesting their treatment inside the inhuman stockade they followed the current pattern of civil disobedience and refused to take orders. Eric Berne's German expressionist paintings captured the barbarity of the situation.

We came up with two other strains for Gutter Puppets: children's theatre and do-it-yourself demonstrations. The kids' Christmas show was fun. Sandy Archer did two seasons. The major job was to find a way to kill Santa Claus. I think one season they managed to change him into a communist.

Bookmobile shows were another attraction. With one little story about a worm who eats books (a bookworm) we fascinated the Library Commission of San Francisco into coughing up a hot three hundred dollars for ten shows at bookmobile locations. Of course, the bookmobile stopped in the racial ghettos. We played for six-through-twelve-year-old brown, black and yellow kids who wanted to get into the action rather than watch it. Skilled people were needed. Not being able to develop a cohesive theory of community action, we let the bookmobile go it alone after ten shows.

The other strain of the Gutter Puppets was the how-to-do-it skits or live Digger papers. Rather than berate the public for its lack of despair over the war in Vietnam or load them with information about the tragedies of American imperialism, taxes and police brutality, we continued our historical role of making people laugh and giving them some information. Curiously, these lesson skits were the first ones we ever performed on the street. We had always done our shows in parks. I tried to cover our street pitching (illegal panhandling) with the sale of underground news-papers, but we didn't make it. The show was too long and the people left before we got to the pitch. In early 1968, the street musicians and artists were not yet around to open the territory to entertainment beggars. We dropped the scheme and went back to free shows in the parks, *with donations.*

The first "lesson skit" was Meter Maid. Punch the Puppet convinced a young girl (live) who was about to put a dime in a parking meter to use a tab top instead so that she could park free. We were right in the pockets of the average viewer. The other puppet show was the telephone credit-card skit. We demonstrated how to make up a fake card and coupled the "cheating" with "why let those large corporations run you down?"

Although we tried, we couldn't come up with any more do-it-yourself skits. There was just so much to tell people and unlike the Yippies we didn't want to further the Digger fantasy of a free society. After the do-it-yourself skits, agit-prop pieces stimulated by particular political events became the dominant theme of the Gutter Puppets.

In 1967 we had been invited to an anti-military ball at Oregon State the day before the ROTC department had its military ball. We did *Olive Pits* and although it was not our best performance, it helped establish an anti-military atmosphere. The feisty liberal math professor who arranged the whole thing asked us to come to the second event in 1968 with a more appropriate piece. We came up with a theatrical image that might irritate the ROTC boys—a women's drill team. The women tried it by themselves for a while and then we found that one of our actors, a six-foot-five giant, had been a drill sergeant and knew all the real stuff. We had him drill the women and at the end

of their drill, they would knock him over or do some reasonably dangerous act to illustrate their role in the new "revolution."

Six women and our giant drill sergeant went off to Oregon State and did the show. Although well received, they came back doubtful about the project. Sandy Archer and Joan Holden were asked to defend the project. Sandy wrote:

TOWARD A WOMEN'S DRILL TEAM
IN THE MIME TROUPE
JANUARY 1969 BEGINNING NOTES

While the movement on the left moves forward historically in epic fits and starts, and progresses slowly toward changing the present United States' capitalistic and materialistic structure, there exists a curious division between the personal and public lives of these vanguard male movers. On the face of the left we see and hear powerful liberating gestures, but it we inspect the private lives, we find a great deal of left-over bourgeois repressive thinking, forcing their personal lives to undergo a confused period of struggle and separation. Some leaders have broken with their "left" wives and children and moved toward specific ties. Community fathers and mothers and other leaders with less private daring make strange marriages of suburban houses and vanguard politics. The serious effect of their confusion lies on the women they leave behind or move toward. In a society of such technological development, in a movement of such grand scope, the problem of infidelity seems incongruous; but it is a psychological problem that most movement people cannot solve easily (we are not dealing with hippies here, but with people who have come from FSM pre-flower days). At most, we find a dangerously cautious "coping."

The Women's Drill Team was formed to bring information and direction to women in and out of the movement. Women in the movement speak of the need for unity and collective actions that will affect the power structure. Women on the fringe of the middle class seek knowledge. How can a woman aid and add to the movement? How can a ghetto mother find out about free legal aid, day-care centers, planned parenthood? *What can we do* is not a question but a cry for action from wives and mothers trapped by circumstance, who cannot "go to the hills" or lead the charge. We have developed a Women's Drill Team to push militantly into lives and communities to give impetus and information on such issues as programs to free women from traditional roles. Marching into their lives, we can demonstrate—street action at its best, go in the daytime to their streets and blocks—what is being done by others and what can be done by them. . . .

Sandy Archer

Striking out in new directions, although exhilarating, is fraught with simplistic images reaching for original insight. The Marching Band's first musical sounds were based on military echoes (more like a Boy Scout drum-and-bugle group) until Charlie Degelman broke it up into something close to folk rock and put in a few Dixieland licks to allow the mountain-of-rags band to sparkle.

The Women's Drill Team fell into the same pattern at its early stage, simple marine-like drill. Given enough time it would have developed out of that repressive stance to another more militant image yet by this time the company was in no mood to experiment. Its life was an experiment and the troupe vetoed the project.

We had as a group moved as one person, a theatrical group functioning as a single artist. With the increased overhead and commitments to a steady company we were in the midst of a changeover from Guerrilla Group to Established Radical Theatre company. The transition is by no means easy, nor has it ever been, even for revolutionary groups.

We were beset by a number of problems inside and outside the company. I tried to get out from the burden and confusion of U.S. genocidal murder and my own personal life coming to a standstill by going to Japan. Hoping to reach a clear place and understand more about the world (and the troupe) I vaulted into another environment. The trip lasted three weeks and I came back to make charts and plan tours.

We were used to claiming new ground, leaping into an area that others hadn't thought of developing and making something work. A leaping schema was a way of getting into action while avoiding questions; however, it became a pattern and then a trap. A leap was not possible—neither to Japan, nor to new forms, while walking steady was unheard of.

The old guard, or the guerrilla vanguard had to change—that was me too—the new troupes had to be introduced to the manner of operations without prejudice. We had an apprentice program that never worked, we couldn't figure out how to institute it, train for what? We wanted to reject our past in order to create anew, yet relied upon our hard experienced expertise to come up with new solutions.

Perhaps as much confusion occurred in my personal life as in the direction of the troupe. Sandy Archer and I had been living together for a number of years not married but as lovers; all around us our peers were getting married! We thought that period of personal life-style had passed but it was coming back with grass and soft-rock music. Perhaps a play on family life would have focused our attentions on some of the undercurrents in the confusion. No one thought of that in those days.

Organizationally we had been a one-or-two-person-lead group with a lot of individual creativity coming forward. As we expanded, the organization of the company became a burden rather than a facilitator. I sensed the change but couldn't figure out what to do about it, others wanted a chance to direct, perform and do the creating. I couldn't give up nor settle down. I was supposed to come up with ideas but was confused. We had a group of people who were willing and ready to cooperate, but cooperate about what? for what? for whom? where? and of course why?

Even though we were blobbing along with lots of ideas and mediocre talent, there were two incidents that demonstrated the old image-making collusion of theatricality and nervy leftism. The Gorilla Marching Band came through the clouds on iceskates and the Wild West Show proved to be a continuation of a long cultural struggle.

Exactly one year after marching into the Peace and Freedom convention and making them stand up and cheer (it was easy), we applied for and received a space to march in the St. Patrick's Day Parade on March 16, 1969. We were often locked off from the straight world, and the long hair began to make it impossible to go out of our circle. However, the St. Patrick's Day Parade was a dream come true. We received our number and went to the parade site early Sunday morning. The difficulty was to make sure that, dressed as we were in rag costumes, playing like we did, known for what we were known for and with a banner, "S.F. Mime Troupe Gorrilla Marching Band," we could stay in the parade.

While we were assembled and waiting our turn to join the main marchers, I went off to look at the rest of the parade. As I watched the Navy,

Army and ROTC units all rigidly pass by, I saw in the middle of the street a kilted, long-haired, bearded man. Heavy boots, plaid kilt and big gloves, he was fantastic! My eyes popped and I began to laugh—a real Scotsman. The cops ran to get him out. It was too mind-smashing to have him walking between military units. I, too, ran to him. He paraded with us—we as his mascot or he as ours.

Two trumpeters, Peter Hennessey (our company photographer) and I, both learned "When Irish Eyes Are Smiling." As we played in or out of tune, the whole troupe of eighteen would stumble in drunken waltz time (the Scot held steady). When the tune finished, we would all regroup and march on. Upon receiving cheers we would flash the "GET OUT OF VIETNAM" banners and then tuck them away and keep moving.

By going into the Parks in '61 and struggling with the Park Commission in '65 we were engaged and committed to confront cultural rip-off in whatever form it turned up. We had founded and supported the Artist Liberation Front, whose objectives were to disrupt, hinder and stop the building of large cultural mausoleums. Although ALF split up there was no great hunk of money put into cement in San Francisco. Rather, an organization called Neighborhood Arts was established which took some of the city money and distributed it locally. We had never attacked the rock scene directly for who would dare face up to the "New Revolution," yet by 1969 the millionaires who had been regular long-hairs a few years ago began to show up on the scene. An announcement appeared in the papers (July 1969) that the Music Council (who?) was to put on the Wild West (what?) in San Francisco (where?). A free rock "festival of life" was to be held in Golden

Gate Park for three days with a paid rock show in the twenty-five-thousand-seat Kezar Stadium each night. The whole park was to be covered by freaks and artists who wanted to do their "thing." Woodstock had just covered the country with its Eastern whirlwind of fortunes when the Music Council announced its plans.

The Music Council was composed of Ralph J. Gleason (*San Francisco Chronicle* rock pusher and now Fantasy Records rock promoter), Bill Graham (Fillmore East and West), Jan Wenner (*Rolling Stone* editor), Tom Donahue (heavy disc jockey and record promoter), Ron Polte (manager of the Quicksilver Messenger Service) and supporting members of the new millionaire rip-off club of the San Francisco sound.

Joan Holden, who had been in the company for many years and knew the history of the Graham/Gleason rise to fame, smiled sardonically and wrote a paper exposing the council. We mimeographed it and went to a Wild West public meeting. We were going into action once again as we had with the Artists Liberation Front. The only difference was at this one we found a new bunch of kids with a positive approach to the whole "festival of free." Twenty-eight communes of the Haight Ashbury were represented and they had decided that a Woodstock rip-off was not going to happen in San Francisco. They demanded the council provide crash pads, food and legal defense for all the young who would show up for the three-day festival. Neither Ron Polte nor anyone else thought there was life in the Haight. A position paper signed by San Francisco Newsreel, the Panthers, Red Guard, SDS, Canyon Cinema, S.F. State Black Students Union, Los Siete, the Mime Troupe and the Haight Communes was printed that called for all of the Haight Commune

demands plus the rights to the films and recordings of the nighttime events.

The rock promoters couldn't understand the political climate of the early part of '68. Mayor Alioto of San Francisco had, upon assuming power, called out the Tac Squad to beat demonstrators at the Fairmont; had poured his favorite Gestapo onto State College, November 6, 1969, to smash any resistance to Hayakawa's program; and had the same bunch shoot up the local Panthers. Haight Ashbury was a mess of narc raids, killings, plantings and media exposure of its despair. The Weathermen had begun bombing, and everyone was into some kind of secret, sometimes important, social work, while the dumb, dumb dollarheads wanted to have a "Festival of Life." The naiveté or unhipness of the West Coast rock combines was shocking. They in their airplanes and meeting rooms at Columbia, Capital, Ashley Famous, etc., had lost contact and couldn't even understand the term "Third World." They didn't even have a token black on their council or out front to cool the crowd.

In some accounts the Mime Troupe was blamed (or credited) with the stoppage of the Wild West. As a matter of fact the filmmakers in the Bay Area wanted a piece of the action (from the film of the Festival of Life), the Haight Ashbury Communes wanted more than a piece of the action, and the Park & Recreation Commission gave the whole thing the coup de grace by taking away its permits for the free use of the parks.

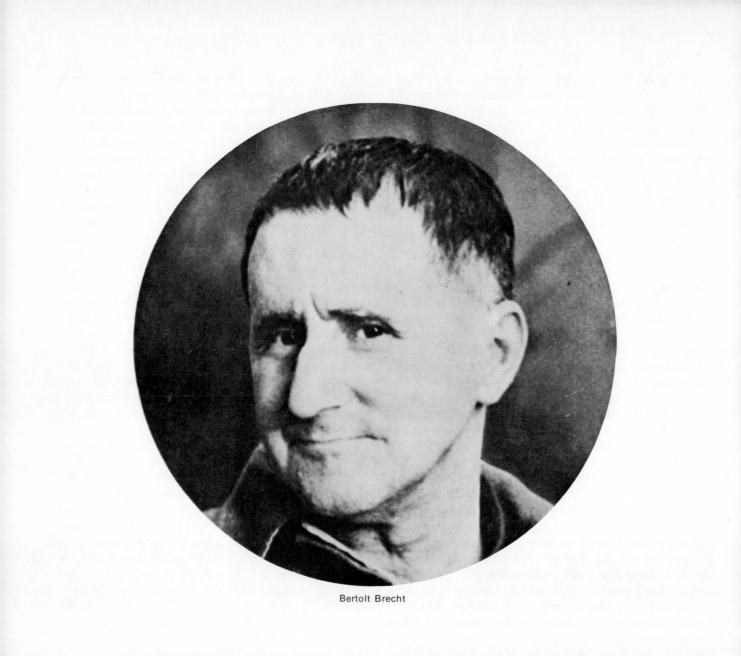

Bertolt Brecht

10

ONE LAST IMPOSITION

For two years I tried to sustain interest in a project that was to be written as we studied the subject. The work had an impressive title—*The Life and Times of Che Guevara as Seen by the Inmates of the United States of America*. It was to be a pageant play on wagons. Once a week we had classes devoted to Latin American history and politics. Each member of the company researched an area and spoke about it and outside speakers gave us a broader analysis from time to time. Kent Minault (ex-Mime Troupe, Digger) agreed to write a scenario based upon his knowledge of the Indians of Latin America. Steve Weissman of *Ramparts* took it on after Kent couldn't go any further. Weissman developed scenes of Che's peregrinations through Latin America prior to his joining Fidel in Mexico. Later Steve Friedman, actor and writer, agreed to complete the job.

My own reasons for insisting on the pageant play were based upon doubts I had during late 1967 and early '68. We needed to examine the concept of "guerrilla" in our rhetoric and come to grips with the historical role of the armed revolutionary. There were many indications that we in

the United States in '68-'69 were not exactly in a pre-revolutionary period. I was revolted by the heavy Maoist dogmatism surrounding us (S.F. Newsreel) and the slogans from underdeveloped countries applied to American technological madness. The gun was more important than the art of the theatre. Didn't the Panthers say so? Didn't the Red Book say so? Didn't every revolutionary say so? I couldn't believe it, nor could I disprove it. Hopefully through the study of the total life of Che we could at least illuminate some of the discrepancies in that "political" line.

The problems were stupendous; a new style, a new form, a new subject and a rational political analysis had to be developed. We tried, but, significantly, we could not come up with a design from the design department nor a script from the writing department. The project was beyond us.

Then Juris Svendsen suggested we produce Bertolt Brecht's last play. He gave me a copy of *Turandot or The Congress of White Washers*. I read his long translation and Sandy Archer did the same. Both of us were mystified by the text and a mite apprehensive about Brecht and the size of the production.

In the past, I had warned against using Brecht as a simple solution for American political theatre. The Actors Workshop's U.S. premiere of *Mother Courage*, done by Blau, was a momentous event which he apologized for after he misdirected it. *Galileo* we have talked about. There were innumerable bad productions of Bentley's apolitical versions. Martin Esslin's book, *Brecht: The Man and His Work*, had contributed to the pollution and tried to extract Brecht from his politics.

In 1964 we had cautiously produced one of Brecht's short plays, *Exception and the Rule*. It

The Exception and the Rule, 1965

The Congress of Whitewashers, 1969

The Congress of Whitewashers, 1969

The Congress of Whitewashers, 1969

was a meticulous production, pushing its original neo-naturalistic style (or Epic European) back on its face and thrusting the whole thing to its roots (Kabuki, Noh). Brecht had used the framework of that Japanese style and I spent much time uncovering and exposing the Japanese details using mimetic solutions for the staging. No matter, the production oozed 1930s images and thoughts. After that production I was never too keen on doing any Brecht because of its European attachment, and the Troupe's concern with immediate answers. I did, however, suggest to three Yale students who came to San Francisco expecting to do outdoor theatre (a "groovy idea") that they would have to relearn their craft because indoor techniques did not work outside and if they wanted to try something daring, "Why not do Brecht outside?" They left town.

The intriguing thing about *Congress of White Washers* was the locale—China. It suggested Chinese opera . . . Chinatown . . . lots of Chinese food . . . Chinese movies . . . Svendsen added that he thought it was probably Brecht's greatest play. We were drinking beer in Berkeley when he laid that one on us. I took another gulp, looked at Sandy, we nodded and decided to do it big and bold. From the first outdoor program:

> After eight years of taking classical comedy outdoors as commedia dell'arte, we take a Brecht play out as Chinese Opera. In China opera used to be done outdoors. Brecht worked on *Congress of the Whitewashers* from 1937 to 1953. The play comes out of a clear incisive, Marxist habit of thought. The Tuis (intellectuals; from Brecht's acronym, *tellektuell-in*) are paid by the system to deform thought, but cannot change the truth or history, which is determined by those the system fails to pay.

Svendsen came and talked to us about Brecht; I had a Chinese actor teach us Chinese opera movement; and we went to Chinatown en masse and saw the blood-curdling, slashing, trash movies from Hong Kong. One in four was worth anything but the Chinese food was good. In the back of my head was a wonderful plan to tour Japan rather than Europe. Americans doing Chinese opera in Japan would come as close as I could think of to doing commedia dell'arte in Italy.

We started work in January 1969 on the entire ninety typewritten pages, six hours a day, and, slowly, ever so slowly, cast eleven people into fifty-five roles. We eventually cut the text, rearranged the scenes and reduced the roles to forty-five, then re-cast, placed the music in the appropriate places, reshuffled and experimented on the production constantly for a year.

Written in 1953, *Congress* was shelved until it was printed after Brecht's death in 1959. It had not yet been performed at the Berliner Ensemble and the only stage production occurred in Switzerland simultaneously with ours. We could study other works of Brecht and the Ensemble through John Willett's books and even some notes from Manifred Wekworth, but we had no production notes as a compass. We were floating on Chinese waters with a Latvian helmsman in a German boat.

Brecht in numerous plays and books explored the role of the intellectual. He spent years crossing over "Tuism" in an unpublished Tui novel, the plays *Der Hoffmeister*, *Good Woman of Setzuan*, and *Galileo*. His own life reflects the risks of an intellectual within the currents of history. The "Tuis" in *Congress* exposed the role of bureaucratic intellectuals who cover the truth rather than uncover it. Good thinking was uncovering the truth; bad was to cover it.

Brecht had in his theoretical writings provided

a little clearer idea of what Epic theatre was—beyond the mere notion of alienation:

Dramatic Form	Epic Form
Plot	Narrative
Implicates the spectator in the stage situation	Turns the spectator into an observer but
wears down his power of action	arouses his power of action
the human being is taken for granted	the human being is object of inquiry
one scene makes another	each scene for itself
growth	montage

These six points are part of thirteen more or nineteen altogether. Alienation, Epic Theatre, was not a matter of simply distancing the audience, nor for that matter merely talking "political." Just as Brecht's ideas—formulated in a society full of growing Nazi Weltzmerz under the heavy mystifying hand of German metaphysicians who could just as easily philosophize one out of reality as commercials do in this country—pose special complications. Epic Theatre cannot merely be replanted in the land of TV, Hollywood movies and newspaper headlines; it must be re-pruned.

We cracked the books and tried to understand how to apply a Marxist or a dialectical and materialist analysis to the scenes. There could be great emotion yet it was directed towards exposing the contradictions in the social conditions. We were not going to perform a dry play. There was power somewhere in the text and we had to find it. The struggle to create an intellectually solid play without falling into the trap of sloganeering and the didacticism of agitprop was uppermost in my intentions.

The first outdoor performance, March 12, 1969, was over two and a half hours long and only the most experienced performers managed to work through the ordeal of heavy wind, cold and text weighted by dialogue. The parks are brutally direct. People don't pay so don't have to stay. During the first months we began with one hundred on the grass and ended with fifty. We attracted many with our colorful costumes and sound, yet couldn't keep them attentive for the length of our exploration. Svendsen's knowledge of performing out of doors was negligible. We were the experts and weren't doing so well either. He, too, wanted to see the entire play produced, so we handled Herr Bertolt respectfully. It took two months to cut sixty minutes and rearrange scenes.

One of the reasons the most experienced commedia performers succeeded in keeping the performance alive on that windy first day was because they had learned to punch each moment and to imprint the essence of the character's reactions. They reacted as well as acted and thus showed the audience what would have happened if they had heard what was being said.

Improvements were slow and laborious; we picked up some Chinese gestures and adapted them to our Western play. Working on a newly designed raked platform was slippery and audience response, if we succeeded according to Brecht, was quiet and reserved—a helluva response for outdoor performers.

To sustain company interest I relied on "the show must go on." On other days, it was a welcome vigilant police force that stimulated the company adrenalin. In a Contra Costa County hippie park, our appearance brought the cops but not the kids. We performed anyway—even trying to make more explicit the repression in the play.

It probably was the first play by Brecht that the Contra Costa police ever saw. They didn't arrest us.

Why continue? Stubbornness and past habit made me cling to the immense production. If we were going out, why not big? A few in the cast kept on learning new things. We changed roles, picked up new gestures, clarified lines and after four months in the parks (weekends only) we went on a tour of the Southwest. Once on the road, performing indoors, the actors gained confidence, pushed around the text and the production became comprehensible to audiences.

What had we done? Had I imposed good thinking on bad thinking? Had we clarified the role of intellectuals in society, East and West? I'm not sure. We made a production that was like Brotwurst Chow Yuk. Only in one or two performances did I see or hear a comprehensive response from the audience. We knew the many innuendos of the lines but were surprised when the audience also understood. A year after I left the company, I saw a motion picture version of our production shot by an Italian filmmaker for Italian television. It was extraordinarily exciting, not only because of the memories but for its explicit utilization of filmic technique. The masked characters, signs, props, banners, all looked comprehensible and the treatment was intelligent. I only saw a rough cut; however, I was left with the impression that we had created a live film, a series of montages. The alienated characters were made more whole through the use of film.

The work was principled yet perhaps improbable. There are limits to theatrical complexities in the open air. The very environment competed with reflection and the patience necessary for great lessons. The company struggled heroically with the obstacles. I think one of my motives must have been to punish the group. "If you're gonna be a revolutionary, then figure out how to perform Brecht and become a Marxist." As I punished them I also punished myself.

We all had a hard time getting on stage inside a mask, covering long hair, losing "identity" and performing a style unclear to any but the most expert. The few who could perform the show well could not articulate precisely what it was we were doing to achieve audience comprehension.

We had tried various organization schemes—loose leadership, company meetings, gerontocracy and finally an elected Inner Core of five members. The social makeup and class of the members of the company plus the life style and history of the Mime Troupe did not help the more democratic organizational plan. Participatory democracy (inherited from SDS) as practiced in the groups of collectives, communes, guerrilla groups, loosely knit action groups, is not likely to lead to revolutionary work nor sustained revolutionary activity. In the theatre, it is likely to lead in the opposite direction—congratulatory participation, amateurism and bourgeois choices.

The failure of the Inner Core from 1968 on to decide the means by which a company member was to be expelled indicated its weakness. Since we didn't hire (we "auditioned") we couldn't fire. Eventually even the hired secretary became a "company member." So, the family image grew until it included everyone and everything and when a member of the family is incompetent and doesn't do the job well, what do you do? Cry, whine, pray or go to Daddy or Mommy. We couldn't figure out how to kick anyone out. In 1970 the Inner Core was voted out.

As distinctions between expertise and will dissolved due to pressure from participatory democracy and idealistic fantasy, the antagonism between professional performer and amateur participating member increased. There was no external aid for the pro either. The use of elite drama forms brought to the public arena was no longer exciting and unique. The parks had been "liberated"; the streets were being used; riots and political tricks of various media freaks took on a phantasmagorical phase and the amateur grabbed center focus.

The society around our theatrical enclave became more and more theatrical. The Mime Troupe had revived the emphasis on the single performer from 1960 to 1965 and made the skilled performer a probability. From 1965 to 1970 the lid was lifted off the big box. The hippies unleashed a surge of incompetence from below and the lumpen middle class wanted to express itself by being. Cooptation rides so fast that *Hair* was out before the scene was over (*Hair* is made up not of actors who imitate but of stereotypes who stand out).

Associated as we were with political factions, we often came under the same false thinking that has permeated American political organizations. Culturally deprived, they emphasize the limited notions of politics as "organizing." To many this means paperwork, files, speeches, and rallies. Cesar Chavez for a long while didn't see the political value of Luis Valdez's Teatro Campesino. How could we expect college kids who only discovered music in the rock century (1964-65) and Newsreel (non-filmmakers) and the underground press (white, middle-class, longhairs, just like us) or *Ramparts* (which finally printed a Mime Troupe play in 1971!) to support the efforts of our small

guerrilla theatre? We could hardly defend our labors as relevant in the face of the culturally deprived "politicos" of the movement while later it became impossible to match the rhetoric of the "revolutionary." To paraphrase Brecht:

> When misery is the politics of the left,
> How can you stand there and make jokes?

The Mime Troupe inherited a do-it-yourself/Horatio Alger/Renaissance man and germinated all sorts of mutants. The Mime Troupe is a microcosm of the movement, thus, its tortuous peregrinations are invaluable in learning about the maze of bourgeois democratic hurdles we had to clear in order to see the historical road.

When the amateurs had as much say, as much right to speak up at meetings (and who would dare say "no"), we lived in a daily burning of passions. Irrationality rose until the fires were too hot and people left. It turned out that both extremes split—the professionals and the politically confused theatrical amateurs. The professionals, the ones with talent and skill, could not take the lack of structure. We saw the dissolution of the dialectic between expertise and participation, between improvisation and training, between a script (written by a talented philosopher) and the actor's freedom to invent. The others had to leave, too—the street hoods, the ones without skills who should not have been in the company. They left, as always, to work elsewhere, not in art but in craft. The middle ground became a "collective." It is too soon to announce the results of that kind of operation. Sandy Archer, who left the company a few months after I did, wrote on the subject:

> When you attempt to break down or break out of
> the divisions of labor, you also begin to break down

the trust and respect that was associated with those divisions. And when those divisions were in terms of skill (or who could do that part of the common goal best) you open the doors to those areas to skilled and unskilled alike, to experienced and inexperienced. While this can bring out innovative ideas or techniques, it primarily focuses on breaking down identities built upon what we would call experienced or professional wisdom. In this way, anyone's opinions become as valid as anyone else's. The extreme result of this would be *individualism*, i.e., total expression of each in all areas. A true collective action, on the other hand, would be based upon emotional and political peers using their specific experience/skills for a common goal.

My own last days were filled with long meetings about program and the meaning of the Troupe. The meetings were held each day for weeks inside a cement-encrusted room we called the Library. Twenty people jammed into a space both physically and ideologically. We argued, some cried, a few left, charts were put up on walls and conversations went on endlessly. I remember one particular night when the forms of reorganization were posted on a wall. About five different plans had been suggested, none of which described the hidden problem of leadership and amateurism or professionalism's self-patronizing labor. The Inner Core did not work and the first impulse was to disband the leadership and create a loosely ordered "collective"—which of course meant a continuous round of meetings. After a five-hour meeting I went home and at 1:00 A.M. worked on a plan that would identify the conditions and make the Inner Core operate.

The elected Inner Core voted on proposals brought to it from anyone in the company, then brought these suggestions to the general company which passed on all programs. The log jam was in carrying out the programs. Sandy and I usually pushed while the other three members of the Inner Core were powers without responsibility. To admit this situation and solve it I suggested that Sandy and I become permanent members, and the other three be elected with specific areas of responsibility and decisive authority; ombudsman (shop steward), publicity (programs and public relations) and production (tech, costume and art). Sandy would continue in finances (budget and books) and I in direction (plays and classes). The plan was designed to identify leadership and require it to function instead of blurring it with participatory jargon and presumptions of collective organization.

The next day I suggested the plan. It was too late. My own will and enthusiasm had been sapped. The troupe was on a path of democratic collectivism that most left organizations were to struggle with for the next two years. In December of 1969 I took a leave of absence to go to Chicago and visit the conspiracy trials. A few months later my "leave of absence" became permanent.

PEOPLE

These articles assume greater meaning when considered in relation to the people who were responsible for the creation of the San Francisco Mime Troupe.

Jonathan Altman
Sandra Archer
Peter Arnott
J. Lani Bader
Steve Bailey
Frank Bardacke
John Barrow
Martin Bartlett
Richard Beggs
Joe Bellan
Rosinda Belmour
Hal Bennett
Peter Berg
Lorne Berkun
Eric Berne
Anne Bernstein
Kelly-Mary Berry
Chuck Bigelow
Marianne Bodian
Lee Bouterse
Bruce Bratton
Jeanne Brechan
Lee Breuer
Ruth Breuer
John Broderick
Emanuel Brookman
Allan Brotsky
Merle Brotsky
Lynn Brown
Willie Brown
Brooks Bucher
Malcolm Burnstein
John Burton
Mia Carlisle
Ronald Chase
Dan Chumley

Peter Cohan
Pedro Colley
Judy Collins
Bruce Comer
John Condrin
Peter Conn
John Connell
Kathryn Cox
Randy Craig
Christian Crawford
Don Crawford
Walter Crockett
Roy Dahlberg
Orville Dale
Susan Darby
Dixon Davis
Ron Davis
Robert Dawson
Charles Degelman
Ken Dewey
Nancy Dickler
Billie Dixon
Rodger Doty
Robert Doyle
June Duggan
Rosemary Eberhardt
Serge Echeverria
Allan Edmands
Paul Ehrlich
Nick Eldredge
Martin Epstein
Ellen Ernest
Sam Erwin
Beryl Feinglass
Jack Feinglass
Robert Feldman

Mike Fender
Lawrence Ferlinghetti
Irwin Fields
Lynn Fischbein
Cindy Fitzpatrick
Barbara Flinn
Jack Floyd
Jay Fox
Jeff Free
Bill Freese
Steve Friedman
George Gauger
William Geis
Ruth Gennrich
Herman George
Jon Gibson
Bob Gill
S. N. Goldberg
William Goodman
Bill Graham
Carl Granich
Francesca Greene
Dawn Grey
Emmett Grogan
Gerhard Gscheidle
Roger Guy-Bray
Roberta Hamble
Elizabeth Hancock
Merle Harding
Elizabeth Harris
Jason Harris
Lewis Harris
Willie Hart
Ann Hatch
Peter Haworth
Fred Hayden

Jim Haynie
Kay Hayward
Wally Hedrick
Peter Hennessy
Darryl Henriques
C. P. Herrick
Roger Hillyard
Victoria Hochberg
Richard Hodge
Ken Hoerauf
Arthur Holden
Joan Holden
Ann Horton
Robert Hudson
Robert Hurwitt
Bollete Jacobson
Melody James
Michael Jason
Becky Jenkins
David Jenkins
Warner Jepson
Zilla Johnson
J. Jeffrey Jones
Jerry Jump
Larry Keck
Sherryl Keyes
Leonard Kline
George Konnoff
Jeanne Konnoff
Harvey Kornspan
Marshall Krause
Gene Kunitomi
Buck Lacey
Carol La Fleur
Barbara La Morticella
Roberto La Morticella

Rob Lanchester
Nina Landau
Saul Landau
Steve Landau
Jane Lapiner
Ken Lash
Robert LaVigne
Norma Leistiko
Arthur Lempert
Cecile Leneman
Felix Leneman
Phil Lesh
Larry Lewis
Carl Linder
Jean Linder
William Lindyn
Sharon Lockwood
Pat Lofthouse
Joe Lomuto
Michael Lawrence
Tomas Lopez
Dave Love
Roy Lowe
Tom Luce
Arthur Lutz
Robert Mackler
William Mackler
David Maclay
Bonnie MacLean
William Maginnis
Sylvia Malm
Joan Mankin
Jason Marc-Alexander
Jerome Marcel
Ephraim Margolin
Van Marsh
Anthony Martin
Julio Martinez
George Mathews
Charles McDermed
Daniel McDermott
Edward McIntyre
Barbara Melandry
David Meltzer

Norma Middlebrook
Consie Miller
Jamie Miller
Robert Miller
Jeanne Milligan
Kent Minault
Robert Moran
Ann Morris
Sara Morris
Bill Murcott
Margo Mycue
Yvette Nachmias
Keith Nason
Robert Nelson
Bruce Newell
Ron Nystrom
Michael Oberndorf
Lynn O'Brien
Terry O'Keefe
Pauline Oliveros
Richard Olsen
David O'Meill
Irene Oppenheim
Mary Overlie
Maruska P.
Gayle Pearl
Diane Pedrin
Verna Pedrin
Nata Piaskowski
Ron Poindexter
Linda Post
Tom Purvis
Judy Quick
Chuck Ray
William Raymond
Ronald Reese
Steven Reich
Fred Reichman
Jim Reineking
Georges Rey
Chuck Richardson
Ann Riley
Valerie Riseley
Dawn Ristow

John Robb
Earl Robertson
Keith Rodin
Elias Romero
Al dela Rosa
Karl Rosenberg
Judy Rosenberg
Susan Roth
Loren Rush
Arlene Sagan
Paula Sakowski
Steve Sanders
Donato Sartori
Richard Sassoon
Barbara Scales
Emmet Scales
Robert Scheer
John Schonenberg
Cornelia Schultz
Betty Schwimmer
Mime Seitz
Shirley Shaw
Ruth Sicular
Marvin Silber
Patty Silver
Marlene Silverstein
David Simpson
Robert Slattery
Jim Smith
Rick Smith
Megan Snider
Peter Snider
Jan Soest
Peter Solomon
Fumi Spencer
William Spencer
Coni Spiegel
Kai Spiegel
Ron Stallings
Marvin Stender
Gary Stephan
Jerry Stephens
Jackson Stock
Caraline Straley

Kathryn Stuntz
Steve Subotnick
Juris Svendsen
Marilyn Sydney
John Swackhamer
Kate Swackhamer
Alan Tabechrikov
Carol Tarble
Dolly Tarquini
Holbrook Tieter
Chris Teuber
Dan Thomas
Charlotte Todd
Mark Truman
Fred Unger
Luis Valdez
Jeanne Varon
Lee Vaughn
Steve Virgil
Hiroshi Wagatsumi
Victoria Walker
Kathleen Ward
Jane Ward
Howard Waxman
Victoria Webber
Erik Weber
Loie Weber
Jael Weisman
John Welke
Donald Weygandt
Shelley Wexner
Jo Ann Wheatley
Norma Whitaker
Jack Wicker
Bill Wiley
Chuck Wiley
Wallee Williams
Ann Willock
Barbara Wohl
Bunny Wolfe
Joan Wright
Ken Wydro

Mime in Action

Flip through the next 26 photos from a 16mm movie of a performance of *L'Amant Militaire,* 1968.

11

RADICAL THEATRES SIX

After I took my "leave of absence" from the Mime Troupe I spent two years alternately blaming myself and wanting to kill the whole bunch who had ruined my conception of radical theatre. In the process of writing this book, analyzing *my* intentions and *our* accomplishments in the era of running survival, my rage subsided into mendaciousness.

On one hand I felt betrayed, yet I couldn't figure out who did the betraying. And while I was at it, who betrayed what? What were the stated objectives that were betrayed, and how was I responsible for clarifying objectives as well as implementing them?

In that period of anti-male-leadership and crude communal—yet sincere—collectivism, the rejected, ejected or self-extracted individual felt guilty; for after all, what was much of the new left of the sixties based on? Guilt was ready and waiting to further obfuscate reason.

I arrived at a realization that although I would have liked to be in control at all times, I wasn't; our social surroundings influenced intuition as well as determined our actions. In fact, if I felt

guilty for failing to make the revolution, or to make the SFMT the center of the storm, then I had neatly elevated myself to a unique position. By pushing intentions and actions back into history and by observing the work of the company from a non-defensive vantage—that is, from outside the group—I could more objectively observe our ten years.

In the study of SFMT history it was necessary to compare what we had done with what else was going on. As of 1974, the Open Theatre (under the direction of Joe Chaikin) has closed down. The Performance Group headed by Richard Schechner still operates in New York City. The Becks—Judith and Julian of the Living Theatre—are said to exist in Philadelphia in the midst of internal divisions; they are, however, expected to perform one or another spectacle. Peter Schumann of the Bread and Puppet Theatre had a closing two-day festival in July 1974 in Vermont, while El Teatro Campesino and the SFMT are very much alive touring and working in their hometowns.

Although books on this type of theatre have lumped all groups under the heading of Guerrilla Theatre or some other catch-all, the best definition of these six groups is still Radical Independent Theatre. The radical theatres are primarily alternatives to the bourgeois world at least in intent, and are all professional. The term professional does not refer merely to union status versus non-union, but to full-time personal commitment.

Just as in political activity there are Marxists who are social democrats and those who are revolutionary, midst the six theatres there is a division between the radical right and the radical left. This is by no means a matter of hairsplitting, for lives have been lost or won or the basis of a few differences, and intentions can be turned into their opposites by misinterpretations.

The left of the radical theatres laughs more, tickles while it fights, engages in picket lines and demonstrations as part of its work, has at its base a mimetic sense of imagery rather than a naturalistic imitation of reality, and has been associated from the get-go with the peace movement, the new left, or the Chicano/migrant workers' struggle. They are Peter Schumann's Bread and Puppet Theatre, San Francisco Mime Troupe, and Luis Valdez's El Teatro Campesino.

The right wing of the Radical Independent Theatres has despaired more at the social setting around it, of its own work, is more closely associated with the educational or entertainment establishment, is an extension or a deviation from the bourgeois theatre, and is closely aligned with the aesthetic avant garde. It consists of the Becks and the Living Theatre, Joe Chaikin and the Open Theatre, and Richard Schechner's Performance Group.

Julian Beck, Judith Malina (The Becks): The Living Theatre

The women's movement has finally brought us to the brink of understanding psychological and personal details in a political or public manner, thus the following account takes into consideration personal and public demonstrations.

I first saw Julian Beck and Judith Malina at their theatre doing *Man is Man* by Brecht. Joe Chaikin played Gayly Gay, and was so impressive that he appeared to be a "Brechtian" actor, even though I had never seen one. He appeared to live the theory. Judith Malina, playing Widow Begbick, was atrocious. I remember her only moment, when she stood before the curtain and gave her Widow Begbick speech:

Interjection by Widow Begbick

Herr Bertolt Brecht asserts: Man is Man
And that is something everyone can assert.
But Herr Brecht also proves that
You can do anything with a man.
Here tonight a man is altered like a car
He is approached humanely and firmly
Persuaded to adjust himself to the course of this world
Letting his private fish swim in the sand.
And for whatever he is rebuilt
On him one can always rely
Man, if we fail to watch over him
Can be turned over night into a butcher for us.
Herr Brecht hopes you're going to see
The ground on which you stand melt away like snow beneath your feet
And realize in the case of the packer Galy Gay
That life on earth is dangerous.
[Translated by Helga Wisalewski]

The speech by Judith was electrifying because I knew she had stood on picket lines, been brutalized by the cops and was a political activist. The aura of her being provided the electricity to the text.

I went backstage to Judith's dressing room to

talk about the theatre. The Living Theatre had become important in the American alternative theatre scene. It struggled for many years in lofts before landing a permanent house on 14th Street in New York. Her dressing room was a little cubicle filled with wall-to-wall pictures of great actresses and actors. I was a bit confused, the progressive political stance of the group seemed to contradict the theatrical tradition in the pictures. I flashed back to a production they did of Picasso's *Desire* at the Cherry Lane Theatre in '55 or '56, which was no more comprehensible than the pictures of the greats of the (commercial) theatre and the beatnik reputation of the group.

My next encounter with the Becks was their production of *The Connection*, a play that talked of junk, fixes and dope, which thrust them into the limelight of national publicity. Chaikin again performed the night I saw it. His character had a boil on his neck and he merely went around doing his job. Could this be Brechtian acting? I found out later that he had a heart murmur and never exerted himself.

Saul Landau and I went to see Julian and Judith in their New York Westside apartment filled with cockroaches, newspapers, and Julian's large paintings on the dimly-lit walls. We heard the scurrying of people in the back rooms. Judith was pasting ads in the scrapbook while Julian sat and talked with us. Condensation of my notes on that meeting, March 26, 1964, with Julian and Judith:

She: Don't come to demonstrations with papers wrapped in newspaper.
He: Castro betrayed the Revolution.
She: Gandhi's Satyagraha the only way . . .
He: Property is theft.

She: I believe in this city and probably not in Robert Williams.
He: I can't kill a cockroach any more.
Both: CNVA (Committee for Non-Violent Action)
She: We did pay a hundred dollars a week to IRS; they closed us on eleven counts related to Federal property.
She: We know a thousand artists in New York.
She: Start with oneself.

Julian gave off the aura of a guru even before gurus were part of the landscape, while Judith came off as practical and politically rational. They smiled and were pleased to hold court.

The Connection was inventive yet had a twinge of the thirties' *Waiting for Lefty* about it. Actors strode in and out of the set. The fake director and fake producer started talking from the back of the theatre and walked up the center aisle to challenge the actors and dispute the play during the play. At intermission fake junkies and real junkies bugged the audience with requests for change and cigarettes. It was a living experience: the thirties' hokiness of Odets's play where actors rose up from the audience joining the "strike" and the more touchy-feely experiences of Ann Halperin's dance group. The mixing of cast and audience and the use of the aisles and stage showed up in the later extravaganza *Paradise Now*.

The last show in New York before their European sojourn was *The Brig*. The story of the filming is as dramatic as the film. The Fourteenth Street Theatre was padlocked and the actors and cameramen sneaked in through the roof. The entire film, shot in one night by Jonas and Adolphus Mekas, captured the energy, the event and the play in one scoop. The presentation is flat. No sexual comment, no overt political or social analysis is made on the activities inside a Navy brig. The Becks presented in all its horror, the exact replica of a brig—social realism.

With the slice-of-life realism of *The Connection* under their feet and the radical pacifism of their own politics in total control rather than the dialectical materialism of *Man is Man*, *The Brig* represents a unique example of the Becks' political and artistic expression. The performance was impeccable and tortuous. After the naturalistic re-enactment of brutality lasting an hour, one question sneaked into my head: "Who would do that to themselves?" Our attention finally focuses on the actors—not on the conditions.

When they were closed down by the IRS in 1964 I never understood if it was because of their own foolishness, governmental repression or opportunism. Were they tired, ready to quit when the IRS bust came? It was rumored that they were ready to fold up their Fourteenth Street tent and the government's padlock offered an opportunity for courtroom drama.

In 1966 I discussed with one of the actors in our company a Radical Theatre Agency that would promote the tours of the Mime Troupe and other groups just coming alive around the country. My friend suggested we call Saul Gottlieb, living in Germany. We placed a call right there

and then from California; fortunately, we didn't reach him. Later I wrote Gottlieb, asking him if he would head up such an agency to promote the left groups and create an alternative booking combine. In '67 when we played New York and were the darlings of the left theatre and radical hippiedom, I met Gottlieb and continued our discussion.

He had written articles on the Living Theatre and was working on a book. He was very interested in solving the Living's problems with the IRS, thereby providing them the opportunity to tour this country. We organized discussions with Joe Chaikin, now at the Open Theatre; people from Gut Theatre, Sixth Street Theatre, Bread and Puppet Theatre, Pageant Players; and Ed Bullins, then with the Lafayette Negro Ensemble. There was general interest because the Mime Troupe had just toured the country on its own hook—booking, playing and scrambling without the aid of a commercial booker.

Saul Gottlieb agreed to take on the job, and the first big fish was the tour of '69, with the Living Theatre repeating the work it developed in Europe. The tour was totally chaotic. The IRS had not been sufficiently cooled and often "seized the box office." Other times the Becks and their international longhairs created more newspaper incidents than they needed, plus a few local arrests for various and sundry infractions of the municipal statutes. As a result, the agency lost money.

When the Becks brought their traveling show to Berkeley, the Mime Troupe went en masse. The first incident of *Mysteries and Pieces* was in the audience. The freeloaders had taken up the front rows and the five-dollar-ticket holders were arguing for their seats. The dispute ensued for

about ten minutes into the opening scene. It indicated complexities that the booking agency, the Becks and the hippie-radical scene had only begun to debate. Charging high prices for a "radical, free, liberating, vertical, revolutionary" product was a little difficult to clarify.

Mysteries and Pieces was a bunch of exercises. Irving Ben Israel, a white heavy with a natural, provided the most interesting performance. I was anxiously watching the show. The Mime Troupe, sprinkled with SDS-ers, was heckling, and although I could see the stuff on stage was touchy-feely, beat, poetic trash, I knew the history of the Living Theatre and wanted to be able to see the show. Finally I split to the balcony, which was empty enough to reflect upon the action on stage and audience. Both parts made up the event.

The next night, with *Frankenstein*, it was much clearer as to what the Living Theatre was about. In the opening scene an actor, sitting center stage, and others in lotus positions surrounding him, are trying to levitate the center person. (The objective is explained over a loudspeaker.) With twenty concentrated yogis counting in English, French, German and Spanish, they fail to levitate the actor. The audience is suckered into the inevitable failure, for if they had ever levitated anyone, we would have heard about it. Yet they persisted in trying despite their constant failures. After this failure, the center figure is taken off stage, put in a coffin, and brought up to an apartment-like structure (scaffolding beautifully lit up) and put through a series of tortures.

The justification for the whole contraption and the two hours of elaborate visual gimmicks is based upon the failure to levitate. It was a paradigm of the Becks' philosophy.

The third production, *Paradise Now*, never happened in Berkeley. The kids had been on demonstrations and just fought off the cops in one or another confrontation, and when the signal to take off your clothes and join the show was given, Super Joel, a red-headed Berkeley hippie activist, was out of his jumper before anyone else. About fifty others got up on stage and within a few minutes were talking to and stomping on the Living Theatre troupe, who were claiming they couldn't travel without a passport, couldn't take off their clothes, and couldn't smoke marijuana. The last statement produced a shitload of joints all over the house. The debacle was unnerving.

After the thing stopped, I went backstage to talk with the Becks. It was court time in the dressing room. As is always the case after a show, the performers are "high" and a bit anxious. What had happened? They couldn't figure it out, but they knew something was different from Iowa. I went up to Julian, asked "How are you?" and if he thought the performance was okay. He said, "What happens, happens; that's part of the show." I asked again if he thought it was okay. He nodded. Then I said that I thought the San Francisco audience might be even more difficult because the Haight Straight Theatre had been doing happenings and spectaculars with rock bands, Kenneth Anger black masses and other such madness that made *Paradise Now* dated. He didn't seem worried. And, in fact, I was wrong. The San Francisco audience, I forgot, was less cohesive and far less politically activist, thereby receptive to participatory experiences in the here and now.

What was the Living Theatre doing in 1969? They brought back the hippie movement from '65, strained through European eyes, ears and crotches. They replaced the games of the street the Diggers had done on Haight and Masonic, and placed on stage in a theatrical atmosphere the events in the pads, streets and parks we had all experienced from '65 through '67, then told us it was new, now, revolutionary, psychedelic, Zen, Hebraic, beat, hip, and anarchistic.

Like *Hair*, the commercial interpretation of hippie life-style, the actors in *Paradise Now* were not actors but people with loin cloths who had only themselves to rely on. As a consequence they were *being* rather than doing. Julian himself, with flowing grey hair and in black jock, was the lean guru, Jesus figure, floating and effective, comforting and controlling the manipulative event. The greatest effect of their '69 labors appeared to be on the middle class and the liberal critics across the country. They disrupted bourgeois conventions in the protective atmosphere of the theatre, where the bourgeoisie had historically demanded that their stage first portray the good life of the rising middle class and then, when the contradictions between surplus value and religious morality were too great, they demanded that the stage (not the church) punish them, kick them in the guts, to provide a cleansing and a cathartic to their corruption. The Living Theatre both hates and works over the middle class, not to change them, only to exorcize original sin.

It was during a lecture by Julian Beck and Judith Malina at the Encore Theatre, reopened in 1972 by Lawrence Ferlinghetti, that they spewed out their pseudo-religious, guilt-ridden, despicable, metaphysical, anarchistic, elitist rap. They had just come back from Brazil, where they had been released through the good graces of thousands who sent coins to help them fight the Brazilian government. While the Becks did improvisational happenings in favellas (barrios of the poor) revolutionary guerrillas were being tortured in Brazilian police stations under AID administration.

I knew that I might do something outrageous, so I asked Richard Lichtman, Marxist philosopher and friend, to accompany me to the lecture to keep my head and outrage in perspective. We later used a tape to recover the exact statements made and recounted our sense of the meeting for a radio program played on the Berkeley Pacifica station KPFA.

Julian Beck [voice]: How can we invent the devices, the mechanisms, the strategies, and put them into action, taking them out of the area of abstract thought and bringing them into the world so that we will no longer be aiding and abetting our oppressor classes? But, so that we are giving our strength and our culture and whatever that culture is able to do to trigger the doors of the imagination to the people so that they can figure out how to get us out of this terrible trap.

Lichtman: If you come into that audience and you feel various kinds of impotence, let's say sexually-politically, all they do is probe the point; that is, they push you where you feel incapable of acting. They're full of the same kind of bourgeois concepts that they mean to criticize when they begin to talk and theorize. One example, for instance, is their use of class terms.

They put the audience down as being bourgeois and, I think, in a few places, really contemptible. But the irony of the situation is that their own analysis of the audience is extremely bourgeois. The theoretical position, inarticulate theoretical position, from which they analyze the audience, is that the audience is made up of a group of affluent consumers. They adopt the standpoint of bourgeois consciousness and bourgeois social theory which tends to conceive of people basically in terms of their consuming functions. . . . They drop out any sense of the audience as made up of people who labor in one form or another; don't really consume commodities but who spent their day reproducing the economic system which is exploitative. They don't take the audience seriously as producers at all, so, consequently, they can't see the audience as having any kind of revolutionary potential.

Julian Beck [voice]: The "people" are those who turn the world—are those people who are producing what man needs. Those people, when I use the term people, I'm talking about that large unified group which is without individuation.

Voice from audience: Just say everybody.

Julian Beck [voice]: I don't want to say everybody because I'm concerned with those people who are producing the food, so that we can eat it, and making our clothes for us to wear or carrying away our shit or making the electricity—who are building—we don't even know how to build a room like this. We cannot lay the bricks and we don't do it. And for that labor that is given us for this privilege we return very little.

Davis: Why does the audience allow him to do that to them? Why do they allow the Becks to lay on this analysis?

Lichtman: Well, this is a place where they share something together. I had the feeling there was a lot of affinity between the audience and them, overall. Even the people who were hostile to them shared a great deal with them. The audience also, I think, tends to regard itself as a corrupt form of bourgeoisification that's hard to get past. The audience sees itself as consumers in large part because it has no genuine control over the productive parts of its life. The only place where its energy can go basically is into consuming. Because it can't make any choice about how it wants to be productive or creative, that's its conception of itself.

Davis: Also something that struck me was the religious tone of his intonations, the Messianic role he felt he had to play which seems to me to fit in with Western civilization's sense of guilt of its own wealth. An American hip audience—an American intellectual audience—is riddled with guilt. These people are the perfect purveyors of that guilt. There were only a couple of people who were outraged when Julian said to his comrades when he was arrested in Brazil, "Cool it, our class will get us out." It was true. Around the world people collected money to get Julian and Judith and the Living Theatre out of jail. One kid got up, outraged, he said, "You punks, you rotten stinkers." It was the moment when I too got furious. He was in a sense slapping you in the face for being human. I never quite believed that the Living Theatre had any dynamic revolutionary role but I believed that they shouldn't be in jail. I could never argue against giving money to get them out of jail, but they were so . . . it's hard to explain how ugly they were about their—about their own friends, their own class, their own followers.

Lichtman: Well, on their own analysis, the act of getting them out of jail had to be another form of corruption.

It's another form of a kind of glorified game where you didn't risk anything. All you did was put up your money, which is part of your corruption. Instead of your suffering in jail the way they did, you got the vicarious thrill of being able to get them out of jail; being a defender of freedom while sitting in your own home just making out a check. I was just imagining what speech you could put in their mouth to make their own position tenable and that's the only thing that would make any sense. But, they condemn the audience at the same time that they rely on it. Absolute cynicism.

Julian Beck [voice]: While I may have great sympathy for your neuroses and your unhappiness or Mrs. Rockefeller's I regard that as a luxury.

Lichtman: Their view is that affluence leads essentially to contentment and misery is the source of revolution so that any act that anybody takes in the short run to improve his own condition moves him further away from being a revolutionary.

Davis: If you enjoy yourself you won't be revolutionary.

Lichtman: The more industrialized the country gets, the less revolutionary it is—there's no strategy for that. Either it falls into a kind of gradualism where if people improve their lot, they become affluent and bourgeoisified and corrupt and if they don't they stay revolutionary. But then the only thing you can look forward to again, in religious terms, is a kind of chiliastic crisis where the world suddenly is sundered and the mobs rise up from their absolute abject misery and simply take power. That's the only scenario that can come out of that analysis. There's no dialectic in it. It has no sense of how people could possibly move from their suffering to any position in which they strengthen themselves. It's like some play on Nietzchian slave morality. The weaker you are, the more revolutionary you are.

Joe Chaikin: The Open Theatre

The Open Theatre is comprehensible as a group when considered as a reaction to the hysterics of the Living Theatre. Joe Chaikin did not join all the activities of the Becks and organized experimental workshops early in '63 with the aid of Gordon Rogoff. Gordon came from *Encore* magazine, the English theatre journal that provided the print for the Angry Young Men of British theatre in the fifties. Rogoff, a soft-spoken cultural activist in commercial and off-Broadway haunts, was supportive of Chaikin's experiments which led to *America Hurrah*.

America Hurrah, the first uptown production, was a result of the improvisational acting explorations within the Open Theatre. It was produced by Beverly Sills, written by Jean-Claude van Itallie, and directed by Jacques Levy. The show provided some embarrassment to the Open Theatre regulars. The performance was a combination of improvisational mirror exercises with dialogue, group therapeutic quick-witted repartée that we can still see in the games of the improvisational theatre groups like the Second City (or their now dead cousins, The Committee and The Premise).

The achievement is one of unified participation, all actors giving and taking without conflict. The actors begin looking and studying each other with concentration on detail and kinesthetic awareness rather than scripts or texts. Theories in the American theatre of self-developed scripts— plays that come from the actors, directors and technicians, rather than playwrights—are a product of the sixties. Both the participatory democracy of SDS and group therapeutic techniques are utilized to create an atmosphere where the whole person (whoever that is) participates in all stages of the creation and becomes the creation. Chaikin's variation on this operation was the inclusion of a writer who improved the scattered intuitive interchanges between characters.

The first time I met Joe was on stage . . . and later at a meeting about the Radical Theatre Repertory (Agency). He was, as always, quiet, concerned, and soft-soled (desert boots in the old days). He is serious, a bit troubled, and if the chance comes to be alone with him, he tells of his heart problem which has gone on for years. The forced limitation of his physical activity made him rely upon his sister, Shami Chaikin, and others to run the business of the group and allowed him time to concentrate on the personal tribulations and the "real truth" in the actor's bag. He was not the producer per se, although he was the strongest influence on the group. He tended to work after other people did something, as Pasoli states:

> Chaikin has a knack for stepping off-center, especially at times of controversy, and people feel their influence within the group to be equal. This is an illusion. Everything actually happens by Chaikin's instigation or sufferance.
> (Robert Pasoli, *A Book on the Open Theatre*)

He shaped and concentrated the labor of others, and in this way he was a good teacher and collaborator.

Of the three pieces in *America Hurrah*, the last was the best. A large, puppet-headed married couple enter a motel room and proceed to scrawl four-letter words on the walls, rip up the sheets and towels, and demolish the room while the hotel manager's piped-in voice tells the rules. It is funny, gruesome, accurate, and a fine image of what we all feel, and some of us do, in motels, as we get ripped off for fifteen to twenty-five bucks a night. The final holocaust, which sounds like an atom bomb attack, is a little gratuitous, but given the company's behavioral and pacifist critique, the only way to end such a perfect depiction of American consumerism is to blame it on outside forces, and the atom bomb appears to them as an "outside force."

For a while I would bump into Joe and Jean-Claude van Itallie every so often, and for a while we wrote letters back and forth. He last told me he had difficulty with my final speech at the end of the *L'Amant Militaire* show in 1967 when I said, "We have learned that this is our country, and it's our duty to change it. If we can't change it, then we have to destroy it." He didn't see where destruction was necessary or helpful, and he couldn't buy that part of the show. I explained that real destruction was not chaotic or anarchistic, rather a matter of knowing the central core of the society well enough to attack it at its root, not smash a few leaves off the dead branches; the best destruction is replacement.

In *Terminal*, ca. 1970, movers clothed in white long-johns went through various activities that seemed clinical. When I realized that Joe had heart trouble, the piece became clear. It was the heart made mimetic. On stage, characters blooped and bleeped like the aorta, ventricles, and the pump of the heart muscles, while others moved around dimly with seriousness, attending to a surgical operation.

Mutations, seen in 1972, was a mind blast of a death trip. I went stoned with a friend of mine, and we couldn't stop talking to each other from the first moment in the theatre. What we saw in *Mutations* was performers playing themselves with a cover of "artsiness." Each person told more or less his or her own story—the football player dressed in numbered shirt did an athletic number; the homosexual did a homosexual dance; the actress did a few lines from some plays; the group leader, Shami Chaikin, did a sputtering incomprehensible patter that indicated "no sense out of reason, no sense out of language." Cleared by high perception, I constantly saw the images of death portrayed on the stage floor, couched in modern dance or pseudo-mimetic movements.

By '72 the Open Theatre had become for the New Yorkers *the* radical theatre. They were doing their own booking. In part the work was principled—that is, written and developed by the company—and they were not doing undressing and sex-titillating drama. Joe had come back from working in England with Peter Brook.

In the fifties actors who performed in naturalistic plays replaced their study of fencing with modern dance, even though they had little use for their developed muscles. Marceau brought a new fad and Decroux followed him with a stint at the Actors Studio. Pantomime became a part of the curriculum and produced more white-faced pedalpushers than actors who could walk in character. By the late sixties, after much rejection of training from anything, Jerzy Grotowski arrived with a mysterious technique of physicalization couched in pseudo-medieval rhetoric. Grotowski's European lineage, Polish mysticism, and disciplined

bourgeois dedication to the development of the "actor" was of course immensely attractive to the naked improvisers who wanted to be, be, be.

Chaikin's use of Grotowski's lessons was related to his previous endeavors; therefore, his use of the new technique was less a fashionable trick than the cooptation of Grotowski jargon by Richard Schechtner of the Performance Group.

When the Open Theatre first received money from the National Endowment Fund, it was used wisely and paid for babysitting and supported less affluent members who couldn't make it into commercials or off-Broadway shows. Joe's words to me late in '72 that "all the political theatre they had done was no good" indicated that he either did the wrong political theatre, or like the good pacifist, despairing, guilt-ridden, kind-hearted soul he is, he needed a show of angst to continue his private labors while fending off any criticism.

Outside the theatre, Chaikin had counseled draft resisters for years. Recently he has worked in theatrical improvisations with prisoners, thus putting his social work consciousness to good use and possibly uniting his political perspective and the suffering in his art.

The contribution of the Open Theatre is more than flash. Robert Pasoli's book on the Open Theatre provides a useful handbook for collective, pseudo-behavioral exercises, gleaned from Viola Spolin, Jerzy Grotowski, and the American actors' need to create something worthwhile for the self.

Richard Schechner: The Performance Group

Richard Schechner, another force in the alternative theatre, has done much more in print than in the flesh, although the Performance Group provided enough flesh to make up for the years of his stage abstention.

I first met Schechner after writing letters and sending articles to his magazine, *Tulane Drama Review.* Schechner took the little journal over from the ubiquitous hands of Robert Corrigan, who had been printing an academic review written by a few professors who went to see English and French theatre in the fifties. Richard wrote in the *TDR* "Comment":

> The American Theatre is in a state of flux, and it lacks significant leadership. Hopefully *TDR Comment will provide this leadership and be a rallying point for those young and eager theatre-workers who are dedicated to an art which has been, in our country, too long the call girl of money and ambition.* In some sense we hope to restore virginity to the theatre, and purpose to theatre-workers.
> —*TDR*, Winter 1962,
> Vol. 7, No. 2, T18

Significantly, Gordon Rogoff also had a comment to make in that issue. He had tried to run *Theatre Arts* magazine—the high-school slick magazine for rising young stars—in a radical fashion, but failed because the publishers read a copy one day and decided to can Rogoff and his staff, return to American Theatre, and stop the talk about the new European stuff. Schechner's first issue, although claiming to represent the virgins in America, had articles on Lorca, Strindberg, coupled with talk of the new English Realism, and that group called "The Becks' Living Theatre."

Plucky and young, he represented the rising criticism of the establishment in America, be it in Washington and Texas, or Broadway and Hollywood. He wanted to support some type of alternative to the entertainment industry.

When I saw him next, he was in San Francisco

and came to see the Actors Workshop. We met in a small house, part-time office, near the Workshop's scene shop in the Mission District. Lawrence Ferlinghetti and I had heard an unpublished *TDR* "Comment" declaring that the new theatre was to be found in the regional organizations like the Workshop, Alley and Arena groups. I remember Ferlinghetti saying right outfront, "That's bullshit; they aren't doing anything new," and I trying to tell him that after my three years with the Workshop I had found that the introduction of new style or collective arrangements was impossible. The Workshop at that very moment was negotiating with the Ford Foundation for increased sums and would eventually make itself available to re-entering the mainstream of commercial, useless culture at the Lincoln Center.

I, too, like Schechner, had come to the regional theatre hoping to create essential theatre in a society crammed with trivia, but found after my three years with the Workshop that the situation was hopeless. No matter what we said, Schechner saw a bandwagon and was in the midst of a hop.

In preparation for the *Minstrel Show* and to catch up on what was going on in the South, I took a trip to New Orleans and Mississippi to see the work of the Free Southern Theater, 1964. I hoped to make some contacts, exchange information with the actors and directors, and possibly see if our notion of taking a black/white minstrel show to the South was at all possible.

I flew to New Orleans and visited with Schechner, who taught at Tulane and lived in the French Quarter. He was on the board of directors of the Free Southern Theatre and had in the main been instrumental in setting up the entire thing with Northern money, liberal attitudes and an off-Broadway consciousness. I saw the Free Southern Theatre do Brecht's *Rifles of Senora Carrar* in McComb, Mississippi. Before the show, while the group was setting up Kleig lights (given to them by Joe Papp) in a run-down movie house, I walked outside and watched a little scene that made Senora Carrar's rifles ridiculous.

An old black man with harmonica was playing something for a group of kids while a taxi driver watched. They got into a little game, and the kids asked him to call a dog with his mouth organ. Dog calling is one of the more useful traits of a small harmonica. The taxi driver, idling in front of the theatre, said he would bet him a nickel he couldn't call a dog with his sound. The old man took the bet and played a few notes and zappo—a dog came across the street to the movie house. The kids jumped and the taxi driver gave up his nickel. I grinned. The kids demanded another dog. The taxi driver laughed but was serious now about the next nickel. The old man played and ever so jauntily a small hairy dog turned the corner and came up to the man with the harmonica. Pandemonium. I can't remember the end of the scene, but I knew that if harmonicas and old black guys doing dog-calls were not a part of

any theatrical presentation in the South, then something must be wrong.

Rifles of Senora Carrar by Brecht is about a Spanish family whose sons and daughters are engaged in the revolution and, finally, after personal tragedy, convince the mother to join their fight. Guns were handed out at the end. The black audience, screaming kids and chattering adults, didn't understand the projections, the off-Broadway or European style, and the issuing of guns, which was completely out of whack with SNCC. and CORE at that time. The vote, integrated transportation and restaurants, and an end to discrimination in the schools were uppermost in everyone's mind. The Free Southern Theater with the help of Richard Schechner was completely out of it—neither politically nor artistically appropriate. They were sojourners in the land of do-goodism, social workers who were working off their guilt.

One could understand the complaints of SNCC when the Northern liberals, white or black, came to town, did their bit, and split after the heavy demonstration was over. The fight had only begun. The theatre group should have acted like guerrillas, not like off-Broadway college types. I tried to show them some of the stuff we had done in the parks of San Francisco, not preaching that our style was right for them, but rather that our material was geared to the people and places we were performing in.

Schechner's next move came some years later. He asked me if he should move to New York or California. He had gotten offers from both places and was trying to decide which place was better for his magazine, *TDR*. I knew he would pick New York, the home of the big deal, although I argued for California. With his feet in the West he

might pick up some radicalism and publish the history of the non-establishment culture in the Western states. People ensconced in New York tend to focus on the East Coast, and I hoped that he would see that the commercial marketplace was not conducive to creative thinking.

Tulane Drama Review grew up, expanded, and became a part of New York University, where once again Schechner became a teacher of drama and continued his search, I presume, for virgins.

When the Actors Workshop went home to Rockefeller's Lincoln Center, the Regional Theatre boom began in earnest. Money, first from Ford, the spearhead of decentralization, then Rockefeller, Carnegie, and all the other national and local foundations, created "cultural centers." The Guthrie Theatre opened with a stipend of two million dollars in Minneapolis, and the big time had arrived for the local intellectual college professors, who were off-Broadway-minded, but didn't want to walk the streets and beat off the hustlers in the East.

In 1967 we performed in New York long enough to visit local dignitaries, and Schechner brought Jerzy Grotowski, his new-found master, to see our show. A group of us went to Schechner's pad in Greenwich Village and stood around to hear the translation of what Jerzy had to say about us.

Grotowski had just come to these shores, made a splash, and was visiting or teaching with his associate and star example of the Grotowski method, Schlesack. Sitting in a low wicker chair, the round, flabby, white-skinned Jerzy, wearing a dark blue suit with black sunglasses, was an ominous figure in the hip pad with a bunch of West Coast, eat-'em-up-alive diggers and iconoclasts.

I gathered after a while that Grotowski thought we were "undisciplined dilettantes" and that our work was negligible. First offended, then proud, I agreed that we were dilettantes. For we believed that the theatre was no more important than the rest of people's activities. We were playing around, yes, with mores, morals, pacifism and American guilt in a way that was not serious for him. Like most Americans, we were more slammers than sluggers, more ridiculous ridiculers than defenders of the faith, and, as visitors to New York, we didn't give a shit for his shit. I didn't like the guy's posture and psychical presence so I left the room to eat up everything on the buffet table.

Richard, on the other hand, became a Grotowskyite, not only in print, but in his forthcoming stage work.

When Joe Chaikin was in Chicago in 1972, I got some of the scuttlebutt about Grotowski, who had, of course, been very popular in America and was less of a sage or theatrical genius in Poland. Grotowski did shows in New York at ten and twenty dollars a head with a hundred seats in the house. Tickets went for a hundred by scalpers, and after this sojourn in the West, he took off for India. While there, I was told, he changed his mind, let his hair grow, lost weight, wore colorful clothes, and went back to Poland to change his monastic, theatrical Polish Theatre Lab into a post-hippie ensemble. I have yet to verify it; however, one can't be surprised by monkish renegades.

Schechner's guerrilla theatre experiments were embarrassing.* While teaching a class at NYU, he was confronted by a group of students who came in and said that Cambodia was being bombed. So he went to a meeting, called for volunteers, and created a guerrilla theatre happening whereby they ran down the aisles of legitimate theatre houses and confronted the audience with "Cambodia is being bombed. What are you going to do about it?" In some places the stage actors stopped, listened, and the audience was attentive, and after the "guerrilla" annoyance left, continued with the show. For, after all, what the fuck is one supposed to do about it?

Schechner himself went off to India sustained by a grant from one of those foundations that want to help us artists understand the world. He continues writing about games, the theory of dramaturgy, and the underlying principles of the collective unconscious.

He has created with the help of others—Erika Munk in particular—a magazine that first spoke for the alternative theatrical groups, although its perspective was academic and liberal. Later they printed materials on cultural activities, inasmuch as the theatre has run off the stage into the streets and parks and now is in the fashion shops.

Schechner moved from college to regional to alternative theatrical groups, hardly ever supporting any political left organization, and remains a

* *TDR.* T47 (1970).

liberal aesthetician similar to Richard Corrigan, the original editor of *TDR* and now the manager of the California Institute of Arts. He has valued his association with the established academic world and hopped around, trying to find some perfect virgin theatrical group that could espouse causes that were so pure that no one would touch them. The failure of this search for purity is like Chaikin's search for meaningful work, and the Becks' search for immediate personal revolution.

That these three throw themselves into their work is no claim to perfection or purity. Herbert Blau (Lincoln Center, CIA and various colleges), Robert Corrigan (CIA) and Robert Brustein (Yale) are no less engaged in their liberal or conservative enterprises. By approaching creation in the theatre from a hop-skip-consumer sense, Schechner will always be a part of the "experimentation" in the theatre, yet of the three right radical groups the least innovative and instructive.

As to radicalism, it would appear that the Becks of the Living Theatre are the most radical. From a liberal point of view they are—Brustein was outraged by the Becks' spectacle in 1969— however, the closer one gets to investigating the claims and practice of the group, the easier it is to see the Living Theatre as a diverting irritant to the bourgeois theatre and a cesspool of ideas. The Becks—Judith, more articulate about politics, Julian, Elizabethan in his description of theatre— espouse undissolved and undigested entities hoping that by accident and occult mystery a synthesis will occur. Zen Buddhism, Hebraic chants, beat poetry, Kropotkin, and rhetoric of the movement's revolutionary heavies spew out of their mouths at a faster rate than anyone else's. For a time in the mid-sixties, the hippies were creating positive examples that answered real needs rather

than "head trips," "vertical revolutionary assaults," and lots of self-aggrandizing horseshit.

The Becks suffer in a grander fashion than Chaikin, and have the capability of catching the publicity in a new event: IRS trials, European confrontations, the fashionable and radical-hunting American press of '69, and, of course, the heroic leap into the Latin American struggle—their sojourn in Brazil and jail. They are truly searching for T. S. Eliot's "ant hill" of martyrdom. And, for that reason, they are the most dangerous and obnoxious, for they suffer in the cause of, and bring out the worst elements of, metaphysical religiosity in the American white middle class.

Upon reflection, the work of Chaikin—focusing on the craft of the actor, utilizing improvisational and psychological techniques—contains a sincerity that pacifists maintain even in the face of obvious personal and group dissolution. The attempt at pure honesty, although simple, is to be respected.

Peter Schumann: The Bread and Puppet Theatre

The leftists, exemplified by Peter Schumann (Bread and Puppet Theatre) and Luis Valdez (El Teatro Campesino) have their own miseries and mysteries to unravel. Schumann is after all more religious and sensitive than Chaikin and the Becks, and whereas they despair, he twinkles at his inventive theatrics.

His heaviness and slow dramaturgy, while a retreat to simplicity and non-technological solutions, have at their core a desire to tell a story. Puppetry is older than bourgeois drama (and capitalism). It was in a conversation with Juris Svendsen in 1968 that Peter Schumann discussed "story."

Juris: But when you put a story on them [the puppets], when and where does the story come from?

Peter: I don't know. That's hard to say. Let's see . . . I don't . . . I don't. That's one of my big misunderstandings with my company, that are constantly advisers on stories, advice from people in the company. And I am not looking for a story whatsoever. Either it comes by itself or I don't want a story. I don't want to look for a story, or read books to find a story or a fable. I really get it from . . . that it comes as an idea, what these puppets are, what their heads are. Like I remember the King's Story, I was fumbling around and doing crazy bits of tryout stories with the children in a high school where I worked at the time. And I couldn't find their story, and it really made me unhappy. I was trying out all kinds of things with these puppets, we played something that was called "Fire" originally with these puppets and it was not good. It was not their story and then one day in the rehearsal I just found it, the King's Story. That it was about him, about the King, and the Red Man and the Blue Man. Before, I had trouble finding names for them. You know, like the guy's red, so what should I call him . . . I used . . . I called . . . Devil? . . . he wasn't . . . and then I gave them funny names, and he was a vegetarian or something. And the Blue Men were tourists in the show, the Moroccan tourists, the tourists from Morocco. And it didn't ever make it, because they were never real, and now, when he was just Red Man, suddenly he was very real, and that was just *it*. To call him that what he was.

Juris: So you called them by their color?

Peter: Yeah. These particular two. Others not. The other one looked like a Priest, so I called him Priest.

Steve: In other words you never have a story where you feel . . . I have to have another puppet . . . and you build one because there's something . . . in other words . . . you have the puppet and . . .

Peter: That's very seldom. I would rather look around in the garbage of the theatre and find something and say, that's the thing, and call it rather than making it up for the story.

Juris: Well . . .

Peter: The Story, I know we talked about that. I find that the hardest thing to talk about, but to a certain degree the story is the inside of any piece of art. It is the telling, the giving away of the inside to somebody else, to the outside to other people. It's done through story, through telling story, and story is just there, in the world, in the world that relates to all people's relationships. You know that's just what we all have and what we all remember. It's our relationship to our relative, our friend, or the things that happen between people. The love stories, the murders, the death of the grandmother, or whatever, these real things. That doesn't need any plotting, you know? That doesn't need, in America they call it plot I guess? And plot is something entirely different. Plot is something artificial, something that you make up that you can play with, like a mathematical formula, you start it somewhere and then you just construct. That's plotting, right?

Juris: Yes.

Peter: And that's very arbitrary, the moves of that, the way that works. And story is not like that. Story is not arbitrary. It seems to be, it's a strange mixture of tremendous exactness and necessity, and tremendous freedom. I don't know whether you notice that in fairy tales, but fairy tales usually have the realness of story. That is, they both feel completely logical and necessary from move to move in that story. And all of a sudden

there's a jump and you don't know where it comes from, you know it's just right, you know?

Svendsen asked about the control the director, Schumann, had over the development of the puppets and the manipulation of the performers of these puppets; but more importantly, he brought the conversation round to the cruelty in the stories.

Peter: Let me say this about what you keep asking me, about death and cruelty. In these plays that you have seen, and in the one that I described, it is probably true because people say that very often. And with children's shows that we did years ago in New York, people held back their children from coming because there was so much of this in the shows. But I ask people who make those complaints to go back to the old stories and to read and find out how cruel the world reflected in stories is. I would say that I can't help it. I'm trying to get the guts of it and get it for real as much as possible. And I can't control whether it's pretty or not pretty. Or whether it is harmonious or gruesome; it is out of my control completely. I can't do that; I can't be outside of my story and look at it as if I was not part of it. Or look at it and say it's all gruesome; that's not possible. You can only do this *in* the story, the works; but not by stepping outside and suddenly recognizing it's cruel. That doesn't work.

Juris: I think you understand that I'm not making this . . .

Peter: No, but it's a genuine question. I do not say it is not.

Juris: It is a question . . . not because this is cruelty, you know that . . . my question is how far do you yourself . . . ask yourself about it. Whether you can, for instance, create a beautiful puppet, and your puppets are beautiful, but people love their ugliness, too, people love their cruelty . . . What would be a beautiful puppet and could it tell a story?

Peter: We have a story that was originally called *Lief in the Moonlight* and now it's called the *Deadman Rises*.

And it's about a woman who goes to a river. The river is a puppet, a person, and she wades in the river, that is, she's being tied to the river and she finds a dead man in the river and she takes the dead man home, and she goes to bed with the dead man and in the morning she opens his eyes. His eyes are taped and she takes the tape away and the dead man rises. Then, they both get up and dance. It's a story done with rod puppets where they players . . . they're on a full open stage where they're inside the puppets and they're walking the puppets. The same system the Great Warrior's built on, but simpler. There's just one rod that they have to handle, the rod that's in the head, just because of that it's more flexible than this thing with the arms.

Juris: And where does that story go?

Peter: It doesn't go anywhere else. It just tells the same story that the big religions tell about their great godly leaders, in terms of a little human but impossible adventure. You see? It's like everybody's craziest dream . . . impossible story. Do you know that there's a film by, I don't know it by title, but a film by Dreyer . . . I've seen it . . . what is it called? It's not called the *Deadman Rises* but it is about a man that brings another man, no another woman, back to life, a crazy man in the village . . . It's all in the setting of a Danish village, about a rich farmer and one of the sons is crazy . . .

Juris: Oh Ordet.

Peter: Is that Ordet?

Juris: I think so.

Peter: And then this son, this Jesus-like son, and he comes in and he brings his sister whom he brings back to life, or his sister-in-law, his brother's wife.

Juris: You don't then want to tell any other stories than those that exist?

Peter: But the one that I just told isn't that one that doesn't exit?

Juris: No that is . . . the story exists in every impulse to bring . . .

Peter: That's right . . .

Juris: To bring someback back to love and back into being

. . . then you're not a moralist. . . .

Peter: No.

Juris: 'Cause everyone else that tells stories is a moralist, 'cause he structures for others, how one has to . . .

Peter: Yes, that's the difficulty. I find it very hard to make a moralistic story, a story which gives truthful advice or that could directly help people to understand something, or to structure a story from that idea of saying something in order to achieve something.

Juris: Yah, that's usually why stories are told, and that's why people who are compelled to tell them tell them, and usually don't understand why they do it. Maybe it's better that you continue to do it the way you have been.

Peter: Yah, I don't know, I think it's a goal to be able to tell it . . . you probably have to sacrifice a lot of your own personal judgment to be able to boil something down to a moral. I don't know what makes it possible for other people to be as simple as moralistic. I didn't have a very good time when I tried it out, when I tried to do that.

Juris: I would think it's usually the lack of love.

Peter: I don't know. Let's look at Brecht's stories . . . *The Three Flyers*, there, the flyers that come down, what is it but one set of being, the death flyers.

Juris: Lindberg flew . . . and he celebrates all those who make the airplane so that somebody can fly it, and he who flies it says that there is more there than me flying in this thing. More than myself, and he asks you to think of those who are not flying and have the experience of it and the glory of it, who work to make the thing possible, not just for others, but basically for themselves. The man who makes the puppet also hopes that somebody else can play it, and not so the puppet can play but that it can be played.

Peter: But Brecht is a moralist now . . .

Juris: Yes . . . and you are not . . . yet.

Peter: But he has the advantage of not really being a moralist but he has enough craziness that it is allowed for him to be a moralist I feel. He's fresh enough. He's sort of the first one in the new role of moralists, and his approach is young and fresh and completely free, the way he deals with a story; and that makes possible for him to be a moralist. For anybody else it could be terribly difficult to be that fresh about stories.

Juris: But what makes it possible for him to be the moralist in your estimation?

Peter: He is a tremendous languageman and poet and he has so much love in himself and so much real care for the people that he knows and he deals with that he wants to tell them something very real and moral, but he's not stuck on that. He doesn't start off and say, "Oh, dear, what do I want to tell the people." He's a real poet and a real warm creator of stories. But he's strong enough to boil it down to a fable.

Peter: Yes.

Juris: And the moralistic aspect is strong because a particular fable can go two ways and he has strength and love enough to try to put it down into a fable and let others work with it . . . He's working to make it into a fable and to do something that is "reproduceable" like your puppets are.

Usually the plays of the radical right are untellable; they are sequences of a montage of events strung to together by formalistic concerns and attempts to bite the tale of immediacy; whereas the best of Valdez and Schumann and the more important and lasting work of the Mime Troupe can be said to revolve around the tellability of performance. It is possible at certain times to recount the performance, retell the story, reproduce it in conversation and life outside the theatre. When this occurs, one grabs at historical roots without ritualization (a religious notion) and in the contemporarizing of the tale, the play is brought right into the mainstream of social conditions.

In his notes for the London tour of the Berliner Ensemble's production of *Caucasian Chalk Circle*, Brecht tells of writing the play in 1944 while in America, horrified by the commercialism of Broadway. He recommends the early Chaplin who was not yet directed to the advance of action in film (action vs. story) and goes on to say:

The pleasure of storytelling is suffocated by the fear of what is not effective. To unbridle the pleasure of storytelling does not mean to let the story run wild. Details will be of great importance; but this means that economy will be important too. Imagination can also be used in the interests of brevity. It is a question of sticking to a subject matter that is rewarding. The worst enemy of genuine play is playfulness. Circumstances are the trademark of a poor narrator. An easy-going, playful manner indicates an inflated ego and disdain for the audience.

The context of theatrical life in America is speed flash, improvisational esoteric arts and commodity theatre. Peter Schumann has used "story" rather than copping to inflated or slick actions as a living force. His stand is pure in that framework. When we examine his stories, however, we find a pacifism on the side of the angels, and angels in America tend to appear on wedding cakes.

Brecht, for example, used story in an epic form within a historical materialist analysis, thereby making a pre-capitalist form modern. Schumann's

bread is like Brecht's soup, yet our American puppeteer fails, so far, to enrich his political context and thus falls prey to radical political accessories.

Luis Valdez: El Teatro Campesino

Luis Valdez and El Teatro Campesino are also organically popular. Although Valdez did a stint in college, his trip to Cuba, his work with the farmworkers, and his religious Chicanismo have kept him away from the mainstream of bourgeois tragedies, traumas and despair of the middle, guilt-ridden class. He was ostracized to his good fortune early, and even though he tried to enter the mainstream through playwriting or college, his brown soul, dirty mind, and intense collective consciousness drove him to Delano. In 1966, he left Chavez, went to Del Rey, and then to Fresno, California, and most recently to a little tourist town kept in the old style, San Juan Bautista.

The greatness of El Teatro Campesino is not only in its work, but in the model it has set for the Chicano community. Each year there is a Chicano festival either organized or supported by Teatro Campesino, in which as many teatros as can fit in a week are gathered to perform and workshop together. Unlike the whites, the brown theatres have not been averse to imitation in their first attempts at performance. Numerous versions of Los Vendidos and other *actos* from Teatro Campesino repertoire showed up at the early festivals of '67, '68, '69. As the groups sifted through their own needs and more sophisticated perceptions developed, criticism of El Teatro Campesino came to the festival also.

Luis Valdez is not only a playwright and director, but a respected cultural leader. He has not refused the mantel; his is ultimately a more responsible position than radical whites who become martyr exemplars and meet with competitive ridicule, rather than critical examination.

Thirty-five groups now exist, some terrible, some good, because of the labor of Danny and Luis Valdez, Augustin Lira, Felipe Contu and Donna Haber—original members of Teatro Campesino. In any Chicano community across the country there is one or perhaps two teatros who perform some of the work of the Valdez group and then make up their own material. These local groups present shows that are naive, energetic, sometimes tedious, but always a lesson for the performers in Chicanismo, identity, and history.

Valdez, like Schumann, puts shows together. They pick out props from their workshops, costume rooms, and houses; utilize everything that is at hand; make some stuff; and generally direct all the shows. Schumann directs (as we found out) without a script and from all indications does not work on actors' technique or for that matter on puppeteering technique. In the early days of the Campesino there was little if any technique to be taught, the performers (not actors) were members of the union, organizers and activists who worked together—improvising without Viola Spolin, performing without Stanislavsky and socially engaged without Brecht. It is significant that the beginnings of both Bread and Puppet, El Teatro and to some extent the Mime Troupe relied upon persons with talent outside of the traditional paths of actors and performers—people that I used to call "people" as different from trained actors.

Recently, however, Valdez has been developing a more disciplined base, training actors, directors, and writers. His brother Daniel tours the country, singing his own tunes and tunes created by Augustin Lira, who runs another teatro in Los Angeles.

Valdez's present situation is one of settling and expanding, yet with his popularity and lack of dialectical analysis (he has plenty of historical material around) and his rejection of the material life of the Chicano (something Cesar Chavez has never ignored), he is prone to utilize liberal ideology, psychological theatrical techniques and listen to academic aesthetes who abound around anyone who has brown skin.

At the start, El Teatro Campesino performed with and for the farmworkers. As Valdez retreated from political associations, first in Delano and then in Fresno, his anti-establishment theatrics have turned into pseudo-religious, spiritual, total solutions. He now purveys the unity of Jesus Christ and Quetzalcoatl: "La vision de Quetzalcoatl era como la vision de Jesucristo."

As El Teatro Campesino expands its association into Latin America, as it is now doing, the influence of the Marxist theatrical groups in Mexico (Mascarones) and Colombia (Enrique Buenaventura's Teatro Experimental de Cali) will pressure Luis Valdez's present National Cultural spirituality to incorporate some concrete materiality.

El Teatro Campesino's swing from social reality to cultural identity is much like the Mime Troupe's alternating between agitprop and political theatre. Whereas the Campesino's present religious turn will be battered by the Marxists from Latin and South America, the Mime Troupe's position in the movement (subject to calls for a guerrilla skit for every radical action) is likely to increase anxiety within the group and thereby produce crude communist products.

The structure of both groups, like other U.S. alternative groupings, is a loosely ordered collective (although El Teatro is patrilineal), or extended family; unable to contain two directions at the same time, they will continue to warble, wobble and waddle.

The model for restructuring and thereby containing broader contradictions rather than instant daily terror of capitalist life-style (or anti-capitalist life-style) is perhaps to study socialist structures from socialist countries and to use this knowledge to re-examine what looked progressive, yet turned regressive, and what appeared as conservative, as truly radical.

APPENDIX

12

GUERRILLA THEATRE: 1965

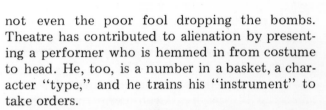

Art is almost always harmless and beneficent; it does not seek to be anything else but an illusion. Save in the case of a few people who are, one might say, obsessed by art, it never dares to make any attacks on the realm of reality.*

Freud defines theatre in America, and Che Guevara tells us what to do about it:

The guerrilla fighter needs full help from the people of the area ... From the very beginning of the struggle he has the intention of destroying an unjust order and therefore an intention, more or less hidden, to replace the old with something new.†

This society, our society—America, U.S.A.—is chock full o'ennui. Distracted by superficial values, and without a sense of humanness, we let machines rule; it is easier to kill from a B-52 than to choke every Vietcong. No one feels any guilt,

not even the poor fool dropping the bombs. Theatre has contributed to alienation by presenting a performer who is hemmed in from costume to head. He, too, is a number in a basket, a character "type," and he trains his "instrument" to take orders.

All businessmen talk of *service*, and know deep in their hearts that unearned profit is the motive. While Lyndon Johnson talks of stepped-up peace efforts, the bombing raids increase. While art and culture are dabbled with, television greys the mind.

Movie and television stars, technical effects, equipment, and the desire for simple packaging are all obstacles to a concept of performer-as-creator in theatre-as-art.

The motives, aspirations, and practice of U.S. theatre must be readapted in order to:
- teach
- direct toward change
- be an example of change

To teach, one must know something.

It is necessary to direct toward change because "the system" is debilitating, repressive, and non-aesthetic.

The guerrilla company must exemplify change

Guerrilla Theatre: 1965 was originally published in *Tulane Drama Review,* Vol. 10, No. 4, 1966. This and the following three essays were published as *Guerrilla Theatre Essays 1* by the San Francisco Mime Troupe in 1970.

* Sigmund Freud, *New Introductory Lectures on Psychoanalysis* (New York: W. W. Norton Co., Inc., 1933), p. 207.

† Che Guevara, *Guerrilla Warfare* (New York: Monthly Review Press, 1961), p. 43.

as a group. The group formation—its cooperative relationships and corporate identity—must have a morality at its core. The corporate entity ordinarily has no morality. This must be the difference in a sea of savagery. There is to be no distinction between public behavior and private behavior. Do in public what you do in private, or stop doing it in private.

For those who like their theatre pure of social issues, I must say—FUCK YOU! buddy, theatre IS a social entity. It can dull the minds of the citizens, it can wipe out guilt, it can teach all to accept the Great Society and the Amaaaaarican way of life (just like the movies, Ma) or it can look to changing that society . . . and that's *political*.

Previous attempts at socially directed theatre since the thirties have been ineffective—with the exception of the Living Theatre, the Actors Workshop (in the fifties, and not since Ford), Off-Broadway in the fifties, Joan Littlewood's theatre, Roger Planchon, and the Berliner Ensemble. What makes this type of theatre difficult? Content, style, and external effects or repercussions.

If the content is too immediate, the art is newsworthy and, like today's newspaper, will line tomorrow's garbage pail. If the content is devious, symbolic, or academically suggestive, the public will refuse to see it, because their minds have been flattened by television and dull jobs.

"To be stupid is a luxury only the commercial can afford."

Social theatre is a risky business, both aesthetically and politically: assuming that the difficulties of style and content have been solved, the stage success can be closed because of "fire violations," obscenity, or even parking on the grass. What do

you do then? You roll with the punches, play all fields, learn the law, join the ACLU, become equipped to pack up and move quickly when you're outnumbered. Never engage the enemy head on. Choose your fighting ground; don't be forced into battle over the wrong issues. Guerrilla theatre travels light and makes friends of the populace.

A radical theatre group must offer more than the commercial theatre; it must be equipped with people and imagination to compensate for the lack of heavy advertising and equipment. Entrenched power is intelligent and artful in its control. Thus operative paranoia is our appropriate state of being. Keep the caliber of performances high—any lack of skill will lose audiences who are ready and willing to attend, but not for charitable reasons. There are too many charities now.

The problem is to attract an audience to a type of theatre it is accustomed to attending and discover forms that will carry the weight of "effective" protest or social confrontation, without turning theatre over to twisted naturalistic symbolism, pop art, camp, or happenings for the chic.

There is a vision in this theatre, and it is not that of the lonely painter or novelist who struggles through his denial years, suffering, and finally breaking into the "big time." The "big time" usually means *Life* magazine commercial success. But in this case it is to continue—I repeat —to continue presenting moral plays and to confront hypocrisy in the society.

Let me make this very clear. It is acceptable to criticize, to debate, to take issue with problems in society, as long as you are not effective—and as long as you gloss over the issues in such a manner as to leave the door open to that soft-pedal

phrase: "There are two sides to every murder." It has been our experience in local dealings with the police and commissioners of parks that when our social comment is clear and direct and not confused by "art" or obfuscated by "aesthetic distance," we have had trouble—arrest, harassment and loss of income.

Ideally, the universities should be examples of socially committed theatre. Yet academic theatre, far from leading, has followed the pattern set by regional theatre companies but is even less experimental and risky. Resident theatres made their stands on repertory, good literature, and the Ford Foundation (not necessarily in that order) and little more is to be expected from this area. The possibility and responsibility rest with the free-swinging independent organizations which are least equipped economically to deal with the complex problems of experimentation. Commercial audiences never taught to think won't buy it—and who in showbiz would want to sell it? It is our obligation to gather audiences and *excite* them into being provoked and confronted, and into returning!

Note: We are talking about the U.S.A. and its theatrical milieu. I do not presume to make universal aesthetic judgments. Theatre and the sense of dialogue are different in this country. Our aesthetic is tempered by what can be done now, and what the actual climate is.

Should we use epic Brecht? Or experiential Artaud?

Epic theatre, culled from expressionistic pre-Hitler Germany, is a historical entity appropriate for its time. To perform historical Epic theatre in a U.S.A. glutted with double-speak, cinemascope, and newspapers, is to rely upon Brecht for help. Yet Artaud here becomes an excuse for intense psychological drama and falls into the American jungle of instant improvisation, instant creation, and instant coffee: all a bit watery.

Should we throw Artaud out to save Brecht? Anything that aids in cutting through the delusions of the American way of life or the morass of missionary ideals that lead inexorably to murder is useful. Use both! But remember that they are European sources, and it is America we are confronting: perhaps baseball is the best inspiration.

Handbook

Find a low-rent space to be used for rehearsals and performances: loft, garage, abandoned church, or barn. If the director sleeps in, it's cheaper.

Start with people, not actors. Find performers who have something unique and exciting about them when they are on stage. For material use anything to fit the performers. Allow the performers to squeeze the material to their own shape. Liberate the larger personalities and spirits.

Commedia dell'arte has been useful for this approach. It is an open and colorful form, uses masks, music, gags, and is easily set up with backdrop and platform. Presented inside, bright lights will do; outside, there are no lighting problems.

For outdoor performances select an intimate grassy area in a park or place where many people congregate, and play Saturday or Sunday afternoons. Go where the people are—street corners, vacant lots, or parks. Set up a portable stage, twelve by fifteen feet, made into eight sections with a backdrop hung on a pole strung along a goal post support. All equipment must be portable and carried in a *borrowed* three-quarter-ton truck. Set the stage so that the sun is in the face of the actors, not the audience. Begin the show by playing music, do exercise warm-ups, play and sing, parading around the area, attract an audience. Use bugles, drums, recorders, and tambourines working with simple folk tunes—rounds well done will do, even Frère Jacques will do. For *commedia* style, the masked characters have to move well to illustrate what they are saying and all must speak out so the audience can hear fifty feet away, over the street noises.

Make sure the ground is comfortable and dry for the audience. Keep the length of the show under an hour, moving swiftly, and adapting easily to accidents, dogs, bells, children. Improvise on mistakes, coincidental noises like police sirens during a chase scene. Use a funny script, adapted for your own purposes (Molière is excellent); cut out excess dialogue, update the language and clearly delineate the action.

A minstrel show is another possible form; it is obviously a good vehicle for civil rights problems. Use old minstrel books, rewriting and updating gags to the conditions of the present. Blackface is a mask too; the stereotyped minstrel will make the mask work. Try to have the actors play the music necessary for a show.

Amateurs can be used if you cast wisely. Rehearse in short, intense periods, keep improving and learning even after the show opens. The show should close better than it began.

Other forms are available: morality plays, burlesque, rock and roll (there *must* be something in rock and roll for the theatre). Use techniques from modern dance, vaudeville, the circus—all these theatrical events focus on the performer.

Ask a painter to do a backdrop or a sculptor to make a prop. For costumes shop the second-hand stores—the Salvation Army helps the poor. If you need program notes or new material, find writers, politicos, poets to adapt material for your group.

When everything is ready to go, play the show for friends, learn from the performances, then take it to the people in the parks, halls, any place. Give it away—anything to build an audience without spending money on advertising.

The group must attract many different types of people. All can help and all can enjoy the co-operative nature of theatre.

Pay the performers from donations received after the show, keep the books open, pay for all materials and anything else that is spent on production. Do not overpay, don't try to match prevailing wages (except in poverty areas). People will work for very little if the work is principled, exciting and fun.

The first steps are necessarily hectic and loosely ordered. Few long-range plans can be made. After an audience and a group have been established (in the second stage) one can begin to think of presenting conventional plays. I suggest you select short, small-cast, one-set plays. Beg, steal, borrow equipment, make your own, and rent only when necessary. Try not to purchase anything other than basic materials that can be

used for two or three shows—when in doubt, invent!

One procedure which the Mime Troupe recently came upon is to join with special groups that need money and do benefits for them: Vietnam committees, SNCC, CORE, children's nurseries. These groups bring the audience and you present the show in their place or a rented theatre and split the take.

The problem of a regularly paid staff is that a constant production schedule has to be maintained to cover costs. But there are solutions: movie series, one-act plays, poetry readings, underground films for the second act. Organization becomes tremendously important in order to save money and energy.

Survival, and with it success, increases the dangers and the responsibility of the directors and the producer. Some traps can be avoided if the group changes its style once a year; during that change, the mind is cleansed and the soul expanded.

Protest at the box office is profitable if it's good. Good theatre can be made meaningful if new audiences are developed, but once you are in the swing of radical theatre, there is no stopping. You must go all the way or the enormity and power of the opposing forces will crush you. Never be caught in a politically aesthetic skirmish with grass in your pocket.

One can learn from the commercial world how to package, sell and expedite. The art world knows how to create. Use both!

It is a slow and arduous path to follow but the people will come to your aid, because your cause is just and your means exciting and full of life. There are hundreds of people looking for some-

thing to do, something that gives reason to their lives, and these are the guerrillas.

13

GUERRILLA THEATRE: 1967

If the eye be jaundiced, pluck it out.
If the society is rotten, rid thyself of it.
If the world be immoral, change it.

BIBLICAL — EXISTENTIAL — BRECHTIAN

The social assumptions which one accepts will determine the type of theatre one creates: street theatre, park theatre, workers' theatre, or warmed-over bathroom theatre. Theatrical discussions must include the socio-political attitudes of the performers in order to comprehend why some believe theatre a tool of change and others "love the theaaaaater."

It is of course entertaining to read quasi-revolutionary statements and scurrilous attacks on the theatre and society for a readership that is outside the mainstream of action; however, we shall continue in hopes that words on paper may communicate thoughts that will lead to action.

My own theatrical premise:

WESTERN SOCIETY IS ROTTEN IN GENERAL, CAPITALIST SOCIETY IN THE MAIN, AND U.S. SOCIETY IN THE PARTICULAR.

This essay originally appeared in *Avatar*, 1967 and in various other newspapers.

The basis of the disease is private property: it puts the value on all things in terms of money and possessions and splits man's personality into fragmented specialties, thus making him useless on the dance floor yet well equipped to run an IBM 1324. The idea of community so necessary to a healthy individual is hemmed in by the picket fences surrounding each patch of earth and the concept of total man has been sutured by idiotic efficient specialization. (This is a simplification of the condition; for further information read: Marx, Freud, Norman O. Brown, H. Marcuse, Regis Debray, C. Guevara, Sun Tzu, Mao Tsetung, Thorsten Veblen, Carl Oglesby, Gary Snyder, etc. etc.)

For the theatre that wishes to change the above and to present alternatives, the problem is in many parts:

PERSONNEL — PROGRAM — PLACE — PUBLIC

The *personnel* (actors, directors, tech, etc.) must come from the class they want to change. If you are middle-class dropouts, you then play for middle-class dropouts, workers for working class, Mexican-Americans for Mexican-Americans, etc. Social work theatre is out; play for your own kind—you understand them, and they identify with you.

The *program* depends upon the ingenuity of the group. It may be rock and roll music or street puppets, but whatever the style of theatre the content has to be a result of the experience of the personnel. To make this more clear: We asked ourselves in the Mime Troupe how we could STOP the war—we then did a satire on our own antiwar pacifism (*L'Amant Militaire* by Joan Holden and others).

The *place* you do it in indicates your style/ your feelings/your attitudes . . . Regis Debray: "The revolutionary in the mountains is different

from the talking revolutionary in the city."

Or McLuhan: "Media is part of the message . . . Location is the platform or the sponge for your program."

The *public* is made up of all those who think they see you in them and all those whom you know; friends, aficionados, tourists, and sometimes peers.

It's all very simple on paper, but the making and the proper use of materials depends upon your own analysis of the needs and possibilities in your own location. To present commedia dell'arte in the middle of Canada may only be a historical exploration. But whatever the presentation, it must engage the common issues, it must become essential to the very existence of the community (i.e., it feeds off and feeds into the community) and it must become a significant moral force.

Success in terms of money, commercial fame, fancy magazine spreads and foundation grants from state, federal or local sources is usually out unless you live in the advanced neo-socialist countries where criticism of prevailing conditions is in order. Viz., Jean-Louis Barrault with *The Screens* (National Assembly almost stopped it) or Kenneth Tynan and Laurence Olivier with *Soldier* by R. Hochuth (censored by the Public Censor). In those less than advanced government-subsidized countries, the theatre as moral force will, as does the single artist, have to live by its wits. To live by your wits is not to imitate the hustler who is a low-class capitalist, but rather the Latin American guerrilla who is a low-class socialist.

The object is to work at a presentation that talks to a community of people and that expresses what you (as a community) all know but what no one is saying: thoughts, images, observations and discoveries that are not printed in newspapers or made into movies: truth that may be

shocking and honesty that is vulgar to the aesthete.

• Prepare to go out of business at any moment

• Prepare to give up your house, your theatre or your troupe, and even your ideas if something more essential comes along

• Travel light and keep in shape

• IDEAS LIKE PROPERTY CANNOT BE PRIVATE

• Nothing is sacred—only sometimes tenderness.

That is the prescription for a theatre company that is meaningful. Like a life that is valuable, you must begin by dropping out, getting away, leaving behind, dumping, junking the waste of dishonorable middle-class institutions, groups, ideas, and debris of years of decay. (They are cynical, bored and depressed anyway.)

The first step may be dramatic; to walk away or drop out from middle-class American (middle-class America is all over the world). Yet the act of creating a life-style that replaces most, if not all, middle-class capitalistic assumptions with a life-style that won't quit, is a full-time job of a full-time guerrilla.

Which of course is the only way to live.

14

CULTURAL
REVOLUTION USA/1968

"One Step Forward"

> Debray in Jail: *"Everyone who aspires to be an intellectual should be a revolutionary, for every real intellectual attempts to recreate the world, in intellectual terms."*

The term guerrilla theatre was first used in 1965 to label the kind of theatre we were engaged in. Since that time, the use of the term has become a catch-all for non-professional theatre groups and becomes presumptuous in the face of historical evidence.

Can the term guerrilla theatre, which describes activity on the cultural front in the USA, actually come close to the activity of an armed revolutionary foco?

In addition to the confusion of "guerrilla theatre" we have the word "revolution" being used in any and every possible way; from the selling of cars to the making of movies. It is time to specify what cultural revolution might be, compare it to armed revolutionary action, and be as dialectical about the realities in this US of A so

This essay originally appeared in *Counterculture*, J. Berke, editor, Peter Owen, Ltd., London.

that if we *do* devise a cultural revolutionary attack then we can have the honor of claiming that we are in the vanguard with the heroes of revolutions around the world.

The romantic nature of guerrilla struggle attracts our minds and we conceive of a guerrilla as one who acts and leads an exciting life—movie-style drama all day! Yet, before Hollywood does in Che by portraying him as some plastic-commodity hero-type, we do know that guerrilla warfare is hard, boring, painstaking, and sometimes fatal.

What is most clear is that, as guerrilla and revolutionary, one commits one's life to the work. There were guerrillas who went home after a few months, or guerrillas who finked and became traitors, but a guerrilla who becomes a revolutionary and stays with it does it for life over death. He often risks his life; he may be called to give it. We who call ourselves cultural revolutionaries are not often killed. The dedication and commitment to the revolution is the first duty of the revolutionary—an obvious fact, but not so easy to translate into cultural revolutionary terms.

We sit in an affluent, industrialized, commodity-conscious society, where liberalism rides the waves and muddies our minds, where radicals who call for dramatic tactics are often lionized in the press and alienated from their constituents, and more lefties are media-conscious than they are community-concious. Militant waving of guns is often a mimicking (not miming) of guerrilla tactics in other countries. Revolutionary activity does not demand that one has a weapon in one's hands to validate one's position—the position is validated by its insight, feasibility and accomplishment; in some cases a gun helps. We have only begun cracking this empire-building ma-

chine, but we must now think of taking power.

In 1967 we traveled across the country and stopped some twenty times to play *L'Amant Militaire* and say:

> This is our society; if we don't like it it's our duty to change it; if we can't change it, we must destroy it.

Some people were frightened by this statement; others understood. To clarify: to destroy something you have to use the correct weapon and replacement is the best destruction. If we simply repress or reject an ideology or a pattern of behavior and do not replace it with something else, we may end up at the same point we began. Opposition to an idea may not be the exact opposite, alternatives do not mean a complete reversal.

Example: the hippie syndrome came out of a rejection of the square and a liberation of spirit in this all-too-suffocating atmosphere. It has now closed itself off from the squares with a circle of simple-minded blast music, Zen-mystical-astrological, bare-assed simplistic fashion show. Whatever socio-political sense the hip scene had was destroyed by its lack of standards, which eventually were supplied by the standards of the rock promoters, the big record companies and the media salesmen. The standards for the hip scene have been determined by the commercial interests that have always run the fashion shows in this country. The hip scene now has its own counter for records, pants, and even long hairpieces (and those jackass sideburns) at the big department stores.

Revolutionaries do not want a piece of the action, not into the scene, not to "make it," but to take it over! And change it!

Power: The cultural revolutionary, just as the armed guerrilla, must want and be capable of taking power.

The radical "analysis" that exposes the system must also lead to indications where the system can be forced to crack, where the loopholes are, where a word, or some activity that can be repeated by anyone will disrupt the monster.

Power is action that can permanently establish a fundamental change in the society one lives in.

Fidel aimed at: (1) conquest of power; (2) the elimination of the army.

Sartre on Cuba: "Gandhi wanted to destroy the caste system."

Nehru said somewhere that this convinced partisan of nonviolence had an intuition that was really revolutionary. He looked for the cornerstone which supported the whole structure; he found it. It was the caste of the pariahs. Castro acted in the same way. The army was the cornerstone he had to break. The army remained public enemy number one.

Just as these revolutionaries recognized the enemy, it behooves us to recognize the enemy in our society. The key to the arch of imperialism, for the cultural guerrilla, is the bourgeois value structure. The middle-class mind with its bourgeois desires and goals of profit, efficiency, specialization, and materialism must be subverted, destroyed, and replaced. If we can destroy this middle-class mentality the monster may withdraw from aggressive suppression. Cultural bombardment must cut into expanding profits and messianic materialism.

If we here have anything to contribute to socialist thought, it is that we can create weapons of culture in the center of the big freezer. But as armed revolutionaries are committed to concrete objectives and tangible realities, we here must think in concrete terms and make our ideas tools/hammers. Not cacophony, but mind-fuck, not only mind-fuck, but alternatives.

We as cultural guerrillas aim at: (1) conquest of power; (2) the elimination of the bourgeois mentality.

Bourgeois Alienation

The varieties of the plague called alienation induce suspicion, despair, isolation, faggotry, and onanism. We distrust people because we have been taught not to trust. When we are cheated, and it begins early, we don't trust THEM—in fact, they tell us not to trust them. We then become like them and don't trust ourselves. (I am not talking about the distrust and suspicion that any guerrilla must maintain for survival, but the disbelief that denies any change in "human nature.") The first obstacle a cultural revolutionary must overcome is his own alienation. Bourgeois radicals are riddled internally with doubts about themselves; doubt from their bourgeois education.

Given: we are all afraid of failure, but tragically good people are afraid of success.

It is necessary to make over the radical who exposes the system into a revolutionary who leads people to change; the revolutionary can be essentially in doubt about the universe, but he trusts himself and believes in *them*.

Alienation crystallizes itself through isolation and Western culture's thalidomization called individualism. Individualism precludes the formulation of revolutionary action which is essentially communal. Because U.S. culture controls so many people, and the masses are so faceless, we have become obsessed with the phony creation of individuals. Those who have made it! Horatio Square. The artist is fucked up by individualism when he begins to sense his "uniqueness." Thus he becomes an object for observation or sale, not for essential use. The artist increases his alienation from the society around him by inventing unique qualities and elite peculiarities. His price goes up.

(We are not talking about *Genius*—which is sweat—we are describing the marketed-individualist.)

U.S. commercially minded culture will pull the Che Guevara out of any historical or group context and make him a hero/saint or a psychotic/die-hard and effectively divest him of his community and social identity.

The "unique" person, this alienated artist, produces work for people he despises or doesn't care to know: elite art for the wealthy. If he wishes to communicate something, the suffering lone artist may develop esoteric tools which can be deciphered only by other esoteric, hip, avant-garde artists. The alienated artist who can only be "appreciated" by a few sells himself through the classics—technique and/or fashion. Eventually he may forget actual content and emphasize style. If he is really avant-garde he can destroy himself.

Example:

Glenn Gould walks onto the stage and bows to the audience.

Threshing machine comes rumbling on.

Glenn Gould puts his hands into threshing machine.

Machine chops them off.

Glenn Gould bows and exits.

Voila! Total Avant-Gardism!

Why play for deaf and empty people? It is just this state of artistic perversion that presides in a milieu where the audience is commodity-conscious.

In the popular field, the imaginative musician becomes a package sold by an A/R man to people who the artist may not even care about. The dim-wits of popular music are legion. We, of course, are impressed with large sums of money and national record sales. Our ears tune in on the kid who is the newest twenty-year-old "genius." The pop version of alienation is to stay stoned so long it matters not what people say, or to fuck up your music because the crowds come to gawk, not listen. Then, too, the artist can make shows for gawkers and the rat race is on with long hair and seven-thousand-dollar amplifiers.

The cold air of death is upon those solo artists, stars, or groups picked up by the commercial press and commercial interests. The demand for freaks and creeps in a dishonest, boring system is great. A freak believes he can't live normally and begins to cultivate all the media ideas of freedom. He further unhooks himself from people, the people, any people.

This profit-driven culture even needs good minds and some good voices to keep it deluded about the reasons for the GNP.

Castro in the hills fought for the campesinos, paid for everything he ate, and bought what he needed.

The Vietcong down the planes, hold a public trial, execute the chief, and then clean up the village.

Alienation from without is first eliminated by acting, working, and helping those you believe in and want to help. It is a mutual association: we help them to help ourselves.

But you cannot ask yourself to do anything you wouldn't ask of others (martyrdom or reverse elitism). The artists must act morally and ethically and ask it of us all. If I act upon myself as I would upon others, then the "people" becomes an abstraction brought to earth. I want to sing—then let us all learn to sing. Mao talked of the revolutionary as a "fish in water." Surrounded by millions of blue ants, he talks of the "single man who crosses the raging waters" and leads the hundred thousand men. Incident: on the long march one bridge was made secure by one man who swam to the other side. Thousands followed. There was no "bravery" in crossing the raging waters: it was one's life one wished to sustain.

In revolutionary terminology the guerrilla foco is the vanguard not the avant-garde; it fights and aims to take power; it educates and fights for others; it fights through itself for others. Contemporary U.S. artists find themselves gathering nuts for themselves, the promoters direct one's interests to self-interest, we must expand the consciousness of self-interest to mean our total social interest. Alienation then drops dead. To stop alienation, to increase the "community" of the healthy:

1. No more working in Hollywood
2. No more working on Broadway
3. No more mass media fillers. *Harpers/Life/ Saturday Evening Post/Eye.* All of them. No more work.
4. No more work for CBS, NBC and friends
5. . . . . (fill in the blank with appropriate names)

Exploitation

By focusing on exploitation of the middle class, the cultural revolution aims at disrupting the very heart of the capitalist society. It is this exploitation that imperialism feeds on.

By raising the burden of the exploited, one gains support of the exploited The middle-class person may eat well and live in semi-material comfort but is made to work at boring jobs, his labor is used for someone else's profit, he is taxed and made to serve his country's imperialist goals. He is used. The middle-class American can be compared to the wretched peasant in any underdeveloped country if we consider the quality of life he maintains and its absurd objectives. (Note that both the rural peasant and middle-class American are conservative, stupid, and suspicious.)

The exploitative nature of corporate liberalism can be exposed, explained and made apparent by alternatives established through cultural means. The ground is fertile. The mind of the middle-class man is riddled with contradictions, hates and fears. He senses he is exploited but opts for more profit, hoping he will get rich quick. He accepts half of what life can offer by excusing himself as the little man. What other than a murderous ideology maintains a person who works forty hours a week, two weeks off a year, at a job that is not productive, that is repetitive or even stupefying. Material rewards are a barbaric return for the soul and energy of a human life.

The Vietnam war has exposed the exploitation and the concomitant irresponsibility. The Little Man and his son or the lower classes and their children, have been told to serve: The professors paid to produce weapons; the military trained to kill and "win"; the politicians given a mandate to expand influence and profit; although the longshoremen object, they load the ships; although some senators criticize the war, they vote for military budgets; although students talk of revolution, they cannot keep any organization alive more than six months.

The community has been divided into segments, each segment tries but cannot control its life. It is exploited, it becomes not responsible, it becomes irresponsible. Thus, no one is responsible. (The parallel to Nazi Germany is annoying.) Exploitation is a two-part problem. Some people *like* to play Uncle Tom.

Certain images are planted in people's heads to make them consume the trivia of American commerce: images of helplessness, incompetence, and inadequacy. The importance and respect given to specialization which "naturally" increases efficiency also produces the sense of incompetence. We are taught, preached, and coaxed into buying

products we don't need and can't fix. We work to buy them and pay to repair them. The American consumer is a basket case who works at some demeaning job to purchase trinkets he thinks he needs in order to stimulate the state of manhood. The alienation from one's work has been talked about by others (Marx and friends); alienation from the *product* is a part of our technological madness. Alienation from the product increases the helplessness in the minds of the purchaser. Power is related to the simple act of competence. If I can fix my car I then have some power, dominion over that machine. If I cannot, then I am at the mercy of AAA, every dishonest mechanic, or the automotive industry's planned breakdown and resale programs. Powerlessness created by the complexity of the machine or the incompetence drummed into our heads by our culture makes for cogs and clods, but it also becomes the main target in the cultural revolution. Images can be changed. We must get people to act, to say no to consumption, to do something to control their lives. The simplest, positive act may lead to larger gains. Example: a puppet show of ten minutes explaining the use of a beer can tab top in parking meters. The puppet explains the use, deplores the illegality, condemns the taxation, but leaves the audience with the image. This activity, albeit small as revolutionary actions go, does cost the city of San Francisco some eighty thousand dollars a year in lost revenue. Many people now use tab tops in parking meters. This could be made into a "revolutionary act" if everyone participated in it. Parking meters are a regressive form of taxation, they provide employment for petty nuisances (called policemen), they become time-consuming harassments if you forget your penny, *and* traffic flow isn't even improved. In participat-

ing, everyone and anyone can enjoy the "political" act of stopping oppression—now. The tab top can do many things: avoid a ticket, save a dime, or jam a meter. So all levels of personal gain are prevalent: it aids the individualistic petty thief or the irate customer who doesn't want to be charged for shopping, or the political revolutionary who wants to make public transportation usable and have it move toward the socialist dream. Admittedly it's a simplistic reaction to a large problem, but immediate positive results in the short range will help. We need things that can be accomplished.

The inability of the bourgeois man to control or change any iota of his life is debilitating and sustains the status quo. "The natural order of the human condition" as depicted by U.S. analysts based upon profit and the "American way of life" establishes an enormous monolithic obstacle to the little man or the debilitated man who sees no way to change anything—he becomes depressed, and eventually mean and regressive. If you can't do anything about the traffic problem on freeways you can become crazy and drive other people off the road.

We must supply people with things they can do

and then they will expand their minds and get closer to the state of consciousness needed to be at least pro-revolution. (We know acid alone doesn't guarantee a revolutionary consiousness, nor does fake religiosity—Leary, Krishna, the Love Merchants' hip dress stores.)

The country needed something to do and Kennedy the First gave us the Peace Corps—a sop, a ruse of imperialism. Yet the revolutionaries must answer the same question: what can I do.

To elaborate on an important point: awareness does not lead to change; activity and actions do. We find that in order to explain ourselves to actors in the Mime Troupe they have to experience the act of performing in front of outdoor audiences. Then they comprehend and may become good performers. They have to do it in order to know it. So too with social change. People have to do it to know it. Something has to be executed. Throw a brick and you begin to understand mass power and even violence. We all learn about our world. Colleges give at least half the story. We learn many facts, we can even learn about radical or revolutionary incidents, but action hardly ever results from the information. What to *do* is not sought for.

To improve conditions, those in power say it is a matter of "personal character" that has to be changed, not the institutions. Those without power wait for a miracle to disrupt the structure; the avant-garde live the post-revolution, and the liberals cynically criticize. All roads lead to the wall mother-fucker, even the mother-fuckers lead us to the wall. What *to do* has to be sought for.

It is better to play the piano poorly than not to play. It is better to fix your house yourself than to work to pay others to fix it. It is better to act concretely in some small way than to wait with

closets full of guns for the telephone to ring and the voice of the unknown leader to whisper: "The revolution will be starting at ten tomorrow . . . get ready."

Fronts I, II, III. Practice of:

Revolutionary art will create a possibility for action for the person picking up on the "message" (specific activity or suggestion) and he must be able to elaborate on it. Many little cultural revolutionaries are needed. Kids have to hum our commercials. People have to regain their own self-respect, become useful to their own immediate community beyond breadwinner restrictives, and we will have moved in on the bourgeois mentality. Remember we are not asking permission "to do our thing"—we want to take power.

The Areas of Operation: Fronts I, II, III. We cannot afford to forget that this cultural revolution exists on the rump of the monster. It must function on different fronts, some not so "pure," more like the Urban Rebel than the provincial guerrilla.

At this stage we certainly must be flexible enough to operate in many areas and open-minded enough to be able to take advantage of accidents and weakness of the "democratic" structures. We then operate as dilettantes to pander to some but not all commercial interests in order to maintain ourselves as examples of the alternative, while we train and educate our gang to be able to assume power eventually. Every step of the way is dangerous, one can "sell out" or be tricked, or become enamored of one's righteousness and lose sight of long-range achievements. Example:

The Mime Troupe does not want to advertise in the commercial press, but we often don't get enough coverage or buy enough space in the underground

press to inform people about our performances and existence. Do we talk to the *Time* man? We try not to, but once you are in *Time* the radical press begins to take notice.

Dilettante or social work front. You go to their house, you play for them, they watch you. As "enemy" they ain't too friendly. You are a social worker helping them get over their fears or hates. One tries to teach but little can get through. They love to see freaks and "obscene" material, they don't understand your "message," it is encased in their own plastic world.

But we go to them with our products to make money to live "independently." We go to subvert if that is possible, we go to expose them. But a good left-wing critic is entertaining as long as he is isolated from action. Exposing the contradictions in their world is important but one should not confuse dialectical exposure with revolutionary action. The simple-minded radical will be convinced by the culture purveyors that one can make a lot of money dishonestly and still create good work.

A sensible human being can only work on the dilettante social-work front so long before he becomes an alcoholic or a madman. You dislike your public so much you eventually either turn inward, becoming hip, esoteric and snide or else you become a cultural terrorist (provo, digger, mother-fucker: NET take-over, Garbage to the Lincoln Center, telling David Suskind he's a pig on David Suskind's show). Terrorism does not make change (Debray, Che) it precedes it; it can loosen the mind and activate people but it cannot create fundamental change. Riots, minor sabotage, can expose the weakness of the system; even violence, as Franz Fanon states, is important to the colonized native. However, Algerian violence did not produce enough revolutionary socialist consciousness. Terrorism may not only backfire but it may use up energy needed to create revolutionaries. The present stage of media sabotage or take-over and confrontation is only social work.

When you go to their house you can move the furniture but you can't move the walls.

II. Example or Life Style. Instead of always going to their house, we have to open our own store. They come, because we're freaky, and then they are on our territory, where we can create an alternative way of life which can be imitated.

Liberated territory means economically independent. Revolutionary rhetoric is being used to sell cars (the Dodge Rebellion); Dylan may have "revolutionized" the pop tune but has also made a fortune for Columbia (or is it Capital), just like Frank Sinatra. To make a fundamental change or be an example of a revolutionary life style, Dylan and some other long-hairs would have to take over the record business just as the French film big names finally came to terms with their own problem and took over the film industry (after the students took over their universities). Examples of liberated cultural territory: the *independent* radical, socialist, revolutionary and/or underground media; free in the parks; the movement coffee houses. We need more: non-profit socialist promotion agencies, galleries, artists, recording companies, film houses, theatres, computer centers. Those ready to change can do as we do, or join us.

III. Revolutionizing the Guerrilla. Father Bonepane who left Guatemala said: "When action is decided discipline is essential." "Revolutionary life style" is too often interpreted to mean "do your own thing"—which in group action is translated as inefficiency and means ineffectiveness. Rejection of parental values is a necessary first step but must not be permitted to condemn the left to perpetual missed opportunities, obscurity, and financial crisis. One exercises one's freedom in choosing to become a revolutionary, and in choosing a revolutionary course of action. To insist on it after that that is to demonstrate oneself still subject to the ultimate parental value, individualism.

Individualism is one of two enemies the cultural guerrilla, almost invariably of bourgeois origin or at least education, has to combat in himself. The other is elitism, an extension of the first: me with my talents and extraordinary awareness, or our group with its hot line, must be replaced as ultimate values by the job to be done. Once these enemies are destroyed the individual is really free to play any of the roles he is called upon by history and necessity to fulfill: to be an actor today, a director tomorrow and next week a writer; a writer today, a publisher tomorrow and next year a book salesman. Che came from the hills and headed the Bank of Cuba; Fidel waters tobacco plants now and talks agricultural technology.

If we can operate on all three fronts, we will not only liberate positive energy, but also destructive energy which will destroy them so that we may take power. We can destroy them ideologically, economically and physically by pushing this democratic monstrosity and libertarian hypocrisy to its limits.

Sun Tzu in 550 B.C. wrote in *The Art of War*, and Mao read him once, "To subdue the enemy without fighting is the acme of skill."

15

RETHINKING
GUERRILLA THEATRE: 1971

Guerrilla theatre was intended to be an alternative
to bourgeois theatre; instead it has become a parallel, slipping in and out of existence, used by the
egocentric, manhandled by the outraged children
of the rich, even expounded upon by the meat-
balls of fashionable theatre. Its original intention
was to describe a radical political perspective for a
type of theatre that would live outside the op-
pressive culture of capitalism. To continue that
direction, it will have to become far more dialectical and less didactic, understand its claims of Marx-
ism, and expel from its ranks the fatheads of
freakdom who incorrectly assume that images will
destroy international corporate empires. In the
hope of creating a more effective radical theatre,
the following essay analyzes some of the vagaries
of guerrilla theatre.

Muddle

Ideas are fluid, but too often they are squeezed
out of context to suit contradictory needs. My

This essay originally appeared in *Performance*, Vol. 1 No. 1,
December, 1971.

1965 guerrilla theatre essay (in the *Tulane Drama
Review*, T32) was a description of what the San
Francisco Mime Troupe had done. The essay was
neither a symbolic definition nor a manifesto: we
declared that we had been involved for five years
in a new mode of theatrical endeavor and we
sounded the alarm for others to take up the
struggle. The gestalt of our activity was guerrilla-
like. The content, form, acting techniques, life-
style, and aims of the Mime Troupe constituted
the guerrilla life of a theatre in an alien society.
Since the publication of that essay, guerrilla
theatre aberrations have been plentiful: Diggers
and Yippies who think politics is a theatrical
splash; liberal thespians who make guerrilla
theatre into a "symbolic action"; and instant
revolutionary-agitproppers who perform, but
ignore the representational nature and requisites
of theatre.

In 1966 and 1967, the Mime Troupe continued
developing its style in the parks and across the
country. In 1968, we ran out of energy and
stopped to examine our progress. Sensing the general misconception of guerrilla theatre, and concerned about the Mime Troupe's developing
pseudorevolutionary rhetoric, I wrote another es-

say, "Cultural Revolution USA . . . One Step—1968," which addressed the problem: "Can the term 'guerrilla theatre,' which describes activity on the cultural front in the USA, actually come close to the activity of an armed revolutionary foco [movement or party]?"

Agitprop

Agitprop is agitational propaganda. Agitprop theatre is made up of skits performed by people who, like their audience, are directly engaged in the content of the skit. For example: Teatro Campesino, when performing in Delano, California, in 1965-67, presented agitational propaganda for the members of the Farm Workers Association (NFWA). Their songs and *actos* (Luis Valdez's descriptive word for social skits with signs: Brecht/Cantinflas vignettes with immediately recognizable characters, placards on chests, who get into political confrontations with other characters) were designed to inform the workers of union negotiations, grievances, and programs. The performers were engaged in organizing work and their *actos* were extensions of that work.

Agitprop done on the street for nonrecognizable yet amorphously familiar audiences is not the same. The conditions have changed when players of the middle class play for unknown people vaguely described as Americans against the war. Still further removed from agitprop are those so-called guerrilla theatre groups who surprise people in the midst of their daily routines by creating a theatrical situation where performers and audience are mixed. Often the skit happens so rapidly that the audience doesn't know it has been hit until the piece is over. The people, mildly duped, are supposed to become conscious of their responsibility and guilt. Acting more like

bandits than guerrillas, and, like newspaper headlines, shouting images rather than telling news, these groups try to "sell" their product through moral suasion and personal confrontation—both ideals of the bourgeois culture (like attacking a balloon with another balloon).

When the Mime Troupe first went to the streets to do short skits, crankies (paper movies à la Peter Schumann), and puppet plays, we didn't try to insult or assault people; we decided to teach something useful. We began by teaching general city-folk how to stuff parking meters with tab-tops, using a simple puppet-and-actor skit to inform them of the free use of parking meters. Another skit in this vein, telephone credit cards, was also designed to teach people something useful. We spoke of telephone numbers of tab-tops, and the people went away smiling and likely to use the information gained. These were our most successful skits and always will be. But this is not revolutionary art.

And even at its best, agitational propaganda is not revolutionary art. It supports rather than examines, explains rather than analyzes. It can be only a temporary form for the group it performs to (farm workers' theatre to farm workers). Didactic rather than dialectical, agitprop often skips over fundamental problems to facilitate immediate gains. Its very particularity limits its usefulness and longevity. The organization's immediate pressures are as constricting as the urgency of immediate explanations. Cesar Chavez often asked the members of the Teatro to return to face-to-face organizing and picket-line work, thereby interrupting rehearsals and sometimes complicating tour dates. When the Teatro began to consider its role as important as the union's, a conflict of interest set in and the Teatro severed its ties with

the union in order to grow politically and theatrically.

The Teatro Campesino left Delano not because it emphatically disagreed with Chavez and the Farm Workers Movement. Luis Valdez, Augustín Lira, and others in the Teatro did not oppose improvements in the farm workers' existence; they all come from the same blood, they understand the oppression. They left because they could not develop their theatre; they could not speak out on Vietnam (the Kennedys supported Chavez and the war); they could not discuss or parody the Catholic Church (the Virgen de Guadalupe led the Peregrination to Sacramento). When the Teatro moved out of Delano, they moved from agitational propaganda to cultural propaganda. They now perform plays or *actos* related to the cultural problems of the larger, more amorphous community of the Chicanos of Atzlan.

Shortsighted political organizing, precisely the kind of political conceptualization that arises in this Protestant, anticultural, antisensual country, fails to recognize that political changes are directly related to the prevailing cultural hegemony. One of the few communists (since Marx) who understood this, the Italian Antonio Gramsci, wrote: "The populace . . . changes concepts with great difficulty, and never by accepting concepts in their 'pure' form, so to speak, but always in some eclectic combination."

Theatre of the Yippies

The Yippies have taken he life-style acting of the Diggers (ca. 1966) and the theatrics of the 1940s and used both for politics. They assume that media actions will make changes: "If it appears in the newspaper, it happened, Ronny,"

Jerry Rubin told me in jest and belief. They read the *New York Daily News*, watch commercial TV and attend Hollywood movies to understand the nature of Amerika. Their intention is to use the information they collect from these sources to create an Amerikan revolution. Their motives are left and unimpeachable—they do use themselves in the fight for change; but we must look at their tactics, not their motives. Do they accomplish what they plan?

McLuhan has defined television as a causal element rather than as a transfer machine. TV, under the umbrella of McLuhan's pop thoughts, made Nixon lose the presidency in 1960 and win it in 1968. Surely, TV must be more principled than that! McLuhan does not consider who owns television. He fails to concern himself with the corporate entities which control programming and the price of images, thus their content. The mass media are not owned by the people, as we should know from the FCC regulations and the content of any TV channel, radio station, or newspaper. Advertisers own it. They rent the space. If you can't rent space, you must do somersaults to obtain coverage. Somersaults create news and created news adds spice to the commercials. The object of privately manipulated mass media is not to distribute news but to create demand for consumer products.

Yippies run into camera range as often as possible because they believe (or believed) the media are a tool at their disposal. Agnew and Nixon believe the same thing, the difference being that Agnew and Nixon have accountable and legal power to follow up their attacks, while the Yippies can only hope the kids are getting the message (or the inside dope). Yippie actions are not guerrilla theatre, but mind-benders, one-liners, image-breakers. When only Abbie Hoffman's voice came over the TV talk show because his American flag shirt had been blacked out, the majority of viewers planned to watch the same "exciting" talk show the next night. Lenny Bruce, the trampoline of the Yippie mind, was not a revolutionary but a brilliant nightclub comic. Lenny Bruce's awesome contradiction was that he was a stand-up comic, a one-man individualistic speedfreak testimonial in a nightclub!! He fell out a window! Dick Gregory, on the other hand, gave up nightclubs. He realized that the content of his political rap was *not* possible in a nightclub. The Yippies fail to recognize the medium of their message. When Yippies assume that Woodstock is their own Nation, it is a conceit made foolish by *Life* and Warner Brothers.

Liberal "Guerrillas"

A liberal like Richard Schechner of the Performance Group feels a twinge of contradiction when teaching a useless course at a large university. An event interrupts his class, so he and others stomp out and purge themselves. He labels this action guerrilla theatre:

One of the basics of guerrilla theatre is that you use

what is at hand. The murders were at hand, and they were used. I found out about Kent State during my seminar on Performance Theory at NYU at 6:00 P.M., May 4. Someone came into the class and handed out a leaflet. ... A general meeting was called for 7:30. ... We decided to start a guerrilla theatre. I got to the microphone and announced that decision. [*The Drama Review* (Spring 1970), p. 163]

Marc Estrin, director of he American Playground (a theatre at Washington, D.C., and Goddard College), another liberal, takes the concept of theatre as politics even further than Schechner. Estrin talks of "infiltration scenarios"; his "actors" infiltrate a public place and bring the "audience" at that location to the point of confrontation and awareness.

SCENE: Any public park across from a public building. ... A man arrives in the park carrying a largish canvas and all the accoutrements of a Sunday painter. He sets up his easel and begins to sketch the building. He is quite friendly to all onlookers and especially friendly to the park police. ... He works slowly and with great accuracy, laying out his lines as if to produce a work for the public library. ... What is important is that he establish beyond doubt his legitimacy in the park, his friendliness with the police and passersby, his solid technique—his existence as a genuine painter who has a right to be doing what he is doing. To as many people as possible: "I'll see you tomorrow," "Come back later and see how I'm doing," etc. Over the course of the next few days ... the painting begins to transform into a scene appropriate to the subject matter—on the White House balcony babies are napalmed, from the roof ICBMs emerge, as a grotesque Nixon and Laird oversee the operations. The painting becomes a mirror reflecting the inner truth behind the marble facade.

The painter attempts to be as friendly to on-

lookers, especially the police, as he was before, but he will find that the nature of their response to him has changed. He may even find that he is no longer allowed to paint in the park without a permit or somesuch. ... He should follow up his expulsion from the park with TV and radio interviews. Money from the sale of the now-famous painting is donated to the Movement. ["The Painter," in *The Drama Review* pp. 72-73]

Estrin is not a revolutionary, but neither is he a rightist provocateur. He would like to make people more aware: "The war is on while you're having fun." When the time comes, he hopes to put theatre and people into the right scenario, the right location, and create a political event. He considered People's Park a good piece of theatre. Estrin—like Schechner, a director who first approached theatre through fantasy and literature—reads newspaper accounts of political activities as *tales;* politics is not connected to reality, politics is theatrical. Liberal thinkers are good souls. Their motives are idealistic and, actually, they are correct in their analyses of U.S. electoral politics. Certainly, the "politics" of Reagan, Murphy, McCall of Oregon (all ex-TV performers) is *tale*, show-biz, image-making. Yet Estrin's analysis is within the framework of American politics, just as Agnew's or Reagan's; he would make the system work better, not overturn it.

Other avant-gardists in theatre and dance point to their efforts to increase communication between viewer and doer as some kind of "revolutionary" new-wave concept. This technical innovation, like improvisational theatre, in bourgeois circumstances not only sustains and increases the empathetic responses of all concerned; it doesn't change consciousness on a conceptual level, nor does it motivate social action.

Radical and Hit-and-Run Agitproppers

If the political Yippies and Diggers are not theatrical, but media mind-benders, and the liberal guerrillas serve only to support the system, what about those radical theatre workers who call themselves guerrillas? Because a theatre group is anti-establishment doesn't mean per se that it is a revolutionary guerrilla group. The theatre we see practiced by radicals is most often agitprop; the current S.F. Mime Troupe, Third World Revolutionists, Pageant Players all give performances that are like briefings before an audience destined for a particular mission. This type of agitprop traditionally supports the existing ideas of its audience; the presentation is like psychodrama. The Chicano followers of the Teatro Campesino, twelve or fifteen teatros over the West Coast, suffer from the same affliction. Rather than a demonstration of insight, we see an expression of outrage, as the groups pseudo-psychologically describe the oppression of the Chicano.

The hit-and-run agitproppers (or instant street-theatre skit groups) which spring up at demonstrations often try to smash complacency and, like the liberals, "spoil people's fun." People engaged in street theatre often rely on slogans which neither clarify their own political position nor present a theatrically interesting event. The act of doing illegal hit-and-run theatrical skits exaggerates this activity's importance. The content is less significant than the "moment." Although this is a step in the right direction, it's only a misdemeanor, not a felony.

There are some publicity stunts which can have political repercussions. For example, the military recruiter who received a pie in the face. Mark Rudd describes the event (in *The New Left Reader*, edited by Carl Oglesby [New York: Grove Press, 1969], p. 292):

> At a meeting of SDS Draft Committee . . . the question came up of what to do when the head of the Selective Service System for N.Y.C. came to speak at Columbia. Someone suggested that SDS greet the Colonel by attacking him physically. . . . The idea was defeated by a vote of thirty to one. . . . It was decided that the Draft Committee would be present at the speech to "ask probing questions." Several SDS members and nonmembers then organized clandestinely the attack on the Colonel. In the middle of the speech, a mini-demonstration appeared in the back of the room with a fife and drum, flags, machine guns, and noisemakers. As attention went to the back, a person in the front row stood up and placed a lemon-meringue pie in the Colonel's face. Everyone split.

The pie incident was gloriously media-oriented. The recruiter was in total focus when his image was blown with lemon pie. But he changed his shirt and returned. He wasn't implacably stopped; his job wasn't taken over, nor was his own relationship to his role seriously threatened. In other words, his power was not touched. The pie thrown to embarrass (a liberal radical pie protest)

did, however, puncture the Colonel's anal holiness and express the outrage of all the students. All the whoop and whipped cream about "do your own thing" or "do something" has, at its base, a positive response to dull speechmaking and dull organizing, but the incident has to be understood. Not all pies work and the overexerted exhortations to act like a madman in politics (the Artaudian disease) don't lead to concrete power. The Yippies get coverage. Liberal theatre-guerrillas make people "aware." Radical theatre-guerrillas protest and agitprop in the wind.

Guerrilla Theatre—What Was It?

In 1965 we declared it possible to create theatre and some life without elaborate buildings and loads of money. But what was the goal of doing this? In 1965, I stated that our purpose was to teach, direct toward change, be an example of change. In 1968, I added the thought: We must take power. In 1970, I stopped and asked: Could we do all the above?

Worried that the call to action might lead to activism for its own sake, soaked with the moral justifications of a "guerrilla way of life," in 1968 I suggested we consider the problem of power in relation to teaching, directing toward change, and being an example of change. I had grown worried because, in the late sixties, we were moving in zippy political and consumer currents; instant revolutionaries, psychedelic visionaries, and rock millionaires impressed all of us and there was little time for reflection. The media became so ubiquitous that the difference between stage and street dissolved. Life-style acting, a slogan of the poetic crude communists, smogged all thoughts.

The Berliner Ensemble is the only example we

have so far of an aggressive, dynamic teaching machine. During Brecht's lifetime, the Ensemble came dangerously close to Antonio Gramsci's idea of truth, rather than Ulbricht's, but who got the lesson here? Bentley? Esslin? While the Ensemble carved a place in history, we were swinging large slogans at square hegemony and calling for revolution of *consciousness*.

The general refusal to abide by commodity living habits found its specific reaction in a rejection of naturalism's bourgeois theatre. Playacting in public for the TV cameras became the main theatre. The mix began in earnest and so, too, the grand confusion. People forgot that for a theatre group, whether it be guerrilla, agitprop, or simply hysterical, *the presentation is the meat of the action*, even though the drama may be a contrived happening, not a literary story, or an adaptation of a play. The action in view is what we learn from. When we actually cross the picket line, punch the cop, throw the real firebomb, tear down the fence, sit in front of a truck, we are not doing theatre. Actors, writers, or directors who confuse theatrical representations with life will struggle desperately to approach reality and become speedfreak schizophrenics.

Onward

The path of relevant political theatre is away from naturalism toward epic theatre. Guerrilla theatre, a reaction to bourgeois theatre, produced a step in the right direction, but the slogans were not meaningful enough to take root and consciousness did not change anything but hairstyles. We have treated our audiences to an ad-agency-like bombardment, by telling the "truth," protesting the "outrages," and showing examples of purity as if our "product" could be sold like cigarettes,

cars, or consumptive goods. The first step is to avoid sloganeering, easy access to information, or one-liners. An audience is more than a group of consumers and we, as performers, are in need of a technique far greater than that of commodity manipulators.

We have not understood or believed the lessons of the past:

> We must come to the inevitable conclusion that the guerrilla fighter is a social reformer, that he takes up arms responding to the angry protest of the people against their oppressors.—*Che*

> There can be no revolutionary movement without revolutionary theory.—*Lenin*

> The truth is revolutionary.—*Gramsci*

What we do next should neither sustain prevailing conditions nor attempt to blow people's minds. Bourgeois conciousness is deep and complex. Radical theatre must bring people to the point of demanding change, through giving them knowledge of the processes of their condition. Imperialism is a far larger tiger than the "bosses," the "Establishment," or the face of Truman/Eisenhower/Kennedy/Johnson/Nixon. Therefore, our weapons must deal with computerized exploi-

tation, as well as rotten personal habits. To become an effective instrument of social criticism or
revolutionary culture, a theatre has to develop a
tangible theory manifested in practice. It must be
conceived with intelligent care and great love. For
those of us who consider revolutionary culture
neither a gimmick nor an extension of bourgeois
careerism, but rather as a process of thought leading to the dissolution of imperialism's hegemony,
dialectical materialism (yeah, Marx) has to become the source of our inspiration.

16

L'AMANT MILITAIRE

from the play of the same name
by Carlo Goldoni
translated by Betty Schwimmer
adapted by Joan Holden
directed by R. G. Davis
As performed by the
San Francisco Mime Troupe, 1967

© 1967, San Francisco Mime Troupe, Inc.

PERSONAGES

Garcia, Generale of the Spanish Armies
Pantalone, Mayor of Spinachola
Rosalinda, his daughter
Alonso, Lieutenant in the Spanish Army
Corallina, maidservant to Rosalinda
Arlecchino, servant to Pantalone
Brighella, Sergeant in the Spanish Army
Espada, Corporal in the Spanish Army
Punch, a puppet

Accents and Characterization: except where otherwise noted, Garcia and Alonso are played as Spaniards; Pantalone as a Jew; Rosalinda, Corallina, and Arlecchino as Italians; Brighella as a Mexican and Espada as a Negro.

Scene: Spinachola, a town in Italy, during the wars of Charles V.

Prior to show

Indoors: portable commedia stage is set up, house lights on.
Outdoors: actors set up stage before dressing. Twenty minutes before performance they begin warming up in costume. They go about their business (looking for props, making up) with no attempt to hide from the audience. There is a quarter hour of singing, clapping, stretching, etc., then the theme of the show is played: an instrumental begun by recorders, picking up a different instrument on each verse until the actors begin singing and parade in a dancing arc in front of the audience, behind the stage, through the curtain, circling off. Breaking off from this circle and beginning before all the others have disappeared, Generale Garcia goes through a long intro:

Signor, Signora, Signorina, Mesdames, Messieurs, et Mademoiselles, Ladies and Gentlemen—Il Troupo di Mimo di San Francisco, presents for your appreciation and enjoyment this afternoon, an adaptation of Carlo Goldoni's *L'Amant Militaire*, translated by Betty Schwimmer adapted by Joan Holden for commedia dell'arte presentation, this adaptation by Joan Holden of Betty Schwimmer's translation of Carlo Goldini's play translated by Betty Schwimmer for Joan Holden's adaptation of a play by Carlo Goldoni entitled . . . *L'Amant Militaire.*

This speech is accompanied by movements and flourishes

to attract the audience. As the Generale shouts the title he is joined by Corallina. They warm up the audience with topical jokes and references and then introduce the characters individually. Each character enters with a line or flourish of some kind. When all the characters have been introduced they start to sing the theme, but Punch interrupts demanding to be introduced. Pantalone orders him to leave, Punch introduces himself, Pantalone chases him off as the actors hit the theme, dance out and Pantalone and Generale enter with Scene i. It is vital that from the first playing of the theme to Scene i the flow be constant: everything is open to view.

Act I, Scene i

Pantalone: After you, signor Generale, Jose Diego Garcia y Vega, the supreme commander of the combined Spanish and Italian allied forces, the supreme commander-in-chief of staff with a black hat and a real sword: after you—boom *[hits a note].*

Garcia: Ah no, my dear Mayor Pantalone, executive head of the civilian population, dynamic leader and chairman of the board of Pantalone International Corporazione, after you—boom, boom.

Pantalone: [recitative] No, no, Generale, in Italy we always put the foreigners ahead of ourselves—boom, boom.

Garcia: [recitative] In foreign countries, my dear Mayor Pantalone, we Spaniards never turn our backs on anyone *[boom-booming music, they tango downstage center; split left and right].*

Pantalone: All right, Generale—what about the *war?*

Garcia: The tide of war has definitely turned. I have received congratulations from Rome and Madrid.

Pantalone: Congratulations.

Garcia: Allied forces have seized the initiative. We have complete control of the cities and towns, and our pacification teams are running over the countryside. The rebels are being rolled back, they're hurting, they're on the defensive, as is proved by the growing number of their attacks.

Pantalone: Wonderful. Just what I wanted to hear.

Garcia: It's going to change, senor Pantalone, because tonight we are launching an offensive that will lead our forces to victory—your loyal Italian troops and my glorious Spanish troops. We have launched tactical offensives, we have launched strategic offensives; but tonight's offensive will be the most offensive offensive of the war! OPERATION GUINEA WRANGLE. The war will be over in six weeks.

Pantalone: [has a heart attack] WHAT?

Garcia: Six weeks.

Pantalone: Generale: I got a lot into this war. I own 51 percent of the shares. I got munitions plants in Milano, I got weapons labs in Torino, I got banks and pawnshops outside of every base—when you end the war, you end the war industry! You murder my markets— you assassinate my economy—you expose me to recession—to depression—to suicide—*[Pantalone stabs himself. Garcia pulls out the knife and arranges Pantalone like a general leading a charge—one hand across his brow peering ahead, one waving a sword; body forward but head still facing Garcia.]*

Garcia: Learn to have ideals, senor. Learn to have vision. Learn to think of the future of your country: *[snaps Pantalone's head around to complete picture]* with this Operation Guinea Wrangle we are creating for you one hundred and sixteen thousand empty square miles—a desert. *[Pantalone snaps out of stupefaction into fascination.]*

Pantalone: . . . It's a parking lot!

Garcia: And you'll have the lease, senor.

Pantalone: And I'll have the lease.

Garcia: And the sole development rights.

Pantalone: The development rights—oh, dio thank you— subdivisions! Housing projects!

Garcia: No, no missile bases. Army, navy, air force missile bases.

Pantalone: Ah, supermarkets.

Garcia: AEC missile bases. Anti-missile, missile bases. Air force academies with no cheating.

Pantalone: It won't work.

Garcia: What?

Pantalone: It won't work. When you win, your troops will leave.

Garcia: Naturalmente!

Pantalone: When your troops leave, the rebels come back.

Garcia: Senor Pantalone, when the Spanish army leaves Italy there will not be one single rebel left alive!

Pantalone: And the next day, Generale, there will be millions of 'em. Swarming over the countryside—perverting the peasantry—committing atrocities; God forbid, murdering dignitaries—expropriating PROPERTY —Oh my God, I can't stand it. Revolution is a cancer you got to keep cutting. What's the good of winning the war if you're going to get *out!*

Garcia: Senor Pantalone, we have to get out. If we were to stay here it would look like imperialism.

Pantalone: We can't have *that!* So Generale—don't win.

Garcia: Senor Pantalone!

Pantalone: Now wait—I didn't say LOSE. When you think about it Generale, we're not doing so bad now. You're fighting, I'm making money, both of us is happy. Well, you take my advice, Generale: win a little, lose a little. That way nobody gets hurt.

Garcia: Senor Pantalone, I am here—Spain is here—against our will—honoring our commitments—fighting to free Italy and fighting to WIN!

Pantalone: Yeah, but Generale, if you win, I lose! What about my business?

Garcia: Ptoo *[spit]* on your business. There are moments in history—not very many—when business interests must yield to the national interest.

Pantalone: Well, when that moment comes, Generale, don't you be surprised to see me looking out for my own interests. Have you considered that I could sell to the rebels? *[Pantalone snaps his right hand in Garcia's face and raises his left in a gesture of triumph. Garcia grabs his outstretched arm and twists it behind his back.]*

Garcia: What do you mean you *could* sell to the rebels? You've been selling to both sides since before the war.

Pantalone: Of course *[Pantalone gives Garcia a karate chop to the throat.]* That's because the rebels is poor, and you're rich. That means you got the cannons and the muskets, they get the broken spears from the crusades. Well, *that* situation could change. Because rather than face the end of my markets, I might lower my prices a little. You think about that, Generale: you think about the rebels with cannons—you think about the rebels with muskets—you think about the rebels with weapons you don't even know about *[Pantalone minces away like a spoiled child, holding his robes up going "Nyah, nyah, nyah, nyah, nyah."]*

Garcia: Senor Pantalone, I thought better of you than that.

Pantalone: You didn't think I was so *smart.*

Garcia: I thought we were partners—friends—allies in el Allianzo del Retrogreso—

Pantalone: Generale, let's face this one fact—this is a dog eat dog world—yip, yip, yip.

Garcia: Senor, es verdad. As Calderon de la Barka said as he faced Alexander Hamilton: *Gr-r-r-r-r.* All those not with us are against us.

Pantalone: Now wait, Generale, I never said that—

Garcia: All those against us, are muertos. Senor Pantalone, we thought that your government was the best Spanish government Italy had. We have assisted it—protected it—helped it to grow; now I find you ready to betray our ideals; ready to sell out freedom to world revolution; bargaining, conniving, consorting with the enemy—

Pantalone: Generale! I didn't do nothing yet.

Garcia: How do I know, senor? How do I know that you're not in their pay? How do I know that we're not being watched? *[Corallina sticks her head out from behind the curtain.]*

Pantalone: That's ridiculous!

Garcia: You could be head of an international conspiracy—

Pantalone: That's enough. This is the mayor you're talking to—eh? If I did something that offended you, I will apologize, Generale—like a man. But it was nothing—nothing, I assure you—it was a slip of the tongue. *[Mime: Pantalone's tongue falls out—this is accompanied by babbling—and falls into Garcia's hand.]*

Act I, Scene ii

Corallina: *[whispers]* Ssst! Signor Pantalone! Signor Pantalone! I've been looking everywhere for you! THE BEE IS IN THE BLOSSOM!

Pantalone: What are you doing here, you whore? Who's watching the house?

Corallina: What I'm doing here is following your orders like a faithful servant—THE SNAKE IS IN THE GARDEN.

Pantalone: Oh . . . what the hell is she talking about!

Garcia: A CODE!

Corallina: THE FOX IS IN THE FOLD!

Pantalone: Will you speak Italian, crow's vomit?

Corallina: Il tenente Alonso e colla sua figlia—Lieutenant Alonso he'sa visiting your daughter!

Garcia: Alonso! He's working for them!

Pantalone: O indelicata! O papa infortunato di una figlia desonorata! Why, God—why? Is this what I sweated, what I starved for for fifty years? Is this what I had children for? Is this *[chokes Corallina]* why you disgraced me in front of the Generale?

Corallina: Run, signor—he just got there; you may be in time!

Pantalone: *[Exit; runs back on "Oh, why does God . . ."* stops, freezing Garcia and Corallina: sees stage is his and breaks into "Blow winds, crack your cheeks" in phony Elizabethan "Is this a dagger that I see before me . . ." Bows to audience's recognition and splits.]*

Act I, Scene iii

Garcia: Just a minute, senorita: I wish to speak with you.

Corallina: Oh, Generale—to me? Well, go ahead—spick!

Garcia: You are a servant in Pantalone's house—is that right?

Corallina: That'sa right, Generale.

Garcia: Lieutenant Alonso is said to have business with your mistress—es verdad?

Corallina: Generale, I'ma jus a poor servant. I'ma wash, I'ma cook, I'ma sew. Generale, for me to know that is to have one hundred ears and two hundred eyes—to be as subtle as the serpent and as wise as the owl—I would have to be everywhere like the poor, and nowhere like good fortune: Generale, a poor, simple, ignorant peasant girl like me why, she would have to *pay* for that kind of information *[right hand out]*.

Garcia: Pay? *[Slaps her hand down. Her left snaps up. Mime: Corallina during Garcia's speech is a turnstile, which Garcia slips through without paying.]* Who would take pay for a chance of serving his country! Every effort for the war effort is an investment in the future of your country!

Corallina: But Generale—people got to eat!

Garcia: Eat?

Corallina: Eat!

Garcia: Eat! Who needs food when he's living on glory? When the war is over, my country will put mountains of pasta in all of your pots. But to win we will need every crumb of information on our fingertips *[licks his fingers]*. Now, my little dumpling, tell me what Lieutenant Alonso is doing with your mistress—remember, this is for the future of your country!

Corallina: You mean, if I could tell you that every Thursday

Garcia: Si

Corallina: At high noon

Garcia: Si si

Corallina: Lieutenant Alonso, in an upturned collar

Garcia: Si si si

Corallina: Wearing dark glasses, sneaks through back streets and climbs over our wall to meet my mistress—you mean, if I told you all that, you mean you wouldn't *pay* me for it?

Garcia: You want me to *pay* to find out that every Tuesday

Corallina: Thursday

Garcia: At three o'clock

Corallina: Noon

Garcia: Lieutenant Alonso, in upturned glasses

Corallina: Collar!

Garcia: Sneaks through the garden

Corallina: The STREETS!

Garcia: To meet with your master?

Corallina: My MISTRESS!

Garcia: Why should I pay for that when I've weasled it out of you already!

Corallina: Shucks! You so smart, I'll give you one more piece of information for free. That's no big secret, Generale, everybody in Spinachola knows it already! It's what comes after that you'd have to pay for. Ciao, Generale *[goes]*.

Garcia: Chow, that's all those wops think of. *[Texas accent begins]* There are times in the life of every country when a half truth matters more than the whole truth. *[background song,* America*]* In the struggle for men's minds, no weapon can be ignored. Senores, the enemy is all around us—they're ruthless, sneaky and uncompromising: and we won't be safe, your children and mine, until every last one of them is wiped out. We are not fighting for Spain alone, senores. We are fighting for the very lifeblood, I say the very lifeBLOOD, of our civilization. *[Whistles. Two actors come in as a horse, connected by an American flag. Garcia throws his leg over them, makes a flourish with his sword and gallops out.]*

Punch: *[appears beside stage]* Hooray for the Generale, hooray for the Generale, hooray for the Generale. Well, now that those creeps are gone, you're gonna see some *real* theatre—you're gonna see a PUPPET SHOW! Judy —hey Judy. Justa second—Judy's a little bashful: I gotta go get her. *[disappears—reappears]* HELP! There's some guy in here's got his hands up my pants! You think that's funny? Listen, I'll give you a real speech, by a real American: "Bolshevism is knocking at our gates—we can't afford to let it in. We must put our shoulders together and hold fast." Al Capone, 1925. Yeah, if you want to laugh, spend a dime and buy a newspaper . . . *[inside only]* How much did you pay to get in here, anyway? *[exit]*

Act I, Scene iv

[The scene is introduced, as are all Rosalinda's and Alonso's entrances, by a flamenco flourish performed by Espada which ends abruptly before the first line.]

Rosalinda: Dear don Alonso, I beg you to withdraw.

Alonso: Why, darling Rosalinda, do you suddenly shun me?

Rosalinda: My father has learned the truth, and threatens to cut off our relations.

Alonso: *[after take]* Well dearest, if he finds us here—es perfecto—then we can get married.

Rosalinda: I accept. But alas, my father will never allow me to marry a Spaniard. And besides *[sob]* I think of the inconstancy of men—I think of the uncertainty of your stay—I think that if I marry you I may never know the joys of a wife—

Alonso: O Rosalinda, then leave nothing to fortune—let's do it today!

Rosalinda: Oh—I think of the hundred perils you're exposed to: I think of bullets, of ambushes—

Alonso: Ambushes, si . . .

Rosalinda: Of widowhood—oh, no one can feel my despair!

Alonso: I feel it, my darling. I feel it, and I offer you my hand in proof of my love.

Rosalinda: Your hand at this fatal point can build a dam against my sorrow.

Alonso: Here it is, my darling, here it is: all yours.

Rosalinda: Dear hand, may heaven make you victorious!

Act I, Scene v

Brighella: [enters with a drum] Aha! Modern war. The hand replaces the sword.

Rosalinda: Who let you in?

Brighella: What do I need, vaseline?

Alonso: Sergeant Brighella, please wait outside.

Brighella: Lieutenant, I've brought your orders. Be armed before evening and ready to march [drum]—we join Operation Guinea Wrangle tonight! [drum]

Alonso: [snaps to attention] Thank you, sergeant. The biggest operation of the war! With Generale Garcia at its head, the victorious Spanish army will sweep across Italy, crushing everything in its path—like the hand of God, striking down evil. Rejoice, Rosalinda, in a matter of weeks, your country will be purified! There won't be a single wop left.

Rosalinda: There is the constancy that you promised me—there is the passion I should have surrendered to—go, since you love glory better than me!

Brighella: Bravo, lieutenant! Never mind, senorita, you're not crying alone. With this news, by tonight, I shall have six women crying.

Alonso: Vanish, cretin. Rosalinda, I ask you to remember that you are the future wife of a Spanish officer!

Rosalinda: I would rather be the present wife of a beggar! O dio—fate has made my first happy moment my last—I can't stand it, I falter, I fall [falls, Alonso catches her]—alas, is Venus then to be ravished by Mars?

Brighella: But Mars has lost his thunderbolt. Leave them in tears, Lieutenant, but always leave them satisfied. [drums; leaves]

Alonso: Oh, Rosalinda—no pain of sword or bullet could possibly compare with the anguish caused me by your anguish; Oh, death would be a kinder sight to me than your tears—

Rosalinda: Then stay—

Alonso: A lover called by duty at the dawn of his happiness goes as sadly as a man called by death in his youth.

Rosalinda: If you loved me you could not leave me now!

Alonso: But an officer who did not rise to the trumpet of honor could no more rise than a dead man to the service of love! [parting] Have courage, my idol. If fortune is faithful, we shall meet in six weeks time—six—if not, we shall meet in eternity. In the meantime, vaya—

Rosalinda: Vaya—

Alonso: Vaya—

Rosalinda: Oh, vaya—

Alonso: Vaya con dios, my darling! [exit—leaves Rosalinda tottering]

Act I, Scene vi

Pantalone: [wailing] Ah, Rosalinda, Rosalinda, if your mamma in heaven could see you now, she'd drop dead from shame. Where is she, the whore? I'm going to beat her and send her to a convent. No—not a convent! And him! Where is he, that viper from Valencia, that Spanish fly? I'm gonna pull out his sting!

Rosalinda: Oh my Alonso! [Pantalone catches her just in time]

Pantalone: My daughter! She's dying. Corallina! Where are you?

Act I, Scene vii

Corallina: Here I am.

Pantalone: Hurry up, do something.

Corallina: [seductive] Why, what happened?

Pantalone: What looks like it happened? She fainted.

Corallina: Poor signorina!

Pantalone: Don't stand there! Bring some vinegar! Arlecchino! *[Corallina leaves]*

Pantalone: Bring some water!

Arlecchino: [inside] Sior si!

Pantalone: Run!

Arlecchino: [inside] I'm coming!

Pantalone: Where is he?

Arlecchino: Here I am! I've come to water the flower children. *[To audience]* Hi, flower children *[throws water on audience and splits].*

Pantalone: O Dio!

Corallina: [enters] Here's the vinegar.

Pantalone: Water! *[Corallina dabs at Rosalinda.]*

Corallina: It don't do anything!

Arlecchino: Here I am! *[back with a douche syringe full of water]*

Pantalone: In that? Dio! Rosalinda! Get away, both of you!

Corallina: I'm not leaving my mistress!

Act I, Scene viii

Alonso: [enters with guitar accompaniment up to "from your side"] Rosalinda—my guiding star, the fixed point of my compass—honor, taking pity on love, has given me leave to retrace the endless journey I made from your side in order that I may clasp you in my arms for one last farewell *[sees others for first time]* —Oh, my God, senor Pantalone—what's the matter?

Pantalone: Oh, signor officer, help us. *[doesn't notice it's Alonso]*

Alonso: Gladly. We Spanish officers know first aid *[crosses to them].* Which one of you is sick? *[All forget Rosalinda, mime: "me, me," displaying various complaints. Alonso takes Rosalinda's hand]* Come, senorita.

Rosalinda: Ai

Pantalone: My daughter! She's coming back!

Alonso: Courage, senorita.

Rosalinda: Alas!

Pantalone: My daughter!

Corallina: Master, I'm gonna throw away this vinegar.

Pantalone: So, nu?

Corallina: Because the juice of Don Alonso isa stronger than this.

Pantalone: Don Alonso!

Arlecchino: Master!

Pantalone: What do *you* want?

Arlecchino: I'm going to take away the water.

Pantalone: I know. For the sickness of my daughter, water is not the cure.

Arlecchino: No, it's not that: it's just that this thing doesn't work—oh! *[squirts Pantalone, leaves]*

Pantalone: Signor Lieutenant, I want to talk to you.

Alonso: Con gusto, senor.

Rosalinda: Aiee *[threatens to faint again]*

Pantalone: Shut up and go to your room.

Rosalinda: Alone?

Pantalone: What do you mean, "alone"?

Rosalinda: I mean I don't feel strong enough to walk.

Alonso: I will help her—

Pantalone: [calls] Corallina!

Corallina: [enters] Here I am.

Pantalone: I want you to take my darling, sweet little NYMPHOMANIAC to her room.

Corallina: C'mon, nymph.

Rosalinda: Alas! We shall never meet again. *[Corallina*

takes Rosalinda, but on "alas" Rosalinda hurries back to Alonso. This leads to a ballet, with all the actors dancing back and forth—going, not going—until they get motion sick. Rosalinda and Corallina exit. Pantalone and Alonso then cross each other in pas de bourree and jete-tour into opposite corners downstage.]

Alonso: Senor Pantalone, I know what you want to say to me. You think that I have abused your daughter's innocence; that my intentions toward her are base—that having caused her to love me, I could abandon her? Fear nothing, senor: although your daughter is Italian, I plan to marry her and take her with me to Spain. *[Falls on one knee.]*

Pantalone: You understand this one thing, Lieutenant. I will never allow my daughter to marry a spick. I'd sell her first. If I ever see you around here again, I will tell the Generale. Addio, Lieutenant. *[Grabs Alonso by the foot; Alonso falls flat.]*

Alonso: Que dice, senor Pantalone? Mira, mira que sin culpa ne condenas. Tacos, senor Pantalone. Enchiladas, tacos, puerco! *[exit]*

Pantalone: Shove it up your guacamole, buddy. If I ever catch you around here with my daughter, I'll take her to the market and I'll SELL her. I'll sell her so quickly —wait a minute—what am I thinking? What am I *thinking?* How to sell my daughter in the market. What kind of man would allow a thought like—how much could I get for the kid? . . . No! I wouldn't do that—no! I'm not that kind of person! *[to audience]* What are you laughing at? You're not beyond reproach. Listen, I wouldn't sell my daughter—there is a very simple explanation: I have, since birth, such a head for business, it thinks quicker than I do. *[exit]*

Punch: Bravo, Pantalone, bravo! Pantalone's a cutie, isn't he folks? Put Lyndon behind a pushcart and you'd love him, too. But you'd never vote for him. Go ahead, Pantalone—sell your daughter. She's worth about 50¢ an hour in the back room of any Saigon bar. Then Alonso won't have any trouble getting her. Well, that's why he joined the army, isn't it? Couldn't get any from

under the noses of the duenas, so he goes off to Italy to cop a wop. Listen, I got a little love song that I'd like to dedicate to Barry Sadler and all our boys fighting under the stars and stripes tonight. *[He is joined by three actors out of mask for:]*

Song

1) Join the army,
See the world,
Burn a gook,
Screw a girl.

2) If at home
You beat your meat,
Go to war
Have a treat.

3) Get the clap,
A purple heart,
Some penicillin,
A brand new start.

4) Join the army,
See the world,
Burn a gook,
Screw a girl.

Act I, scene ix

Brighella: [enters, goes through manual of arms, accompanied by drummer at side. Drummer: "Yay, Humboldt State ROTC! Yay!" He leaves.] This government I work for, she's crazy. Ten years we been fighting in this stinking country, and we got to stay here till we *win.* Then we go fight in another stinking country. We could move now: there's nothing left to steal, and this Italian food makes us all sick. And the women either don't have nothing to do with you, or they cut your throat afterwards. But without victory, the generales don't get no satisfaction . . . With the weapons we got now, they may finally get some, too. Blast you full of holes, melt your flesh off—pretty soon somebody going to get hurt. But not me. I got a way out. *[calls]* Hey, Espada.

Espada: [enters, gives himself commands and drills, ending: "Yeah, sir!"]

Brighella: Hey, Espada.

Espada: How you doin, Sarge? [elbow nudging]

Brighella: Corporal Espada, tonight we are launching Operation Guinea Wrangle, which will bring the Spanish forces to victory.

Espada: Oh, yeah Sarge.

Brighella: And for this operation the Generale has requisitioned one-hundred new recruits.

Espada: Oh, I'se hip to it, Sarge.

Brighella: And for every wop that we recruit we get five pesos.

Espada: Yeah, sure Sarge.

Brighella: And so, us two is goin to be the two biggest recruiters in the whole army.

Espada: Yeah, sure Sarge.

Brighella: In that case Espada, how many recruits we got?

Espada: How many wops we got? Les see, we got Rossini, Toscanini, Paganini, Zucchini, eeny, meeny, [etc.: ad libs]

Brighella: ESPADA!

Espada: Yeah [counting toes and fingers finally] fo!

Brighella: Fo?

Espada: Fo!

Brighella: Espada, do you know that the Generale has placed us in a position of great responsibility?

Espada: Responsibility!

Brighella: Do you understand the responsibility placed upon us as Spanish soldiers in Italy?

Espada: The responsibility!

Brighella: And do you understand the responsibility we have as recruiting officers?

Espada: The responsibility!

Brighella: And do you understand that when the orders come down to go to the front line, *you'll* have to go in their place?

Espada: The responsibility?

Brighella: THEY'LL BREAK YOUR ASS!

Espada: My ass? My ass! Ooh the responsibility. [Brighella kicks him.] My ASS!

Brighella: Now look Espada, you and me, we in a pretty

tough jam [Espada concurs] BUT as Barnum and Bailey said to General Hershey—there's a sucker born every minute.

Act I, scene x

[Arlecchino enters singing, dancing: Brighella and Espada join the song]

Brighella: Hey senor, you want a drink of wine?

Arlecchino: Wine? Sure, I love wine.

Espada: [pounces on Arlecchino] Hey, buddy, you wanna join the army? [Arlecchino spits the wine in his face, struggles free.]

Brighella: Espada! AtenHUT! [Espada snaps to attention.] You can't put a man like that in the army.

Espada: Why not? I don see nothin wrong wid him.

Arlecchino: There's nothing wrong with me!

Brighella: Espada, you and me are going to have a little lesson. Think carefully now and tell me: who goes in the army?

Espada: Now, sarge, wha you ask me dat fo? You know evvybody go in de ARMY, less dey bin to pison o else done funk de tes—

Brighella: Everybody *you* know goes in the army—everybody *poor* goes in the army, because for them the army represents a step upward—decent pay, respect [inaudible objections from Espada], the adoration of women—right?

Espada: I guess dats right.

Brighella: But there are others, Espada: [oratorical pose

and accent] men who may be limited in their physical capabilities, men who may be frail or unadroit, but men who nonetheless possess a surfeit of *intelligence* which can be channeled into the mainstream of the political, cultural, and scientific progress of this nation TODAY! *[Arlecchino and Espada fall down.]*

Arlecchino: Like men who can ravel the ravioli, and ministrate the minestrone.

Espada: Yeah, like men dat can make it wid de president's DAUGHTER!

Brighella: That's the hard way. I'm talking about men who work with their *brains.*

Arlecchino: With their brains?

Arlecchino and Espada: How?

Brighella: The kind of brains that'll get you a three day work week.

Arlecchino: Fourteen hours a day, every day

Brighella: The kind of brains that land you 500 piastros a week

Arlecchino: 2 piastros—that's what *I* get

Brighella: The kind of brains that gets you a secretary who will tickle your fancy.

Arlecchino: Nothing from my Corallina!

Brighella: You and me, Espada, in the army, we think we're pretty well off. But this senor got education, opportunity, money—

Arlecchino: I want to join the army.

Espada: Oh, noo, senor—you can't do dat—you got to get yoself one of dem 2-S deferments—latch onto one of dem dere HIyuh degrees, land yoself dat job at General Dynamics, get you dat new Lincoln Continental and you's on de ROAD. Why, if you was to join the army now, you'd be obstructin the free flow *[mime: jacking off]* of IDEAS.

Arlecchino: Please, sergeant—take me?

Brighella: Oh, no, senor, I couldn't do that—and deprive society of the benefits of your education?

Arlecchino: Please, sergeant—please take me—I'll do anything—I'll even

Espada: *[lower]* Quiet, son—I'm tellin you we got to work within the powuh structure.

Arlecchino: PAY *[Espada and Brighella talk unintelligibly.]*

Espada: How much?

Arlecchino: 5 piastros, that's all I get: *[pays Brighella]* Uno, dos, tres, cuatro, cinco piastros.

Brighella: Well, senor—remember you talked me into it. Sign your name here in this little book. *[Arlecchino makes a big X.]*

Brighella: Hey, what's your *name?*

Arlecchino: *[spade accent]* Arlecchino X. *[They hit him.]* Battochio.

Brighella: Want your pay now, or later?

Arlecchino: Why put things off?

Brighella: You're a wise man, senor. *[pays him]* Uno, dos, tres, cuatro, cinco piastros—

Arlecchino: Cinque piastros! I'm rich!

Brighella: *[Takes it back, coin by coin.]* Pero, cuatro. One for the uniform. Tres. One for the soldiers retirement fund. Dos. One for the entertainment committee—next week, we get Nancy Sinatra and the Fascist Fandango Five.

Arlecchino: Due piastros!

Brighella: QUARTERMASTER! *[Quartermaster brings uniform, hands it to Espada who dresses Arlecchino.]* Aten-HUT! *[Espada and Arlecchino snap to attention.]* That's pretty good, private. I think I'll go tell the Generale about you. *[leaving]* Remember what General Hershey replied back to Barnum and Bailey: "You think *you* got the greatest show on earth?" *[exit]*

Arlecchino: Hey Corporale—let's go over to the barracks and tell dirty stories! *[no response]* Corporale! *[Espada remains frozen at attention.]* Hey, Corporale! *[Checks Espada all over; becomes a dog, sniffing; finally takes a big sniff and sneezes. On "Choo" Espada marks time. Arlecchino experiments, marches Espada around with Ah-choos; finally gives a bugle call, then a fart, and Espada charges out yelling "Kill! Kill!"]*

Act I, Scene xi

Corallina: [enters, sees Arlecchino] Santa Maria!

Arlecchino: Corallina! Come celebrate. How do I look?

Corallina: Is that what you meant when you promised to marry me?

Arlecchino: Why shouldn't I marry you?

Corallina: You're gonna march with the army tonight and leave me behind!

Arlecchino: Beautiful Corallina! You can follow the troops!

Corallina: You may be crazy, but I am not. Why did you do it?

Arlecchino: To have plenty to eat and drink, to have shoes and a uniform, to do nothing—but mostly, Corallina, I did it for the respect.

Corallina: Wonderful! Ha, ha!

Arlecchino: Ha, ha, what?

Corallina: In the winter in the snow, and in the summer in the sun, you're gonna be on the walls with a rifle on your shoulder, saying "Who goes there?" You'll sleep on straw, march till you're half dead, and if you make one mistake you'll be beaten.

Arlecchino: Beaten?

Corallina: Like a dog. Then they'll send you into battle: you'll run through the sand, with the air full of bullets; you'll lie in the mud, bombs falling all around you; you shoot—

Arlecchino: Bang!

Corallina: *[Arlecchino mimes action in this passage, finally dying.]* And never know what you hit; they shoot—bang—the first one misses you; bang—the second one; you're still alive; bang—the third one: you see red—then white—then black, then it's all over. *[pause]* Arlecchino? Arlecchino. Arlecchino! E morto! Mi Arlecchino e morto! *[cries]* No! No more dancing in the streets! No more singing in the meadow! No more laughing in the sunlight—and I was gonna fix him some pasta tonight, too—pasta con pesto, just the way he likes it. With a little bit salami on the side—a piece of mortadella—a couple slices American cheese, a bit of provolone *[Arlecchino lifts his head—she spots him]*—and just a little, tiny bit *baloney.* *[Bursts into exaggerated grief and ignores Arlecchino's mimed protests.]*

Oh mi, Arlecchino! Mi Arlecchino e morto! E morto! He ain't gonna have none of that! And I was going to meet you tonight, too—at 7, under the cherry tree! But you won't be there Arlecchino—because you're dead, that's why—because that cornuto army, it'sa kill you! I'm gonna go say a prayer for you in the church. *[cries]* Goo-bye. *[leaves]*

Arlecchino: Arlecchino, you so dumb, sometimes I don't think you're an Italian at all, I think you're a Sicilian. *[This becomes an argument between his body and his ghost, until Espada marches on zombielike, as he left in Scene x.]*

Act I, Scene xii

Arlecchino: Eh, sior Corporal! I changed my mind. Here's your uniform—here, take your due piastros *[etc. Espada marches. Finally Arlecchino jumps on his back; talks in his ear.]*

Brighella: *[enters]* Halt, Corporal. Private, dismount. *[Arlecchino jumps down behind Espada.]* What did you do with my private?

Espada: Your private? I sent him down to headquarters to have his head quartered.

Brighella: Well then, where's my five pesos?

Espada: Sarge, if I was your five pesos, I'd be headed for the door *[Grabs Arlecchino as he takes the hint.]* Say buddy, you got a fin for my man?

Brighella: Ah, there's the private. Hello private.

Arlecchino: Sgt. Brighella *[saluting].* I've been looking everywhere for you. My mama is very sick. I have to leave the army—goodbye.

Brighella: Oh, su madre infirma—que miseria—but private you doin ok—you got your hat, a new uniform, you got a little money in your pocket, you signed the papers—so you're screwed, wop.

Arlecchino: [to Espada] You understand—no hard feelings, Corporale. Addio. *[Espada slams hat back on his head.]* Ya greasy spick!

Brighella: What? Insulting a corporal? Beat him. *[They beat him.]*

Arlecchino: I retract.

Brighella: Get up.

Arlecchino: I can't move.

Brighella: [kicks him] Get up. Do your duty.

Arlecchino: I'm assassinated. *[gets up]* What do I do?

Brighella: Thank the man who beat you.

Arlecchino: Thank him? The dirty spick, I'm gonna—

Brighella: Stretch him out. *[They repeat.]* Fifty blows.

Arlecchino: [in crucified position on floor] Mea culpa, mea culpa. My God, my God, why hast thou forsaken me? *[Soldiers do a take to each other, then tack his hands down.]*

Act I, Scene xiii

[As Brighella and Espada finish crucifying Arlecchino, Garcia enters in horseback mime, rides around.]

Garcia: I've come to brief you. It will be short. Our forces: our Spanish forces and their loyal Italian forces will line up along both coasts of Italy. When I give the signal, both columns will start marching toward the center, assisted by cannons, siege engines, rock crushers, earth movers and every chemical, biological and pathological weapon known to man. Mountains will be transformed into deserts, deserts into oceans and oceans back into mountains! *[notices Arlecchino]* What's that?

Brighella and Espada: [stumbled explanations]

Garcia: Well pick it up, give it a pair of legs and put it on the front lines! Remember every man, woman, and child is your enemy. We march at sundown. You've got your orders. *[He charges off, they march off as spirit of '76.]*

Punch: [sings] "From the halls of Montezuma" *[etc.]* Powerful! Devastating! Good old hard-hitting *realism!* Dig it: the system forcing that poor slob into the army —hah! What a cop out—hey who puts this show on, the communist party? Listen—nobody *has* to go into the army. There are lots of ways to get out. You blow up the draft boards, commit a crime, go to jail, pour blood on the records, stay in school for twenty-seven years— or you can psych out. Very easy—see you get yourself good and loaded and stay up for three nights. And then you go down there and write with your left hand (that's if you can still see the paper) then, you let them know that *you* are a leading *prevert*, you don't come right out and tell them—you just let them know. Then, when you finally get in front of the shrink, you put your head down on his desk and cry. *[cries: Wa-a-aah!]* You don't like that method, huh? Too all-American to be crazy? Just stand up and say "Hell, no—we won't go!" *[Corallina as pom-pom girl—off stage—leads audience in cheer.]* Some of you people don't know how to cheer! I know what you're doing: you're protecting your records, so you can have a civil service job when you're forty years old. There's nothing I can do for *you*—you're in the army already. *[exit]*

End Act I

Act II, Scene i

Rosalinda: [announced by guitar] Snatched from the very pinnacle of happiness—deserted at the very door of bliss! Alonso, I shall not long survive your departure— each moment promises to be my last! *[Corallina approaches Rosalinda crying. They start crying in response to one another, segue into musical comedy, then back.]* This tender blossom withers, consumed by despair! *[They cry harder.]* Ah, Corallina, my child— how happy you look. Your cheerful face is like a ray of sunlight in this the darkest midnight of my life! *[Coral-lina chokes]* Oh! Farewell Alonso! Oh—welcome, death—

Corallina: Farewell, Alonso: death welcomes you.

Rosalinda: Farewell, Alonso, until we meet again.

Corallina: Farewell, Alonso, we'll never see you again.

Rosalinda: What do you mean, we'll never see you again?

Corallina: Because he ain't coming back.

Rosalinda: What do you mean, he ain't coming back?

Corallina: Think of it, signorina: a brave soldier like the Lieutenant, he wouldn't *permit* himself to return alive. Be proud, signorina! Rather than risk the disgrace of survival, your lover will greet every bullet like a mistress—

Rosalinda: Corallina!

Corallina: And embrace death like a bride!

Rosalinda: Dio! No!

Corallina: I can see him now, with his arm and his leg shot off *[mimes all this]*.

Rosalinda: Oh

Corallina: And his guts spilling onto the ground. He grows weaker, lungs burning, gasping for air; he calls for water, nobody hears; with his last strength he turns his face to heaven and sees—vultures. He falls back

Rosalinda: Criminals!

Corallina: . . . with his last breath, whispers—Rosalinda!

Rosalinda: Murderers! Flesh-eating monsters!

Corallina: Si

Rosalinda: Hypocritical warmongers, slaughtering innocents!

Corallina: Si.

Rosalinda: Has history ever seen such injustice?

Corallina: *[grotesque]* Hey, lady, ya gotta dime for a poppy?

Rosalinda: Corallina, we've got to stop them!

Corallina: You're right, signorina, you're right! And I—simple, ignorant peasant girl that I am—have a plan.

Rosalinda: A plan? Corallina, how wonderful! Signori, see the beauty of the practical mind! Oh, my Alonso, I will see you again—I will gaze into your eyes; you will embrace me *[etc., etc.]*

Corallina: Signorina—

Rosalinda: Presto, presto—what is it?

Corallina: It's a bit rough, signorina!

Rosalinda: I'm ready for anything!

Corallina: Okay. First you go to your room and close all the drapes and the blinds, and don't let *no* Venetians in. You light a candle, you let down your hair . . . put on your best nightgown, and now—get in bed with a Bible. I dress as a nun. I go to the Generale. A lady must see him, it's her dying request. In the name of religion, he can't refuse. I lead him through back streets. I bring him to your room. You smile very faintly, but you're too weak to talk. Fascinated, he leans over closer . . . and closer, to catch your last words . . .

Rosalinda: And? *[Corallina whispers in her ear]*

Corallina: And then I break his balls!

Rosalinda: What?

Corallina: I chop him up in little pieces, and I kill him!

Rosalinda: No, that's murder!

Corallina: No! It's war!

Rosalinda: That's what's wrong with it! We can't fight war with war!

Corallina: Why not?

Rosalinda: Because that way the chain of killing would never be broken—the curse of blood would never be lifted—the heritage of horror would only be passed on.

Corallina: Signori! Now you see the beauty of the sensitive spirit.

Rosalinda: There is only one way to stop war.

Corallina: How?

Rosalinda: With words!

Corallina: Words?

Rosalinda: Words! Speeches, books, articles, leaflets, petitions! We will speak to them, we will speak to them, Corallina, and the sweet voice of reason will silence the thunder of battle.

Act II, Scene ii

Pantalone: *[enters]* HCHPTOOO! *[spit]* Hello, hello, hello. Rosalinda, my daughter: with the chilly fingers and the hot pants, how are you?

Rosalinda: Papa! This war is wrong!

Pantalone: Poor baby, got a fever.

Rosalinda: It violates *everything!*

Pantalone: You're a fine one to talk about that!

Corallina: [*as John Wayne, ready for two-handed draw*] Signor, the Spaniards got no business in this country.

Pantalone: [*same*] You're right Corallina, and that lieutenant got no business in my house!

Rosalinda: Papa! The people don't want the war.

Pantalone: The people. So *nu?*

Corallina: [*encouraged*] The rebels only want land.

Pantalone: That's *all!*

Rosalinda: Young men are dying!

Pantalone: They are?

Rosalinda: Little children are starving!

Corallina: Italy is in ruins!

Pantalone: [*crying*] It's true! It's a tragedy—it should never have happened!

Rosalinda and Corallina: SO . . . . . .

Pantalone: [*country club accent*] We've got to make the best of it and invest in the future.

Rosalinda: But papa!

Pantalone: Don't worry, papa takes care. A little sacrifice today brings a happy tomorrow. Remember that Rosalinda. For example: tonight I invited the Generale to our house for dinner.

Rosalinda: The Generale!

Corallina: [*chippie accent*] Listen, Rosie, ya ain't gonna try that crap on the Generale!

Rosalinda: [*same*] Honey, I gotta! Al's behind the eight-ball!

Pantalone: For that I sent you to private school? A little patience today is a new contract tomorrow. Tonight the Generale is coming to my house for dinner—and listen Rosalinda . . . I just found out I got to go some place, so I want you to *entertain* him till I get back.

Corallina: Is this what you sweated and starved for twenty years?

Pantalone: Who asked you, pigeon spit? Get in the kitchen.

Corallina: I know when I'm not wanted. [*Spits at Panta-*

lone and leaves. Pantalone chases her to right curtain— she pops her head out left and gets him again.]

Pantalone: Rosalinda—

Rosalinda: Yes, papa?

Pantalone: Shut up. Tonight the Generale is coming to my house for dinner. This is the most important night of my life! I want everything *perfect*, you understand! *Perfect.* The atmosphere should be *light!* Jokey-jolly, a few yuks! [*slams fist into palm*] Get it?

Rosalinda: Yes, papa.

Pantalone: Shut up. He's tired, he's had a hard day: it's not easy to kill a hundred thousand people every day.

Rosalinda: The poor man!

Pantalone: Oh, boy. I told you to shut up and you talked back to *me!* You talked back to your father! Your father, the boss! Your father, the ruler! Your father, the master! [*becomes MGM lion*] ROAR!

Rosalinda: But, papa.

Pantalone: Roar.

Rosalinda: What about the Generale, papa?

Pantalone: What *about* the Generale?

Rosalinda: The Generale is coming and the table isn't even set!

Pantalone: [*has an attack*] Why isn't the table set?

Rosalinda: [*imitates him*] I was waiting for word from the boss. [*exit*]

Pantalone: [*yells after her*] Don't use the cheap silver! [*pause*] Use the cheap silver! If I pull this off, it'll be the biggest thing I've ever done. Marry my daughter to Garcia? A marriage of industry and the military. I'll have the army in my pocket, I'll have free war contracts wherever he goes—Bolivia—Guatemala—Peru— and it couldn't fail—it couldn't fail, because nobody could keep his hands off my Rosalinda! . . . But suppose he don't want to marry her? What if he tries to weasel out of it? What if he just wants to diddle and split? I gotta warn her! He don't get nothing till she sees a ring. The Generale don't get nothing: nothing, not bare elbow! [*exit*]

Punch: Haven't you sold your daughter yet, Pantalone? Well, it's for sure the Generale isn't going to marry her.

The thing to do is hire the Generale and put him on your board of directors. General Dynamics has 52 ex-generals on its board of directors and they get over two billion a year from the government. Eisenhower warned the country about the military and industry having a complex but JFK went right ahead with his New Frontier. JFK said, "Go west, get more land," so who do you think's in Saigon? General West . . . more . . . land. *[exit]*

Act II, Scene iii

Alonso: *[enters announced by guitar]* Mi siento a la muerte. I may not live to be killed. The war of love and honor that is raging in my breast is deadlier than the war around me. Love bids me, "Stay . . ."

Two Flower Children: *[enter, offstage right]* Stay . . .

Alonso: ". . . the future is uncertain . . ."

Flower Children: The future is hard/uncertain

First Flower Child: *[they argue]* How can I think with a flower in my hair? *[exeunt]*

Alonso: While honor cries, "Life without glory is death." The thought of Rosalinda kindles my blood, but to desert the cause of freedom would consume me with shame.

Corallina: *[enters]* Signor Alonso!

Alonso: Es posible? An angel. A messenger from heaven—a ray of light in the darkness. Corallina, your arrival is as that of a mother to a lost child; a ship to a drowning man; a holy missionary to the humble, miserable savage . . .

Corallina: Grazie, signor, I . . .

Alonso: What does my goddess send to tell me? Oh, don't say it: I know—that the anguish of our parting assails her tender breast with a thousand spears—that her eyes from limpid pools have become gushing fountains—that her soul, to follow me, is deserting her body—don't tell me these things Corallina: I don't think I could bear them.

Corallina: I won't signor, because she didn't send me. I . . .

Alonso: Rosalinda didn't send you?

Corallina: No, I . . .

Alonso: Oh! Heartless, cruel, inconstant! A goddess of stone. Gone one hour, and I'm already forgotten. Replaced, no doubt, by some deserter, some effeminate fop without obligations to duty or honor! Bueno—from this moment, my heart is at peace. Love has no place there, honor reigns alone. I march . . . *[Marches. He is now 7 years old.]*

Corallina: Signor Alonso! *[yelling]*

Alonso: *[marching]* Shut up!

Corallina: You forgot your skate key and your frog.

Alonso: I'm not interested.

Corallina: My mistress—

Alonso: Your mistress!

Corallina: My mistress, Rosalinda—

Alonso: I don't care!

Corallina: My mistress, Rosalinda, SAYS—

Alonso: *[stops]* SAYS, Corallina? What? What does she says? My very life may depend upon your words—digame.

Corallina: My mistress says that this war is wrong.

Alonso: This war is *[gags]* . . . no. I cannot say that word.

Corallina: Wr-r—malo.

Alonso: Stabbed in the vitals of my honor!

Corallina: Malo!

Alonso: Poisoned in the bowels of my principles . . .

Corallina: What'd you have for breakfast?

Alonso: . . . murdered in my machismo by the woman I love! Rosalinda, you could not have found a better way to kill me! *[Cries. He is now four years old]*

Corallina: *[like fast slaps]* Malo, malo, malo, malo, malo! Wait, signor, that's not the bad part. The bad part is, she's gonna take that information and she's gonna tell it to the Generale!

Alonso: . . . swords! Daggers Thunderbolts! Storms at sea!

Corallina: I knew you'd see the danger, Moby Dick!

Alonso: Danger? That is *insanity!*

Corallina: That's it signor, she's crazy . . . for you!

Alonso: To say that to the Generale—on the eve of a great battle—it's appalling! A disaster! We've got to protect him!

Corallina: Who?

Alonso: Whom.

Corallina: Him?

Alonso: Si. Imagine the pain that a great man must feel, when those for whom he has sacrificed everything turn —*[mime: stabs Corallina, turns the sword]*

Corallina: Good evening, ladies and gentlemen, and now the news on ABC.

Alonso: [pulls the sword out, switching her off] against him. "Et tu, Brute"—it was grief that killed Caesar. And Socrates—Coriolanus—Our Lord—Richard Nixon— alas, Corallina, history groans with examples of greatness betrayed by the mob!

Corallina: [as a mad dog] Rabble, rabble, rabble, rabble, rabble.

Alonso: I would gladly give my LIFE to spare my Generale that pain!

Corallina: . . . You would?

Alonso: Si, I would.

Corallina: Well then, why don't you run right now to our house, signor? Because you're the only one who can stop her.

Alonso: Stop her? *[light dawns]* I will stop her! I, Lieutenant Alonso, will stop her, and I will save my Generale!

Corallina: This way, signor—

Alonso: Think of it—I, Lieutenant Alonso—I throw open the door—I rush in there—I seize Rosalinda—I embrace her and I SAVE my Generale!

Corallina: Please, signor?

Alonso: History will thank you for this, Corallina.

Corallina: VAYA!

Alonso: It will thank you. As Lope de Rueda once said, Corallina—*[going]* history will thank you for this. Gracias *[sweeping bow]* de nada.

Corallina: [at curtain] History certainly works in very strange ways: Ebbene, so long as it *works. [exit]*

Act II, Scene iv

Garcia: [enters] Why has Pantalone invited me to his house? That is unnatural for a wop. It could be he wants to speak to me on some private business. But— this is the house where Alonso makes those visits. Perhaps it is some kind of a trap. *[guitarist introduces Rosalinda]*

Rosalinda: For Italy and Alonso!

Garcia: Senorita! Your beauty is your introduction. This rare blend of nudity and charm can belong only to the esteemed daughter of senor Pantalone.

Rosalinda: This—warlike vision—clearly announces the valorous Generale Garcia, crusher of continents.

Garcia: I was looking for your father.

Rosalinda: My father has most unfortunately been detained, and cannot join us until later.

Garcia: [aside] It is some kind of a trap. *[Guitarist rushes in on false cue. Garcia scares him off.]*

Rosalinda: His absence gives me the opportunity to speak to you on a matter of gravest importance.

Garcia: Con mucho gusto.

Rosalinda: You may not agree at first with all I have to say, Generale, but I know that you will give my remarks due consideration in the fair spirit of public debate.

Garcia: Senorita, I shall be honored to hear whatever responsible sentiments you wish to express. You know and I know, and it cannot be repeated too often, that our freedom-loving society is based upon public debate. As Lope de Vega said to Thomas Jefferson, hablo, hablas, habla; hablamos, hablais, hablabamouth! Freedom of speech is our most valued principle—nay, our most vital domestic policy. Whenever foreign leaders ask me how our country avoids revolution, I tell them that we have—freedom of speech!

Rosalinda: Well then, Generale, I want to point out that all the goals toward which human nature naturally aspires—progress, happiness, and prosperity—require for their fulfillment one fundamental condition, namely peace.

Garcia: They do, indeed, senorita; that is why the fundamental policy of the Spanish government is to pursue peace with every available weapon.

Rosalinda: And no country has the right to interfere in the internal affairs of another!

Garcia: And therefore my country is prepared to take over any country that any country tries to interfere with.

Rosalinda: It's especially unjust for a large and powerful country to impose its will on a country that is small and defenseless.

Garcia: That is why the countries that my country takes over are usually small and defenseless ones.

Rosalinda: Generale, the Bible and the laws of all civilized countries tell us killing is wrong.

Garcia: Es verdad.

Rosalinda: War is killing, raised to an infinite power—

Garcia: Es also verdad.

Rosalinda: Therefore war must be infinitely wrong!

Garcia: Well argued, my dear little hippy. The Spanish government is pledged to fight wars wherever and whenever they break out.

Rosalinda: Generale! Spain is making war in Italy!

Garcia: Spain is combating a war in Italy.

Rosalinda: Spain is interfering in Italy with force and violence!

Garcia: Spain will never abandon Italy to the forces of violence. Senorita, the job of world peace officer is a hard job, a lonely job, a job that only Spain, with its unique tradition of freedom, is equipped to perform. There are few things that can make this job any easier, but one of them is the gratitude of those who are saved. Gracias, senorita; muchas gracias, senorita; gracias muchas, senorita.

Rosalinda: THE SPANISH WAR IN ITALY IS WRONG!

Garcia: Como, senorita?

Rosalinda: THE SPANISH WAR IN ITALY IS EVIL, IL-LEGAL, IMMORAL AND WRONG!

Garcia: You have expressed a little too much.

Rosalinda: It's the truth!

Garcia: That's treason. The fact that our freedom-loving society is based upon public debate does not mean that you can stand up in public and inform the enemy that the people are not 100 percent behind their leaders!

Rosalinda: Who *is* the enemy? Who's killing thousands of young boys on both sides everyday?

Garcia: I'll tell you, senorita—it's *you* creeps, who stand up in public and say that the government is a liar—the society is rotten—you aiders and abetters of the enemy, it's *you* who are killing our boys!

Rosalinda: Madre di dio!

Garcia: [Texas accent] And how do you think it makes those boys feel [sob]—to know they are being murdered by their sisters and sweethearts!

Rosalinda: Dio—pazienza!

Garcia: But we are here, senorita! We are here: Spain is here, and we are going to defend those boys and defend the Italian people against traitors like you if we have to wipe out the whole country!

Rosalinda: I CAN'T STAND IT! [snatches Garcia's sword and raises it to stab him]

Garcia: Cabron!

Rosalinda: No—murder—that's war—rather the ultimate sacrifice! [With an effort, she turns the sword on herself.]

Garcia: That's not good enough. Why don't you BURN YOURSELF?

Act II, Scene v

Alonso: [rushes on preceded by guitarist, who can't stop. Every time Alonso begins his speech, guitarist starts over. Finally actors rush from backstage and drag him off.] Rosalinda, my dearest! I know, my darling, know how intolerable your pain is, and that is why I have rushed from the ends of the earth—to prevent you from doing what you would certainly live to regret! [turns, sees Rosalinda and Garcia for first time] Oh, my God.

Garcia: Et tu, big mouth. [takes the sword] So—Lieutenant Alonso. Every Tuesday—

Alonso: Thursday, senor.

Garcia: In upturned glasses—you meet with the enemy to plot the place, the fatal hour, the coldly calculated moment of your Generale's death. But you arrived—haha, no crime without a flaw—you came one moment too soon—one moment too soon to see your Generale sprawled on the floor, his blood staining the carpet! You forgot to synchronize your WATCH!

Alonso: But, senor—I don't have a watch!

Garcia: I was right! *[whistles "Forward march." Brighella and Espada enter]*

Rosalinda: [fainting] Alonso! *[Brighella and Espada drill, badly; finally stop facing curtain. During Garcia's speech they mime passing a joint.]*

Garcia: It's heartbreaking, Lieutenant, to see one of our strong Spanish youth infected and corrupted by foreign propaganda: to see one who has enjoyed all the privileges of our unique way of life—isn't that right, boys?

Brighella and Espada: [holding the smoke in] Si, si, Generale.

Garcia: To see one of our boys become the tool of an enemy power. I don't know what to say.

Alonso: But Generale—my Generale—I don't understand.

Garcia: I was right. Arrest them. *[Espada and Brighella arrest Alonso and Rosalinda.]* To the stockade, march! *[Soldiers march prisoners across stage, they line up at left and mark time.]*

Act II, Scene vi

Arlecchino: [enters with a dress over his costume, singing ingenue song in falsetto] I finally figured out how to get out of the army! But—now the soldiers is after me now worse than ever. One of them came up to me and he said, "Buenas noches, senorita. You wanta come on over to the barracks and let me sock it to ya?" One of them put his hand on my leg. The next one put his hand on my culo—si, but the *next* one—I got to get out of here! *[He sees the others and tries to hide behind them; all march off except Espada, who has seen Arlecchino, and Arlecchino, who thinks he is safe.]*

Espada: Hoo, look at dat. Now, honey, it ain't right for a pooty young thing like you to be out heah all by yoself—you needs some company, and I is here to give it to you.

Arlecchino: [falsetto] Oh! It's a soldier!

Espada: Thass right, I is—every inch a soldier. Hee, hee, hee. They say march, I marches. They say shoot, I shoots. They say, go out there and git yo ass killed, I gotta go and git killed . . . But 'fo I do . . . I'se gonna get me some.

Arlecchino: [falsetto] My mother told me never to talk to soldiers.

Espada: Don you worry yo purty little head bout no *talkin'*. *[handles Arlecchino]* Come on, I knows all you wop chicks make it. Hey, an' I thought you all suppose to have them big pannetones!

Arlecchino: AHCHOO!!! *[Repeat sneeze—march lazzo. But Espada makes his final charge at Arlecchino.]*

Espada: [grabs Arlecchino] I KNOW YOU. Private Battochio, ain't you?

Arlecchino: Oh no! My name is Serafina Battochio!

Espada: You mus be dat Batokyo Rose! Come on, Battochio, you an' me's gonna have us a little fun! We's goin on down to headquarters an' collect us 30 pesos reward for turnin' in a desuhtuh! But while we's on the way, we's gonna do a little marchin' in time! *[Exeunt. Mime: Espada is committing buggery upon Arlecchino.]*

Punch: That was a pedestrian bit of pederasty. That's enough of this bullshit. If these actors had any guts they would stop right here, with Alonso arrested, with the Generale screwing Rosalinda, with Brighella screwing Corallina, and Arlecchino executed. You know the war is just a little bit tougher than this clown show. Why, if we really wanted to do something about it we might drive on over to our local gun shop . . . pick up a mortar . . . drive on over to Port Chicago . . . set up the mortar in the backyard of a nice little house, barbecue a few ribs, open a couple of beers, lob a mortar over into a napalm depot and BLO-O-O-M—*enlightened democracy.* Bye-bye. I'm leaving for some country with a good puppet government. *[exit]*

End of Act II

Act III, Scene i

[Death march. Arlecchino enters at gunpoint, Rosalinda

and Alonso as prisoners; soldiers, Garcia. Espada lies Arlecchino.]

Garcia: The kings, the armies, and the peoples of the allied kingdoms, Italy and Spain, charge you with espionage, desertion, insubordination, and the unnameable crime against nature. Corporal, read the evidence. Espionage.

Espada: Trying to pass as a civilian.

Garcia: Desertion.

Espada: Concealing your uniform.

Garcia: Insubordination.

Espada: Trying to deceive an officer.

Garcia: Unnameable crime against nature.

Espada: Bein dressed in drag.

Garcia: How do you answer the charges?

Arlecchino: I haven't been asked yet.

Garcia: Guilty or not guilty?

Arlecchino: Time off for good behavior?

Garcia: All crimes are punishable by shooting.

Arlecchino: Let's say I was running away, and you can shoot me in the foot.

Brighella: Let's say it was a crime against nature.

Garcia: You admit you were dressed as a woman?

Arlecchino: When was that?

Garcia: This afternoon.

Arlecchino: Oh no, this afternoon I was out behind the church smoking geraniums!

Garcia, Brighella and Espada: GUILTY!!!

Arlecchino: Guilty?

Brighella: If you weren't guilty, we wouldn't be about to shoot you.

Garcia: I am going to read a press release. The Spanish army is not in Italy to make war on the innocent. Everyone we shoot is either a spy or a deserter. One rotten barrel can poison all the lousy apples—what is this?

Arlecchino: I didn't do it.

Garcia: In time of war there is no place for sentiment. Nevertheless, since the prisoner is clearly retarded, I am determined to make him an example of our mercy.

Arlecchino: Oh, grazie, signor Generale—a saint . . .

Garcia: One shot will do for all four crimes. Corporal, ready— *[Espada takes aim]*

Arlecchino: Wait! . . . what about my children?

Garcia: How many do you have?

Arlecchino: That's the point—I didn't have them yet.

Garcia: Let's go. On your Marx, on your Trotsky . . .

Act III, Scene ii

Corallina: [appears over curtain as Pope and blows bugle] I'ma da Pope. *[Everybody freezes.]* But first, I'ma sing a little song.

> SONG *[all]:* "When the moon hits your eye like a big pizza pie dat's amore" *[stops—all fall down]*

Laudo, laudavi, laudotomy, lobotomy, op. cit., loc. cit., id., est, et cetera, tempus fugit, time flies.

Rosalinda: Il papa!

Alonso: Who?

Corallina: I'ma da Pope, dope.

Garcia: [rises] Welcome, Holy Father, on behalf of the defenders of religion. This visit, at the opening of the biggest operation of the war, inspires us with a fresh sense of the rightness of our cause. We are about to launch—

Act III, Scene iii

Pantalone: [staggers on, doesn't see Pope] Generale—per favore—don't kill my daughter—she's a dummy but I love her—*[Pope blows bugle at him.]* Who's *that?*

Brighella: That's the Pope.

Pantalone: That's a nice piece of merchandise he's got on—oy *[flops]* Holy Father, forgive a poor miserable sinner who's never done anything wrong—ever!

Corallina: PACE—

All: Pace, pace, pace, pace, pace

Corallina: Our children. We, the Pope, have an announcement to maka.

All: Maka, maka, maka, maka, maka

Corallina: THE WAR IS OVER. PEACE IS DECLARED.

Garcia: Caramba!

Corallina: No! Peace. Pacem in terris. Now, my children.

We want to hear no more lies and we want to see no more destruction. We stop it because there's nothing in you to stop it with. You empty, and you country is empty. And you try to fill it up by expanding into other people's countries. You can't fight yourselves by destroying other people, my friends. You can't fight a holy war against the enemy—you can't because I didn't say that you could! (See my other papal bull, publius proclamento.) Because the real enemy, my bambimi, is *ignorance.*

Pantalone: [country club accent] YES!

Corallina: The real enemy is boredom

Pantalone: [same] YES!

Corallina: The real enemy is PRIVATE PROPERTY!

Pantalone: Wait a MINUTE!

Corallina: You got to learn to create inside yourselves, expand you minds, expand you selves and then maybe you won't go around destroying other people. In nomine patrium, fillilili spiritu sanetum—his will be done—we'll begin right now: you will all quit the army!

All: [sounds of rejoicing—except Garcia]

Corallina: Lieutenant Alonso—you will marry Rosalinda.

Alonso: Es posible?

Corallina: You will live in the country

Alonso: Oh, si, senor Pope

Corallina: Raise bambini—and grapes. And Lieutenant Alonso—

Alonso: Si

Corallina: When you know something:

Alonso: Si, senor Pope—in my heart, si—

Corallina: Don't say it—write it.

Alonso: Que alegria! Que perfeccion!

Corallina: I said write it!

Alonso: That is exactly the life I would have chosen for myself, [drops accent] had it not been for my misconception of the role of the soldier in modern society. [All applaud ten times.] Danke gentlemen, danke. Rosalinda—querida—

Rosalinda: Since it is God's will, I accept.

Pantalone: I'll kill her! I'll—

Corallina: Signor Pantalone. Come here, signor—come

here to your Popey-Wopey. Signor Pantalone, you see how we saved your daughter's life—

Pantalone: Yeah I see!

Corallina: You see how we restored your political powers

Pantalone: Yeah?

Corallina: You see how we spared your factories—

Pantalone: Yeah—thanks Pope.

Corallina: Now, we gonna take those factories and change them back from guns to olive oil.

Pantalone: No, Pope—we can't do that.

Corallina: We gonna do it, signor. We gonna institute a guaranteed annual wage, a three-day work week for all those who *want* to work, and no more buying Pirelli-Minetti products, and recognize the union,[1] and huelga,[2] and sabotage the revolution! And free food in the parks every day, and the Grateful Dead every Sunday!

Pantalone: Oy—my profits—my babies—strangled in the cradle—

Corallina: To guard you against that temptation of oversized fatty profits, signor Pantalone, we—the Pope—appoint Brighella you accountant.

Pantalone: Morto— [faints]

Brighella: Sere rico! Spread the wealth, senor. It ain't socialism, but it's creeping.

Corallina: Corporal Espada, you can go home.

Espada: Thank YOU, missuh Pope. I don think this heah Italy need me too much anyhow. I'se gon take mah gun on back to de home funt.

Corallina: What is you native country, my son?

Espada: Oakland. [or Detroit, Newark, etc.]

Garcia: [insane] Basta! Miscegenation! Socialization! The Pope has been subverted by the enemy!

All: S-s-s-s-s-s-s-s

Corallina: Get 'em, seraphims! Get 'em, cherubims!

Garcia: There is still one country that will never stand by while civilization and religion are trampled on—one nation that will carry the flag of freedom to the end of the world! Arriba! [into the audience] There are still more Democrats left—follow me! [ad libs]

Corallina: He'll be back when you want him; he's just

gone to have a talk with Cardinal Spellman. Now, our children, we have done all we can do for you. Signor Pantalone.

Pantalone: Oh, boy.

Corallina: Embrace you son-in-law.

Alonso: Senor Pope, I will say one thousand Hail Marys—

Corallina: Kiss him! *[they embrace]* *[Corallina through a bullhorn]* You're both under arrest ... Now go an prepare for the wedding. Domino nabisco— *[etc.]* *[Others march off, singing wedding march; Pope disappears.]*

Pantalone: *[as he goes]* A wedding—why didn't I think of that—I could hook it up with a bar mitzvah, cater them both. I could make a fortune.

Act III, Scene iv

Corallina: *[enters, still as Pope]* Arlecchino.

Arlecchino: Arlecchino. Oh, it's so dark; I must be dead— and it's all on account of that cornuto army.

Corallina: Get up, Arlecchino.

Arlecchino: O Dio—who's that?

Corallina: This is GOD, Arlecchino. Come on, uppa, uppa, out of you grave!

Arlecchino: Oh, no! *[cries]*

Corallina: Come on, Arlecchino, we gotta march on another picket line!

Arlecchino: I'm floating up to the giant picket line in the sky.

Corallina: You gonna be so happy!

Arlecchino: I hope so

Corallina: But first, you got to open you eyes.

Arlecchino: *[looks]* Oh God, it's Dio! Oh Dio, I'm dead.

Corallina: No, cretino! Get up—look—it's me, Corallina! *[they hug]* What you think this was, a fairy tale? *[steps forward]* Listen, my friends—you want something done? Well, then, do it yourselves! *[whole cast returns on opening line of:*
    SONG
    "Marat we're poor" *[from* Marat/Sade*]*
Recorder starts theme which accompanies bows.]

End

Notes 1 and 2 refer to the California farmworkers' unionization drive.

CHRONOLOGY

DATE	MIME TROUPE HISTORY	RELATED EVENTS
July 3, 1958	R. G. Davis arrives unnoticed in San Francisco, post-beat and pre-hip	
October 29, 1959	R. G. Davis Mime Studio and Troupe presents *Mime and Words* at the S.F. Art Institute; performers: Dawn Grey, Susan Darby, R. G. Davis and Robert Doyle.	
March 1960		Actors Workshop production of George Bernard Shaw's *The Devil's Disciple*.
1960		Peter Schumann arrives in New York City and founds Bread and Puppet Theatre.
May 20-22, 1960	R. G. Davis Mime Studio and Troupe performs mimes at Pacific Coast Arts Festival, Reed College, Arthur Holden (student) chairman; skits: Man with a Stick, White Collar Day, Wanna Play?, Arlecchino & Brighella, Cars, City Dweller, Bird in Flight, The Circus; performers: Dawn Grey, Susan Darby, R. G. Davis, Robert Doyle, Norma Leistiko.	
September 23-25, 1960	Troupe performs same program at the Monterey Jazz Festival.	
December 11, 1960– June 28, 1961	R. G. Davis Mime Studio and Troupe offers 11th Hour Mime Show, Sunday nights at 11 p.m. at the Encore Theatre; the above programs were offered as part of this series.	
1961		Bread and Puppet Theatre's first American production of *Totentanz* at Judson Memorial Church, New York City.
April 25, 1961	Mime Troupe production of *Act Without Words II* by Samuel Beckett (part of 11th Hour Mime Series); performers: R. G. Davis, Robert Doyle; performed with Actors Workshop productions of Yeats's *Purgatory* and Beckett's *Krapp's Last Tape*.	

DATE	MIME TROUPE HISTORY	RELATED EVENTS
November 18, 1961	*Event I* (Part of Midnight Mime Show series at the Encore); performers: Mia Carlisle, R. G. Davis, Larry Lewis, Norma Leistiko, Barbara Melandry, Yvette Nachmias, Ron Poindexter, William Raymond; sculpture by Robert Hudson; costumes by Judy Collins; lighting by Lynn Fischbein; sound by Lee Breuer; special lights by Wally Hedrick and Mike Fender; stage manager Tom Purvis; assistants Atheline Wold and Barbara Flinn; helpers: Bill Wiley, Cornelia Schultz, Ann Horton, Ken Hoerauf, Lowell Picket, Ken Lash, Ken Dewey; upstairs man Carl Linder.	
1962-63		Bread and Puppet Theatre performs in the tradition of wandering troupes of medieval Europe, wandering throughout New York and New England wherever an audience could be found.
January 20, 1962	*Dowry* (Mime Troupe's first Commedia dell'arte production); performers: Joe Bellan, Ruth Breuer, Mia Carlisle, R. G. Davis, Susan Darby, William Raymond, Ronald Reese; costumes and masks: Ann Horton. Premieres at the Encore and goes on to be the Mime Troupe's first summer production in the parks—two performances.	
Easter 1962		Bread and Puppet Theatre performs its *Easter Play*—first in a series of Easter performances in New York churches through 1967.
June 1962	"Method and Mime" by R. G. Davis printed in *Tulane Drama Review.*	
June 13, 1962	Beckett's *Act Without Words II* and *Who's Afraid* by Jonathan Altman presented at Poetry Festival, S.F. Art Museum; performers: R. G. Davis, Robert Doyle.	
June 13-14, 1962	*Dowry* presented at the Spaghetti Factory; Mime Troupe moves out of Encore.	
September 10, 1962	R. G. Davis Mime Studio and Troupe moves to studio at 3450 Capp Street.	
December 25, 1962		Bread and Puppet Theatre performs *Christmas Story*—first in a series of

Christmas performances in New York through 1967.

Actors Workshop production of *Galileo* by Bertolt Brecht.

December 1962–
January 1963

. . . 1963   *Plastic Haircut,* film by Robert Nelson, Bill Wiley, Robert Hudson, R. G. Davis, Judy Rosenberg; sound by Steve Reich.

January 1963   R. G. Davis Mime Troupe severs all connections with Actors Workshop, abandoning security, renouncing establishment success and losing most of the company except R. G. Davis.

January 11, 1963   *Event II* at the Tape Center; cast: Ruth Breuer, Susan Darby, R. G. Davis, Daniel McDermott, Judy Rosenberg; set by William Wiley and Karl Rosenberg; film and tapes by R. G. Davis and others.

May 25, 1963   *The Root* from a play by Machiavelli; adapted by Milt Savage from an adaptation by Bart Midwood; directed by R. G. Davis; cast: R. G. Davis, Victoria Hochberg, Arthur Holden, Daniel McDermott, Jamie Miller, Tom Purvis, Donald Weygandt; masks by Ann Horton; costumes by Judy Davis; music by William Spenser and David Jenkins. Premiered at Capp St. Studio; second summer in the parks—five performances.

August 15–
November 2, 1963   San Francisco Mime Troupe presents *Ruzzante's Maneuvers* by Milton Savage at Capp St. Studio after premiere fiasco at the San Francisco Museum of Art; produced and directed by R. G. Davis; cast: Joseph Bellan, R. G. Davis, Victoria Hochberg, Joe Lomuto, Jr., Daniel McDermott, Marvin Silber, Norma Whittaker; masks by Ann Horton and Bruce Newell; costumes by Marina Sender; music by Steven Reich and William Spencer.

late 1963   Bread and Puppet Theatre settles in at Bread and Puppet Museum on Delancey St., N.Y., where it performs through 1966 numerous puppet, mask, and mime productions; improvisational shows, sidewalk shows, pageants, parades, political and anti-war shows; and constructs 10-12 foot puppets for plays and parades.

December 11-29, 1963   *Ubu King* by Alfred Jarry; directed by R. G. Davis; performers: Sam Erwin, Victoria Hochberg (Mere Ubu); Arthur Holden, Jerry Jump, Joseph Lomuto, Jr., Judy Rosenberg, Marvin Silber, Kai Spiegel (Pere Ubu), Fred Unger, Norma Whittaker, with Mark Truman, Jeanne Brechan, Georges Rey, Richard Olsen, J. Jeffrey Jones; sets, props and costumes by William Wiley; music composed by Steve Reich; film by Robert Nelson; special thanks to Saul Landau, Jean Varda, etc. at Capp St.

January 25, 1964   *Mime(s) and Movie* at Capp Street; a retrospective show consisting of R. G. Davis in *Mime(s); Plastic Haircut;* and Beckett's *Act Without Words II* with Tom Purvis and R. G. Davis.

February 27, 1964   *Event III (Coffee Break);* projections by Elias Romero; sound by Steve Reich and Phil Lesh; movement by R. G. Davis and Fumi Spencer. Presented with *Along Came a Spider* by Kenneth Lash; directed by R. G. Davis; cast: Jeanne Brechan, Don Crawford, Jerry Jump, Dave Love, Tom Purvis, Judy Rosenberg, Erica Rosqui, Fred Unger, Norma Whittaker. At Capp St. studios. Sets by John Barrow.

April 22, 1964   Mary Ann Pollar presents the S.F. Mime Troupe in *Tartuffe* at the Veterans Memorial Auditorium; production marks the end of Mime Troupe's habit of playing to small audiences in its studio and an acceptance of the need to rent larger halls to get to more people.

May 14– July 25, 1964   *Chorizos,* adapted from Saul Landau's scenario by Tom Lopez; directed by Tom Purvis; cast: Jeanne Brechan, Jerry Jump, Buck Lacey, Joseph Lomuto, Jr., Tom Purvis, Judy Rosenberg, Mark Truman, Norma Whittaker. Third summer in the parks—eight performances.

July 24, 1964–
March 1965

Tartuffe, adapted from Moliere's play by Richard Sassoon; directed by R. G. Davis and Nina Serrano Landau; cast: Sandra Archer, John Broderick, R. G. Davis (later replaced by Bob Lanchester), Jerry Jump, Joseph Lomuto, Jr. (later replaced by R. G. Davis), Dan McDermott (replaced by John Robb), Marlene Silvers, Jo Ann Wheatley (replaced by Billie Dixon); sets by Richard Beggs; masks by Francesca Greene; music by Steve Reich; lyrics by Saul Landau. Premiered at S.F. Mime Troupe Theatre, 3450 20th Street.

August 28–
September 1, 1964

Tartuffe tours Los Angeles.

September 1964

Free Speech Movement begins with small picket line in front of the administration building (Sproul Hall) on UC Berkeley campus to protest administration crackdown on student political groups. Movement quickly grew in response to increased repression to include some 10,000 students and culminated in a massive sit-in, Dec. 2, in Sproul Hall in which over 800 students were arrested in a pre-dawn raid. The Academic Senate voted to support the students' immediate free speech demands and the administration gracelessly capitulated and settled in to the long bureaucratic process of co-opting faculty radicals (those whose tenure prohibited dismissal) and whittling away the rights the students had won.

October 6, 1964

Mime Troupe begins casting for a minstrel show.

January 1965

Palace of People's Culture pipedream; shareholders: Alvin Duskin, Saul Landau, R. G. Davis.

May 18, 1965

Tartuffe at San Jose State College; Luis Valdez sees performance, interviews R. G. Davis and decides to join Troupe himself.

May 7, 1965

Bill Graham presents the San Francisco Mime Troupe in *The Exception and the Rule* by Bertolt Brecht; translated by Eric Bentley;

directed by R. G. Davis; cast: Peter Berg,
Manny Brookman, Nick Eldridge, Judy Gold-
haft (Rosenberg), Merle Harding, Fred
Hayden, Bollette Jacobson, Jerry Jump,
John Robb; music by Pauline Oliveros and
Jeanne Brechan; sets by Fred Reichman;
masks by Francesca Greene and Sara Morris;
presented with "The U.S. War in Vietnam,"
a talk by Robert Scheer. Premiered at the
Gate Theatre in Sausalito, May 7.

May 21-22, 1965

Vietnam Day teach-in on the UC Berkeley
campus, marking the beginning of the
Vietnam Day Committee which became the
major focus of the movement in Berkeley
until the Spring of 1966. Major activities
included attempts to stop troop trains from
passing through Berkeley (successful) and
three large marches in the Fall of 1965.
At the last of these the Mime Troupe presented an inconsequential skit using large
puppets.

June 1, 1965

Robert Scheer's report on U.S. intervention
in Vietnam appears in *Ramparts.*

June 17, 1965

Bill Graham presents the S.F. Mime Troupe
in *A Minstrel Show or Civil Rights in a
Cracker Barrel;* written by Saul Landau and
R. G. Davis from original, traditional and
improvised material; directed by R. G. Davis;
Minstrels: John Broderick, Willie B. Hart
Jr., George Matthews, Jason Marc-Alexander,
Julio Martinez, Malachi Spicer (Kai Spiegel);
Interlocutor, Robert Slattery; musicians:
Carl Granich and Chuck Wiley; movie (*O
Dem Watermelons*) filmed and edited by
Robert Nelson; music by Steve Reich.
Premiered at Commedia Theatre, Palo Alto.

Summer 1965

Bread and Puppet Theatre works with a
community project in East Harlem,
sponsored by Spanish Catholic Action.

July 1965

S.F. Mime Troupe moves to 924 Howard St.

July 25-
September 12, 1965

Candelaio, an adaptation by Peter Berg from
a play by Giordano Bruno; directed by R. G.
Davis; cast: Sandra Archer, Nick Eldridge,
Kay Howard, Jerry Jump, Lomuto, John
Robb, Shirley Shaw (replaced by Judy

Rosenberg), Luis Valdez; music by Pauline Oliveros; set and costumes by Coni Spiegel; masks by Francesca Greene. Premiered at Washington Square Park, S.F. Fourth summer in the parks—12 performances.

August 7, 1965   R. G. Davis steps into Luis Valdez's role for special arresting performance of *Candelaio* in Lafayette Park—busted for performing in the parks without a permit.

August 11, 1965   Atheneum Arts Foundation cancels performance of *Candelaio* at Mt. Tamalpais after it is declared "unacceptable" by Gordon T. Kishbaugh, Superintendent of District 2, California State Division of Beaches and Parks.

October 14, 1965   Bill Graham presents the S.F. Mime Troupe in *Chronicles of Hell* by Michel de Ghelderode; translated by George Hauger; directed by R. G. Davis; cast: Sandra Archer, Peter Berg, Serge Echeverria, William Freese, Jerry Jump, Lomuto, Kent Minault, Terry O'Keefe, Chuck Ray, John Robb, John Schonenberg, Robert Slattery, Ken Wydro; sets by William Geis III; costumes by Kathryn Stuntz; sound by Pauline Oliveros; presented with Lawrence Ferlinghetti or David Meltzer reading from their own work. Premiered at the Commedia Theatre, Palo Alto.

November 1, 1965   R. G. Davis found guilty of performing in the parks without a permit.

November 1965   El Teatro Campesino founded by Luis Valdez and members of the National Farm Workers Association with the NFWA, to dramatize the issues of the Delano grape strike and urge farm workers to join the union.

November 6, 1965   Appeal I, rock dance benefit at the Howard Street Studio; among those contributing their services for the benefit of the Troupe were Sandy Bull, the Committee, Allen Ginsberg, the Jefferson Airplane, John Handy Quintet, the Mothers, Peter Orlovsky.

November 19, 1965 Gate Movies (Nelson/Graham)

December 10, 1965   Appeal II, rock dance with light show at the
                      Fillmore Auditorium: Great Society,
                      Jefferson Airplane, the Warlocks (Grateful
                      Dead), Mystery Trend, the Gentlemen's
                      Band, Jeanne Brechan, the VIP's—and the
                      John Handy Quintet which never got to play
                      due to a dispute with Bill Graham. This was
                      the first such dance to be presented at the
                      Fillmore.

December 17, 1965   R. G. Davis sentenced to 30 days suspended
                      and one year's probation. This conviction
                      cost the Mime Troupe its first and only grant,
                      an annual $1,000 from the City's Hotel Tax
                      allocations for the arts.

1966   Bread and Puppet Theatre conducts
                                                                        community projects in the South Bronx
                                                                        and central Harlem, sponsored by New
                                                                        York parks dept. and the council for
                                                                        parks and playgrounds; also presents
                                                                        weekly children's workshops, experimental
                                                                        plays and music sessions in space provided
                                                                        by the New York Shakespeare Company
                                                                        in old Astor building.

January 14, 1966   Appeal III at the Fillmore; produced by Bill
                      Graham; Grateful Dead, Mystery Trend, Great
                      Society, The Gentlemen's Band.

January 14, 1966   Movies at the Gate Theatre . . .

January 5-22, 1966   *Minstrel Show* plays the Encore alternating
                      with a second program of R. G. Davis *Mime*,
                      Jane Lapiner & Co. *Dance* and P. Oliveros
                      Sound.

January 26–   The Actors Workshop presents the S.F.
February 6, 1966   Mime Troupe: *Act Without Words II* by
                      Samuel Beckett; directed by R. G. Davis;
                      cast: Jerry Jump and John Robb; *The
                      Exception and the Rule* by Bertolt Brecht;
                      directed by R. G. Davis—same cast as
                      before with Peter Berg replacing Nick
                      Eldridge; produced by Bill Graham.

February 1966   *What's That, a Head?*, puppet play for
                      children; written by Barbara LaMorticello;
                      directed by Sandra Archer; cast: Peter

Berg, Jeanne Brechan, Judy Goldhaft, Robert LaMorticello, Norma Middlebrook, Kent Minault, Ann Willock; puppets by Robert LaMorticello; music by Jeanne Brechan.

February 11, 1966 — ACLU files a civil suit against the San Francisco Park and Recreation Commission to show cause why the S.F. Mime Troupe should not be granted a permit to perform in the parks.

February 1966 — Bill Graham leaves his position as Mime Troupe booker and business manager to rough it at the Fillmore.

March–April 1966 — El Teatro Campesino accompanies NFWA pilgrimage from Delano to Sacramento.

April 1966 — *Minstrel Show* tours Northwest; Minstrels: Peter Cohon, R. G. Davis, Willie B. Hart, Jr., Lomuto, Jason Marc-Alexander, Chuck Richardson; Interlocutor, John Robb; musicians: Bill Freese, Jim Haynie, Arthur Lutz; understudies: Joe Bellan, Robert Hurwitt, Tom Luce.

April 3, 1966 — *Minstrel Show* performance at St. Martin's College, Olympia, Washington, closed down in mid-performance.

April 16, 1966 — S.F. Mime Troupe presents The Traps Festival, benefit for the Bob Scheer for Congress campaign: *Jack Off!*, A Girlie Show; choreographed and directed by Judy Goldhaft; dancers: Sandra Archer, Judy Goldhaft, Jane Lapiner; projections by Erik Weber; music by Charles McDermott; design by Karl Rosenberg and Barbara Scales; *Mirage*, a film by Peter Weiss; *Centerman*, an interpretive dramatization of Wolfgang Borchert's short story "The Dandelion"; written and directed by Peter Berg; cast: Jim Haynie, Jerry Jump, Lomuto, John Robb, John Schonenberg, Malachi Spicer; set by John Connell.

May 1966 — First urban performance of El Teatro Campesino at Committee Theatre, San Francisco.

May 2, 1966	Mayor Shelley's newly appointed Art Resources Development Committee of the S.F. Cultural Board holds first meeting, a luncheon at the Crown Zellerbach Building. Luncheon is crashed by members of the S.F. Mime Troupe, dressed in a variety of costumes from minstrel to commedia and playing musical instruments. This demonstration leads directly to the formation of the Artists Liberation Front; the position paper, read by R. G. Davis to the assembled dignitaries and drafted by Peter Berg, foreshadows the early Digger papers which were disseminated toward the end of the following summer.

May 7, 1966 — California State Senate Fact-finding Subcommittee on Un-American Activities hits S.F. Mime Troupe in annual Burns Report for obscene gestures and Marxist neighbors.

May 31, 1966 — With Assemblyman Willie Brown in the chair, actors, directors, dancers, painters, poets, publishers, musicians, producers, sculptors, novelists, entrepreneurs, reporters, et al. meet at the Howard St. studio of the S.F. Mime Troupe to form the Artists Liberation Front dedicated to their collective defense and offense. Among those present: Lawrence Ferlinghetti, Kenneth Rexroth, Bill Graham, Ralph J. Gleason.

June 5, 1966 — *Olive Pits* (first version), a commedia dell'arte adaptation by Peter Berg, Peter Cohon & Co. of a play by Lope de Rueda; directed by R. G. Davis; cast: Sandra Archer, Anne Bernstein, Peter Cohon, R. G. Davis, Joe Lomuto, Judi Quick; costumes by Judy Rosenberg; masks by Ann Willock and Francesca Greene; technical director Charles Herrick.

June 19, 1966 — Teach-On LSD/etc., a benefit for the Timothy Leary Defense Fund, with Big Brother and the Holding Company, the Sopwith Camel, David Meltzer, Allen Ginsberg, Michael McClure, Richard Alpert, and Timothy Leary speaking on "The Politics and Ethics of Ecstacy"; panel on "Drugs and Society," moderated by Ralph Gleason, with Richard Alpert, Allen Ginsberg and Patrick Hallinan; projections by Erik Weber and Elias Romero; S.F. Mime Troupe premieres *Search and Seizure,* a cabaret play, written and directed by Peter Berg; cast: Steve Bailey, Peter Cohon, Emmet Grogan, Arthur Holden, Tom Luce, Jeanne Milligan, John Robb, Caraline Straley; in the Colonial Room of the Saint Francis Hotel.

July 2–
September 1966

The Miser, from a play by Moliere, adapted by Frank Bardacke; directed by Joe Bellan; cast: Peter Berg (replaced by Lomuto), Peter Cohon, John Condrin (replaced by Robert LaMorticello), Roger Guy-Bray, Robert Hurwitt, Bill Lindyn (replaced by Arthur Holden), Gayle Pearl, Judi Quick (replaced by Sandra Archer), Malachi Spicer (replaced by Emmet Grogan), Anne Willock (replaced by Val Riseley); assistant director George Konnoff; adviser R. G. Davis; set design by John Connell; music by Gayle Pearl and Davey Jenkins; costume design by Judy Gold-haft; masks by Francesca Greene and Anne Willock. Premiered in an empty lot at the corner of Laguna and California. Fifth summer in the parks—19 performances.

July 17, 1966

Artists Liberation Front benefit at the Fill-more with Allen Ginsberg, Sopwith Camel, and the only public performance of the S.F. Mime Troupe's rock band's smash hit, "I Got Fucked in Vietnam."

September 8, 1966

Minstrel Show busted after second performance in Phipps Auditorium, Denver, Colorado, after second performance in that city to kick off the Troupe's first midwestern tour; show is under the direction of Peter Cohon; John Condrin, Peter Cohon, Willie B. Hart, Jr., Bill Lindyn, Jason Marc-Alexander, Earl Robertson: cast; Interlocutor: Robert Slattery, musicians and understudies, Kent

	Minault and David Simpson; technical director C. P. Herrick. Cohon, Robertson and Lindyn busted on public obscenity charges and freed on $700 bond.	
September 19, 1966		*Lomuto Reads* opens as Lomuto strikes out on his own to make it big on the college poetry reading circuit.
September 27, 1966	*Out Put You*, a cabaret play written and directed by Peter Berg; cast: Joseph Bellan, Emmet Grogan, Arthur Holden, Judi Quick, Val Riseley.	
late summer 1966	First Digger papers begin to appear, tacked up on the walls and doors of the Mime Troupe studio. The papers are manifestos of radical art calling for structural reorganization of the Troupe. By September the Diggers have turned their focus onto the community at large and their papers are being distributed in Haight-Ashbury.	
October 8, 9, 15, 16, 1966		Artists Liberation Front free fairs are put on in the ghetto parks throughout the city, organized by Yuri Toropov & Barbara Wahl. They feature rock bands, games, painting, etc. for young and old.
December 1966	Gargoyle Carolers hit the streets of San Francisco.	
December 16, 1966	Gargoyle Bust: Gayle Pearl, Jeanne Milligan, Ann Willock, Paula Sikowski, Johnathan Altman, William Freese, Orlin Vaughan, Arthur Holden, Roger Guy-Bray, and Jane Lasch are arrested on begging charges.	
January 7, 1967– February 1967	*The Condemned*, an adaptation of Jean-Paul Sartre's *The Condemned of Altona* with the assistance of Cecile Leneman, Felix Leneman MD and Martin Epstein; directed by R. G. Davis in association with Peter Berg and Juris Svendsen; cast: Sandra Archer, Lynn Brown, R. G. Davis, John Robb, Robert Slattery; design by Gary P. Stephan and Jim Reineking; films and projections by Erik Weber; costumes by Judy Goldhaft; lighting by C. P. Herrick; presented at the Geary Temple.	
February 6, 1967	Minstrels Cohon, Lindyn and Robertson	

	acquitted in Denver trial—sterling performances by attorneys Walter Gerash and Leonard Davies.
February 15, 1967	Gargoyle trial ends in hung jury, a victory for attorney Dick Hodge in his first appearance on the defense side of a trial.
March 1967	Minstrel Show takes off on a last quickie tour of points East and back across Canada.
March 9, 1967	*The Vaudeville Show* opens at the Geary Temple; acts: "The Henriques Quartet," Daryl Henriques & Co.; "Natasha," Paula Gilbert (Sikowski); "Dr. Kronkite," Joseph Bellan, William Lindyn, Ann Willock; "Boris and Natasha," Paula Gilbert and Roger Guy-Bray; "Punch and Judy," William Lindyn and Ann Willock puppeteers; "Bodies," a dance choreographed by Jane Lapiner, with Lynn Brown, Judith Goldhaft, Lomuto, Mary Overlie, John Robb; "Wanda and Her Birds," Joseph Bellan; poetry by Lomuto; Richard Brautigan reading from his own works.
March 14, 1967	*Minstrel Show* busted in Calgary, Alberta; Royal Canadian Mounted Police get their men and preserve the purity of fair Calgary; R. G. Davis, Lee Vaughan and Ron Stahlings locked up in Spy Hill Gaol without bail pending trial on pot charges. Protests begin in New York and San Francisco.
March 22, 1967	Lee Vaughan, the only defendant out on bail, has his $1,000 bail revoked (forfeited) when he is late for a court hearing after being detained at the border as an undesirable alien—being a narcotics suspect and all.
March 25, 1967	Appeal Party and Bail Benefit for the Mime Troupe held at the Geary Temple with The Bearing Straight, Freedom Road, Virgil Gonsalves, films, etc.
March 28, 1967	Davis and Stahlings finally get bail and Vaughan is released on condition that he immediately leave the country. All three follow that advice.
April 12, 1967	Appeal IV at the Fillmore (courtesy of Bill Graham): Jefferson Airplane, Moby Grape,

	Grateful Dead, Quicksilver Messenger Service, Loading Zone, Andrew Staples Group; produced by Robert Hurwitt; poster donated by Mouse Studios.	
April 1967	By executive fiat the 59 member Troupe is cut down to 14 full-time members.	
May 12–	*L'Amant Militaire* from a play be Goldoni; translated by Betty Schwimmer; adapted by Joan Holden; directed by R. G. Davis and Arthur Holden; cast: Sandra Archer, Peter Cohon, R. G. Davis, Charlie Degelman, Kay Hayward, Darryl Henriques, Arthur Holden, Kent Minault; set designed by Wally Hedrick; masks and puppet by Ann Willock; Punch by Bill Lindyn; costumes by Ann Willock; Sixth summer in the parks —46 performances (alternating toward the end of the summer with *Olive Pits*).	
June 16, 1967	S.F. Mime Troupe invades the turf of El Teatro Campesino in Delano, with: *Olive Pits* (second version), adapted by Peter Berg and Peter Cohon from a play by Lope de Rueda; directed by R. G. Davis and Sandra Archer; cast: Sandra Archer, Peter Cohon, Ellen Ernest, Darryl Henriques, Arthur Holden; set design by Jerome Marcel.	
June–August 1967		El Teatro Campesino goes on national tour with performances in The Village Theater, New York, Newport Folk Festival, and the Senate Committee on Migratory Labor, Washington, D.C.
Summer 1967		Bread and Puppet Theater performs at Newport Folk Festival and Expo '67, Montreal. It performs numerous slapstick and antiwar plays for community groups in the New York area; tours Eastern colleges; appears on National Educational Television; produces woodcut antiwar banners, papier mache doll puppets, and antiwar newspapers.
August 22, 1967	San Francisco Mime Troupe defeats *Ramparts* in baseball.	

September 1967		Establishment of El Centro Campesino Cultural, a farm workers' cultural center, in Del Rey, Calif., with El Teatro Campesino.
October 10– December 6, 1967	S.F. Mime Troupe goes on national tour with *L'Amant Militaire* and *Olive Pits* (Marilyn Sydney replacing Kay Hayward and Ellen Ernest); performing and demonstrating and chasing Dow recruiters across the midwest and into the cultural havens of the East Coast.	
January 1968	Lew Harris is working as company manager.	S.F. Tac Squad (Black Shirts) attack demonstration at the Fairmont Hotel.
January– February 1968	Mime Troupe undertakes short Los Angeles tour.	
January 26, 1968		We receive leaflet about Fred Gardners Coffee Houses alive.
January 28, 1968	Obendorf, tech manager for 1967 tour, quits.	
January 25, 1968	California State College at Fullerton faculty council and student senate vote to deny S.F. Mime Troupe use of the campus Quadrangle for a free performance of *Olive Pits* to be given on February 7. Drama professor George Forest leads opposition to the ban. Troupe decides to play anyway as Forest goes to court to reverse the ban.	
February 4, 1968	Judge James Judge rules in favor of the campus ban against the Troupe. President Langsdorf grants Forest permission to have the Troupe perform for his drama class, and only his drama class, providing Troupe members personally accept injunctions against performing before they do so.	
February 7, 1968	S.F. Mime Troupe presents *Olive Pits* in an orange grove across the street from the Cal State Fullerton campus. Controversy over the performance and the ban becomes a major campus cause. Professor Forest quits the college.	
February 1968		Haight Street riots; Tac Squad takes over.
March 16–18, 1968		Peace and Freedom Party founding conven-

		tion in Berkeley. S.F. Mime Troupe's Gorilla Marching Band debuts.
Spring 1968		Bread and Puppet Theater goes on first European tour to France, Germany, Holland and England.
April 5, 1968	*Ruzzante or The Veteran* from a play by Angelo Beolco; translated by Suzanne Pollard; adapted by Joan Holden; directed by R. G. Davis; cast: Steve Friedman, Arthur Holden (replaced by Keith Nason), Marc Ling (replaced by Eric Berne), Boris Morris, Gayle Pearl (replaced by Melody James); set by Wally Hedrick; technical director Kerb Feeler; masks by Dan Chumley after Donato Sartori of Padua; costumes by Joan Wright; premiered at Chabot College, Hayward, Calif.	
April 1968	Gutter Puppets perform. Built and written by members of the company; puppets by Ruth Sicular and Megan Snider.	
April 26, 1968	*Ruzzante* presented on the campus of Cal State Fullerton.	
April 28, 1968	*The Farce of Patelin* adapted by R. G. Davis and Jael Weisman from a 15th century French farce; directed by Sandra Archer; cast: Eric Berne (replaced by Jael Weisman), Lee Bouterse, Daniel Chumley, Charles Degelman, Gary Rappy (replaced by Michael Alaimo), Ruth Sicular (replaced by Gayle Pearl), Jael Weisman (replaced by Lorne Berkun); sets and costumes by Megan Snider; masks by Daniel Chumley and Donato Sartori. In this play the Mime Troupe incorporated a Cranky, a device borrowed from the Bread and Puppet Theater and designed for the Troupe by Daniel Chumley. Premiered in Canyon, Calif. Seventh free summer in the parks (alternating with *Ruzzante*)—124 performances.	
May 1968		Gut Theatre, mainly Puerto Ricans of East Harlem, begins performing under the direction of Enrique Vargas.
May 25, 1968	13th Annual Village Voice Off-Broadway (Obie)	

May 25, 1968	13th Annual Village Voice Off-Broadway (Obie) Awards: S.F. Mime Troupe cited for "uniting theatre and revolution and grooving in the park."	El Teatro Campesino awarded Obie for "creating a workers' theatre to demonstrate the politics of survival."
June 13, 1968	San Francisco Mime Troupe beats *Ramparts* at baseball.	
June 18, 1968	Carl Oglesby visits the Troupe, plays tuba, and leaves.	
June 21-23, 1968		SDS Southern Regional Conference. Klonsky (RYM II) presides.
July 1968	Kent Minault, Steve Weissman work on "Che Pageant."	
August 1968	San Francisco Newsreel takes offices in S.F. Mime Troupe Building.	El Teatro Campesino produces its first full-length play in conjunction with the Radical Theatre Festival: *The Shrunken Head of Pancho Villa* by Luis Valdez.
October 1968	Peter Solomon and Roy Dahlberg are bookers for the Troupe.	
September 25–29, 1968	Radical Theatre Festival at San Francisco State College: Bread and Puppet Theatre, El Teatro Campesino, San Francisco Mime Troupe, Gut Theatre, and Berkeley Agit-Prop. Festival featured performances by all participating troupes; films (*Have You Heard of the San Francisco Mime Troupe?; Reiteration* [Bread and Puppet]; *O Dem Watermelons*); parades, open rehearsals, improvisations and workshops; panels with Sandra Archer, R. G. Davis, Jerry Rubin, Peter Schumann, Luis Valdez, Juris Svendsen. *Shrunken Head of Pancho Villa* premieres at Festival.	
October 1968	*Patelin* and *Ruzzante* tour the midwest.	
October 1968	R. G. Davis visits Japan.	
October 31, 1968		Fred Gardner writing *Zabriskie Point* for Antonioni. Coffee Houses continue
November 1968		Living Theatre begins tour of the U.S.
November 5, 1968	Luise Aliamo secretary to Mime Troupe.	
November 6, 1968		San Francisco State strike begins; runs six months.
December 1968	Children's Christmas play; kill Santa Claus.	

December 23, 1968	Idea for Telephone Credit Card Puppet skit.
January 1969	Women's Drill Team notes, Sandra Archer.
February 1969	*Patelin*, with Gutter Puppets, tours Northwest and Vancouver.
February 14, 1969	S.F. Mime Troupe's Ladies Drill Team performs at Oregon State University, Corvallis, Anti-military Ball. Telegram sent: Dear Ladies Drill Team, . . . Forward, . . . Marx! Don't Turn Right. Lenin and the Staff.
March 3, 1969	Bookmobile Puppet Show opens.
March 16, 1969	S.F. Mime Troupe marches in S.F. St. Patrick's Day Parade.
March 29, 1969– March 12, 1970	*Congress of the Whitewashers*, from a play by Bertolt Brecht; translated by J. M. Svendsen; adapted by the S.F. Mime Troupe; directed by R. G. Davis; design by Megan Snider; actors: Sandra Archer, Lorne Berkun, Daniel Chumley, R. G. Davis, Steve Friedman, Melody James, Sharon Lockwood, Michael Lawrence, Joe Lomuto, Jael Weisman; technicians: Peter Snider and Chris Teuber; musicians, Randy Craig, Cindy Fitzpatrick and Jefferson Free; music by Leonard Kline; lyrics by John Flores and Juris Svendsen; costumes, props and masks by Nancy Dickler, Larry Keck, David Maclay, Susan Roth and Caralie Tarble. Premiered in Live Oak Park, Berkeley. Eighth free summer in the parks—110 performances.
Spring 1969	Bread and Puppet Theatre departs on a second and more extensive European tour.
April 1969	*Patelin* and Gorilla Marching Band tour the Southwest; with Gutter Puppets.
April 6, 1969	Administration of Navajo Community College, Many Farms, Arizona, cancels Mime Troupe performance of *Patelin*—no arrests.
April 7, 1969	Navajo Community College, Many Farms—S.F. Mime Troupe ejected.
May 30, 1969	Gorilla Marching Band marches in People's Park Parade, Berkeley.

June 1969	Civil Suit filed by ACLU; Robert Adams filing civil action against Hayward Area Recreation District for refusing permit to S.F. Mime Troupe to perform.
June 1, 1969	S.F. Mime Troupe defies ban against performing in Earl Warren Park, Contra Costa County; perform *Congress of Whitewashers* before an all-cop audience.
July–August 1969	*Congress of Whitewashers* in Bay Area parks.
August 28, 1969	Wild West dead through the combined efforts of Haight Communes, ex-Mother Fuckers, Newsreel, S.F. State BSU, Red Guard, Los Siete and other third world liberation groups; kill an attempt at an S.F. "Woodstock."
October– November 1969	Northwest tour with *Congress of Whitewashers.*
October 15, 1969	S.F. Mime Troupe Marching Band marches in Moratorium Parade, Pullman, Washington.
December 22– January 3, 1970	First Radical Theatre Workshop at San Jose State College.
December 23–24, 1969	Christmas Puppets; New Santa Claus, Jack and the Beanstalk, Red Herring; with Sandra Archer.
December 24, 25, 26, 1969	Davis in Chicago visits Conspiracy.
March 12, 1970	*Congress of Whitewashers* ends; Davis leaves the company.
April 1970	Mime Troupe, Marching Band, Gutter Puppets with Robert Scheer tour Southwest, Midwest, perform *Congress of Whitewashers.*
May 16, 1970	*A Man Has His Pride or Independent Female* opens at Ash Grove; directed by Sandra Archer; written by Joan Holden.
June 6, 1970	Rosenberg Foundation grant for children's shows.
August 1970	"Eco Man" and "Telephone" (puppet play) published in *Ramparts.*
August 1, 1970	Sandra Archer leaves S.F. Mime Troupe to

make film in Chile with Saul and Nina
Landau and 30 others.

Mime Troupe now called a collective,
produces "Seize the Time," on the Chicago
trial of Bobby Seale, tours with Tom Hayden
in the East, produces various skits on Soledad
Brothers trial, oil in the bay, drugs and the
war.

BIBLIOGRAPHY

BOOKS

Jotterand, Franck. *Le Nouveau Theatre Americain.* Paris: Editions du Seuil, 1970.

Kourilsky, Francoise. *Le Bread and Puppet Theatre.* Lausanne: La Cite Editeur, 1971.

Lesnick, Henry, ed. *Guerrilla Street Theater.* New York: Bard/Avon, 1973.

Schevill, James. *Break Out! In Search of New Theatrical Environments.* Chicago: Swallow Press, 1973.

Taylor, Karen Malpede. *People's Theatre in Amerika.* New York: Drama Book Specialists, 1972.

Weisman, John. *Guerrilla Theater: Scenarios for Revolution.* New York: Anchor/Doubleday, 1973.

FILM

Have You Heard of the San Francisco Mime Troupe? 1966. Donald Lenzer & Fred Wardenburg. 16mm/60 min./color. From: BFA Educational Media, 2211 Michigan Ave., Santa Monica, Calif. 90404. (213) 829-2901.

ILLUSTRATIONS

INDEX